THACKERAY
THE NOVELIST

THACKERAY
THE NOVELIST

BY

GEOFFREY TILLOTSON

CAMBRIDGE
AT THE UNIVERSITY PRESS
1954

CAMBRIDGE UNIVERSITY PRESS

Cambridge, New York, Melbourne, Madrid, Cape Town,
Singapore, São Paulo, Delhi, Tokyo, Mexico City

Cambridge University Press
The Edinburgh Building, Cambridge CB2 8RU, UK

Published in the United States of America by
Cambridge University Press, New York

www.cambridge.org
Information on this title: www.cambridge.org/9780521175968

First published 1954
First paperback edition 2011

A catalogue record for this publication is available from the British Library

ISBN 978-0-521-17596-8 Paperback

TO

MY MOTHER AND FATHER

CONTENTS

PREFACE   *p.* ix

BIBLIOGRAPHICAL NOTE AND
  ACKNOWLEDGMENTS   xiii

CHRONOLOGICAL NOTE   xiv

ABBREVIATIONS   xv

I 'TO DEFINE THE THACKERAYAN
   ONENESS'   *p.* 1

The method proposed, *p.* 1. Encouragement from bibliography,
p. 3.

II THE ONENESS OF THE MATERIALS   *p.* 5

The consanguinity of the personages, *p.* 5. The stretch of scene
and time, *p.* 8.

III THE ONENESS OF FORM AND MANNER   *p.* 11

The lack of a formal plot, *p.* 11. Continuity, *p.* 20. Continuity:
certain methods, *p.* 25. Continuity: the method of imagery, *p.* 35.
Continuity: the method of epic imagery, *p.* 41. Intercommunications, *p.* 49. Continuity: prose style, *p.* 50.

IV THE CONTENT OF THE AUTHORIAL 'I'   *p.* 55

The limits of self-expression for a novelist, *p.* 55. Thackeray and
the content of the 'I', *p.* 56. The limits of autobiography, *p.* 66.

V THE AUTHOR'S CONDUCT OF HIS
   COMMENTARY   *p.* 71

The novelist as dramatist or historian, *p.* 71. 'Panorama' and
'scene', *p.* 82. The status of the thing seen, *p.* 85. An addition
made to the scene, *p.* 88. The commentary in the action, *p.* 90.
The action in the commentary, *p.* 97. Time standing still, *p.* 108.
Variety, *p.* 110. The links with the shorter writings, *p.* 111. Story
and musing, *p.* 112.

CONTENTS

VI THE AUTHOR'S TRUTHFULNESS OF

PERSONAGE AND ACTION *p.* 115

'This person writing strives to tell the truth,' *p.* 115. Truthfulness
of personage, *p.* 116. Complete truthfulness of personage, *p.* 123.
Milly Costigan, *p.* 137. Beatrix Esmond, *p.* 144. Character
various within itself, *p.* 148. The puzzle of character in time,
p. 151. The ruling passion, *p.* 155. Surprise of character and
actions, *p.* 157. Few 'tricks of art', *p.* 164. Fragments of formal
plot, *p.* 172.

VII THE AUTHOR'S PHILOSOPHY *p.* 175

Lack of logic, *p.* 175. No lack of thought, *p.* 179. Truth about
the whole range of society, *p.* 182. On conditions of authors,
p. 196. New truth about emotions and moral character, *p.* 198.
The 'form' of truth new and old, *p.* 204. 'We may never forget
truth', *p.* 206. Commentary, early, middle and late, *p.* 209.
Sermonizing, *p.* 216. A constant attitude to truth, *p.* 220. Truth
and 'the ordinary man', *p.* 228. 'The world of all of us', *p.* 229.
The authorial person and the ordinary man, *p.* 235. Indecisive
moralist, *p.* 240. The author's estimate of himself, *p.* 248. The
author and human frailty, *p.* 251. The core of truth, *p.* 255.
A summary, *p.* 266. 'The chords of all his memory', *p.* 267.

APPENDIX I. THACKERAY'S PERSONAGES AND

HIS FRIENDS *p.* 273

Biographical infiltration, *p.* 273. Historical criticism, *p.* 277.
Weighing the evidence, *p.* 283.

APPENDIX II. THACKERAY AND TWO LATER

NOVELISTS *p.* 288

'Shakespeare is a great poet', *p.* 288. Thackeray and George
Eliot, *p.* 289. Thackeray and Henry James, *p.* 296.

INDEXES *p.* 307

PLATES

Thackeray as drawn by Richard Doyle *facing p.* 62
Thackeray's 'portrait' of himself *facing p.* 63
Thackeray's design on the wrapper of
the parts of *Vanity Fair* *facing p.* 63

PREFACE

At the present day the place of Thackeray's novels in the regard of Englishmen, and perhaps also of Americans, has its interest for any historian of literary reputations. Most of the critics whose work achieves print dislike or slight them, and give us the impression that they speak for everybody. Having come to like them very much in recent years, I expected to meet polite disapproval—that glaze of the eye behind which the well-disposed mind seeks to turn the conversation—when I admitted to writing on them; only to find that the embarrassment was on my side alone. Not one of a dozen or so people but voiced either respect or warm liking for Thackeray's novels. On the chance evidence of this dozen people, most of whom do not teach English literature, one of whom is an American, who are of various ages (I show in my book that age counts in a reader of Thackeray) around and above forty—on the evidence of these people, his novels are still honoured and read. I recall the experience of Neville Cardus, given us in his autobiography; at a time when printed criticism assured him of a due arrest, probably a death, in the passion for the novels of Dickens, his inquiries for them at the local public library always found them 'out'. To be in and out of the turnstile of a public library is, I claim, a proof that a novel is alive, and well alive. Of Thackeray's novels, *Vanity Fair* and perhaps *Esmond* would by that test be found still in motion. Probably *The Virginians* also—the British Broadcasting Company presented it a year or two ago as a serial radio-play, and this caused some people, I understand, to read the original. But where we are concerned with novels that have been popular for much, if not all, of a century, a further test is to be made before the certificate of death is signed. Of the millions of copies printed during their long heyday, tens of thousands, inherited perhaps and dingy, survive on private shelves. I have made no enquiries of public libraries, but if they do little traffic in Thackeray, private copies, on my evidence, still have their devoted readers.

This may mean—I take the opportunity to draw a moral for the public at large—that, given a proper send-off, people would be ready to rescue and piously furnish the house in Young Street, Kensington—double-fronted, bow-windowed, handsome as domiciles go in this London of makeshifts and accommodations—the house where most of Thackeray's greatest work was done. There it stands, ninety years after his death, empty, black and glum, discoursing in tones Dickensianly heavy on his old theme of vanity of vanities. It could live again and blossom—yes, with the freshness of his novels—as the London houses of Carlyle and Dickens now blossom, and the house of Keats, whose poetry Thackeray was one of the first to welcome into the circle of great literature.

As to the method used in my book, I am aware that the argument would proceed at a smarter pace had I interposed fewer quotations in support of it. Their amplitude may be allowed in fairness to Thackeray since he is not now read universally; and by the same token in fairness to some of my readers.

I wish to thank my wife who introduced me to the critical writings of William Caldwell Roscoe, and who, at the penultimate stage of its career, read my manuscript, making valuable suggestions. I am also indebted to the book she has recently written on the novels of the 1840's, and in particular for her help in interpreting the Preface to *Pendennis*.

G. T.

BIRKBECK COLLEGE
UNIVERSITY OF LONDON

July 1953

BIBLIOGRAPHICAL NOTE AND ACKNOWLEDGMENTS

The quotations from Thackeray's writings are taken from the most authentic editions I myself possess. To make amends to my readers, who will probably possess different editions, I have referred the quotations to the chapter of the novel they come from, taking the chapter numbers from the Oxford Thackeray. The text used for *Philip*, *Lovel the Widower*, *Denis Duval* and *The Roundabout Papers*, is that of *The Cornhill*, where they first appeared, and that for *Vanity Fair*, *Pendennis*, *The Newcomes* and *The Virginians* what in a rough and ready way I may call 'the first edition in book form', not inquiring too closely into issues and variants, which may be safely assumed to have no pertinence for my present purpose. The text used for *Esmond* is that of the Oxford Thackeray, from which all other writings of Thackeray are quoted.

There are advantages in quoting from the original or early texts, advantages which are reduced when a later edition corrects a slip committed in the turmoil of quick writing, or misprint, or when it records an authentic new reading. Such errors I have silently put right, but I have not troubled to collate quotations from early texts with the last of the author's lifetime. Perhaps, therefore, an improved reading has not always been honoured.

For permission to quote from Thackeray's letters I thank Mrs Hester Thackeray Fuller, the editor, my friend Mr Gordon Ray, and the publisher, the Harvard University Press. I am grateful also to Mrs Hilda Spear, who helped to check many of my quotations.

G. T.

CHRONOLOGICAL NOTE

The following are the dates of the works of Thackeray most frequently referred to in this book.

[1811 Thackeray born.]

1839–40 *Catherine*, periodically in *Fraser's* (May 1839– Feb. 1840).

1843 *The Ravenswing*, periodically in *Fraser's* (April– Sept.). 'Dennis Haggarty's Wife', *Fraser's* (Oct.)

1844 *The Luck of Barry Lyndon*, periodically in *Fraser's* (Jan.–Dec.); revised edition, *The Memoirs of Barry Lyndon, Esq.*, 1856.

1846 *Notes of a Journey from Cornhill to Grand Cairo*.

1846–7 *The Book of Snobs*, periodically in *Punch* (Feb. 1846–Feb. 1847).

1847–8 *Vanity Fair*, in parts (Jan. 1847–July 1848).

1848–50 *The History of Pendennis*, in parts (Nov. 1848– Dec. 1850).

1852 *The History of Henry Esmond, Esq.*, 3 vols.

1853–5 *The Newcomes*, in parts (Oct. 1853–Aug. 1855).

1857–9 *The Virginians*, in parts (Nov. 1857–Oct. 1859).

1860–3 *The Roundabout Papers*, periodically in *The Cornhill* (Jan. 1860–Nov. 1863).

1860 *Lovel the Widower*, periodically in *The Cornhill* (Jan.–June).

1861–2 *Philip*, periodically in *The Cornhill* (Jan. 1861– Aug. 1862).

[1863 Thackeray died.]

1864 *Denis Duval*, periodically in *The Cornhill* (March– June).

ABBREVIATIONS

Allingham	*William Allingham: A Diary*, ed. H. Allingham and D. Radford (1907).
The Brontës	*The Brontës: their Lives, Friendships and Correspondence*, 'Shakespeare Head' Brontë, ed. T. J. Wise and J. A. Symington, 4 vols. (1932).
Brownell	W. C. Brownell, *Victorian Prose Masters* (New York, 1902).
Greig	J. Y. T. Greig, *Thackeray: a Reconsideration* (1950).
Johnson, *Lives*	Samuel Johnson, *Lives of the English Poets*, ed. George Birkbeck Hill, 3 vols. (1905).
Ray	G. N. Ray, '*Vanity Fair*: One Version of the Novelist's Responsibility,' *Transactions of the Royal Society of Literature*, New Series, xxv (1950), pp. 87–101.
Roscoe	*Poems and Essays by the late William Caldwell Roscoe*, ed. R. H. Hutton, 2 vols. (1860).
Ruskin, *Works*	*The Complete Works of John Ruskin*, ed. E. T. Cook and A. Wedderburn, 39 vols. (1903–12).
Saintsbury	George Saintsbury, *A Consideration of Thackeray* (1931).
Thackeray, *Letters*	*The Letters and Private Papers of William Makepeace Thackeray*, ed. G. N. Ray, 4 vols. (1945–6).

CHAPTER I

'To Define the Thackerayan Oneness'

The work of every author cannot but round itself into a unity, of which every reader achieves his own sense at his own rate. As we read, our sense of this unity improves in strength and clearness. The process of improvement, however, does not receive much of our attention during the first stages of reading. It is the differences between one work and another that we notice first—the differences between *Love's Labour's Lost* and *The Winter's Tale*, even between *Hamlet* and *Lear*, the differences between *An Evening Walk* and the *Lyrical Ballads*, even between *The Prelude* and *The Excursion*, the differences between *Pickwick Papers* and *Edwin Drood*, even between *Our Mutual Friend* and *Bleak House*. As we read on, finding the author's work 'before, behind us and on every hand', we come to feel more at home in it. The mass shrinks to a whole that is manageable. And our sense of this whole being the maturer achievement, the criticism we value most is that which best helps to express it, which comes nearest to naming the foundation of all the writings in the one mind that produced them, which has deciphered and described the one stamp that seals every page of the tens of thousands, which has enriched for us the content of such generalities as the 'Shakespearian', the 'Wordsworthian', the 'Dickensian'.

The critic of Thackeray's novels has little power of choice, as I see it, over the method he adopts. From an early stage he must seek to define the Thackerayan oneness. Inevitably, he is first struck by the separateness of the novels. Having its own FINIS, each of them calls for treatment by itself, treatment such as Saintsbury gave each in turn when he wrote those vigorous prefaces to the Oxford edition—later collected in *A Consideration of Thackeray*. As first encountered, each novel differs enough from its fellows to tempt the critic to play the impressionist, calling *Esmond* the prince among them— that novel which is at once rapid and melancholy, a thing of silver and fire—calling *Vanity Fair* the one most 'lively on the wires', *The Newcomes* the most golden, *Pendennis* and *The Virginians* the most delightful (as the Pastoral is the most delightful of the symphonies of Beethoven), the unfinished *Denis Duval* the most Dickensian (if we bear *Great Expectations* in mind), that long *nouvelle*, *Lovel the Widower*, a great bell scribbled all over with personal jottings, giving out a deep note; *Philip* the most indolently lordly, and, if the thinnest in matter, containing imagery and description unmatched for scorching richness outside pieces of late Shakespeare or Ruskin—for these later novels belong to the later years of the shortish life of Thackeray, not years of decline but of an older age which, begun almost in youth, was, as Longinus would say, the older age of Thackeray. Some things certainly may be said for the novels one by one. But if, accepting the account I began with, we are on the watch for the dawning of a sense of the Thackerayan oneness, we may be surprised at the speed with which it comes upon us. For Thackeray is an author who encourages it to dawn early. His works, planned to be as alike as possible, implore us to take them together. 'Of few writers', Saintsbury asserted, 'can it be said with so much confidence as of Thackeray, that he is all of a piece.'[1] Or, to quote the

[1] *Corrected Impressions*, 1895, p. 8.

testimony of another critic, 'A writer like Thackeray, who is throughout his career so true to himself, cannot properly be judged by samples.'[1] Our sense of the Thackerayan coherence soon becomes dominant, and we cease to be much aware of differences, ceasing to attend to the chronology of the novels, or, if we are reading his work in all its kinds, to the differences among articles, essays, lectures, sketches (literary and pictorial), stories, *nouvelles*, novels, verses, letters—though I shall be mainly concerned with the six long novels.

2

I find something to my purpose in the very bibliography of the long novels. Their format encouraged his first readers to see them as a batch. Thackeray did not give those readers anything like the material objects we read him in. On one occasion he spoke ingeniously of 'lisping in numbers'.[2] It was in numbers, in monthly parts, that four of his six long novels were first published. He responded, that is, to the cue of Dickens, who had gathered readers by the tens of thousands, giving them his long expensive novels in spaced-out pieces they could conveniently afford to buy. Thackeray saw his chance, though not to rival or to beat Dickens; he was always keenly and amusedly aware of the gap between the degrees of their popularity; when he crowed that 'Mrs. Perkins's Ball' had brought him 'very nearly' the popularity of Dickens, he ended broken-windedly:

that is Perkins *500* Dickens *25000* only that difference![3]

Seeing his chance, Thackeray published *Vanity Fair*, *The History of Pendennis*, *The Newcomes* and *The Virginians* in parts, eighty-nine parts in all, each part

---

[1] A. A. Jack, *Thackeray: A Study*, 1895, p. 17.
[2] *The Virginians*, ch. xxxv.   [3] *Letters*, II, 258.

1-2

wearing the yellow cover that came to be associated with him as the cover of green or duck-egg blue with Dickens. Of the other two novels, *The History of Henry Esmond, Esq.* was published at one go in three bound volumes; but the 'jaundiced livery'—the conscious phrase is Thackeray's[1]—was not denied to Philip Firmin: *The Adventures of Philip*, and also the six instalments of *Lovel the Widower* and the four of the unfinished *Denis Duval*, appeared in numbers of *The Cornhill*, which under Thackeray's editorship, and later, sported the old saffron. At the end of his busy career, then, Thackeray stood before those of his first readers who had not called in the services of a binder as a shelf of pamphlets, like a long run of numbers of a magazine. With the modest air of being no more than ephemera—or their monthly equivalent—of all being alike and of the same importance or unimportance, they wore the appearance of uniformity.

This bibliographical coherence is the emblem of my present study. The Thackerayan unity is a thing felt strongly, however many separable virtues and faults contribute to its formation. And because what we feel strongly we see as magnificent—that at least is how I see it—the Thackerayan oneness is worth investigating.

[1] *The Virginians*, ch. xxxv.

CHAPTER II

The Oneness of the Materials

Thackeray did what he could to give his fiction a unity that is obvious.

In the first place he was at pains to link his novels by the consanguinity of the personages. The author of *Joseph Andrews* had invented a new member of the family invented by Richardson, but Thackeray, like Balzac and to a lesser degree Disraeli, promoted such transferences into a practice. His novels hang together like a dynasty. If, unlike Balzac and Trollope, he did not group them, or some of them, under one name, it was not for lack of choice. *Esmond*—to neglect chronology of composition as we do in arranging the line of Shakespeare's history plays—leads on to *The Virginians*. Arthur Pendennis, who is the centre of *The History of Pendennis*, is the supposed editor of the materials that make *The Newcomes*, and with his family participates in the action of both. And though at the close of *The Newcomes* we are invited to see him 'disappear...as irrevocably as Eurydice', he returns to share and record the adventures of *Philip*. Lady Kew, important in *The Newcomes*, is the sister of Lord Steyne, who is important in *Vanity Fair*, reappears in *Pendennis* as the friend of Major Pendennis, and is mentioned in *The Newcomes* and *Philip*. By means of *The Newcomes* we learn the later history of some of the personages of *Vanity Fair*. The links between novel and novel are sometimes so fine as to declare themselves all the more as placed deliberately. Even in *Lovel the Widower* the Rev. Charles Honeyman and the dubious Sherrick,

5

prominent in *The Newcomes*, get a passing reference. And though the great novels fall into two main groups, those groups themselves are not without their family interconnection. The Warrington of both *Pendennis* and *The Newcomes* is a descendant of the family into which the daughter of Henry Esmond marries. He is also mentioned in *The Virginians* and *Lovel the Widower*. The truncated *Shabby Genteel Story*, which Thackeray foresaw, I think, as a long novel, provided the situation out of which with a little juggling of dates sprang, a generation later, the action of *Philip*. Most of his novels are about the same families. The curious reader may consult the *Thackeray Dictionary*, compiled by Isadore Gilbert Mudge and M. Earl Sears, a fascinating work of the pious sort which, when the novelist is Thackeray, serves a critical purpose.

Thackeray picked up a personage in an earlier novel for use later. If he had foreseen this usefulness he would no doubt have introduced more of them earlier; Clive Newcome reappears in *Philip*: if Thackeray could have gone back, the family might have been introduced in some corner or other of *Vanity Fair*.

Chesterton, I find, has put all this very well in a passage contrasting Thackeray with Dickens:

The habit of revising old characters is so strong in Thackeray that *Vanity Fair*, *Pendennis*, *The Newcomes*, and *Philip* are in one sense all one novel. Certainly the reader sometimes forgets which one of them he is reading. Afterwards he cannot remember whether the best description of Lord Steyne's red whiskers or Mr. Megg's rude jokes occurred in *Vanity Fair*, or *Pendennis*; he cannot remember whether his favourite dialogue between Mr. and Mrs. Pendennis occurred in *The Newcomes*, or in *Philip*. Whenever two Thackeray characters in two Thackeray novels could by any possibility have been contemporary, Thackeray delights to connect them. He makes Major Pendennis nod to Dr. Firmin, and Colonel Newcome ask Major Dobbin to dinner. Whenever two characters could not possibly have been contemporary he goes out of his way to make one the remote ancestor of the other. Thus he created the great house of Warrington solely to connect a "blue-bearded" Bohemian journalist with the blood of Henry Esmond. It is quite impossible to conceive Dickens keeping up this elaborate connection between all his characters and all his books, especially across the ages. It would give us a kind of shock if we learnt from Dickens that Major Bagstock was the nephew of Mr. Chester.[1]

The practice was approved, as we might expect, by Browning, who met it in Balzac:

for *you* [Elizabeth Barrett], with your love of a "story", what an unceasing delight must be that very ingenious way of [Balzac], by which he connects the new novel with its pre-decessors—keeps telling you more and more news yet of the people you have got interested in, but seemed to have done with...they keep alive, moving—[is it] not ingenious?[2]

'People you have got interested in'—a novelist would do well to satisfy himself that his personages have caught the interest of his reader before he brings them round again. This proviso underlies a complaint Ruskin made a quarter of a century after Thackeray's death:

may I be allowed to express one of the increasing discomforts of my old age, in never being allowed by novelists to stay long enough with people I like, after I once get acquainted with them. It has always seemed to me that tales of interesting persons should not end with their marriage;[3] and that, for the general good of society, the varied energies and expanding peace of wedded life would be better subjects

---

[1] Dickens, *Edwin Drood & Master Humphrey's Clock*, Everyman ed., pp. xvii f. The fourth word of the quotation should perhaps read 'reviving'.

[2] Letter of 27 April 1846: *Letters of Robert Browning and Elizabeth Barrett Barrett*, 1899, II, 107.

[3] This had been Thackeray's opinion: see below, p. 19.

of interest than the narrow aims, vain distresses, or passing joys of youth.

I felt this acutely the other day, when the author[1] to whom we owe the most finished and faithful rendering ever yet given of the character of the British soldier, answered my quite tearful supplication to her, that Mignon and Lucy might not vanish in an instant into the regions of Praeterita and leave me desolate, by saying that she was herself as sorry to part with Mignon as I could be, but that the public of to-day would never permit insistence on one conception beyond the conventionally established limits. To which distrust I would answer—and ask you[2], as the interpreter of widest public opinion, to confirm me in answering—that for readers even of our own impatient time, the most beautiful surprises of novelty and the highest praises of invention are in the recognised and natural growth of one living creation; and neither in shifting the scenes of fate as if they were lantern slides, nor in tearing down the trellises of our affections that we may train the branches elsewhere.[3]

Thackeray, happier in an earlier time, had every confidence that reappearance would be welcome. Nor should we contrast times so much as the power of novelists. Were there any complaints, I wonder, when the Christina Light of *Roderick Hudson*, who before that novel ended had married the Prince, reappeared in *The Princess Casamassima*?

2

There is also a geographical and historical principle of unification. The action of the novels occupies often the same named places—various districts of London, Brighton, Brussels, Baden-Baden, 'Pumpernickel', Virginia. And whether the same or not, all share the

---

[1] Mrs Arthur Stannard, who produced popular fiction under the name of John Strange Winter. For further annotation see Ruskin, *Works*, XXXIV, 615 and XXXVII, 592 f.
[2] The editor of the *Daily Telegraph*.   [3] *Works*, XXXIV, 615.

same map, which is as fixed, externally documented, indivisibly one as the stretch of public history to which all the novels also relate themselves. This geographical, as well as temporal range is indicated in *The Virginians*, where after the encounter of the French and British at Duquesne, 'where the great city of Pittsburg now stands', Thackeray comments:

It was strange, that in a savage forest of Pennsylvania, a young Virginian officer should fire a shot, and waken up a war which was to last for sixty years, which was to cover his own country and pass into Europe, to cost France her American colonies, to sever ours from us, and create the great Western republic; to rage over the Old World when extinguished in the New....[1]

And moreover, in time at least the stretch of the novels is even wider than this, since near the heart of *Esmond* lies much of the Stuart-Hanover conflict. Nor must that word 'stretch' imply any tenuity or sparsity of furniture; along the stretch historical detail is sown thick, and almost always it is accurate. The delicacy of this historical detail was noted early on; one contemporary reader, for instance, noted that Thackeray

constantly uses names known before, and almost in the same state of life. Thus Miss Pinkerton [of *Vanity Fair*] keeps a school at [Chiswick], and corresponds or has corresponded with the great lexicographer. Now Pinkerton is a name well known as that of [an antiquary and historian, 1758–1826] and it is really not improbable but that his daughters [who did not in fact exist] might have kept the school;

and the writer goes on to instance, apropos of Becky's father, an artist of the name of Sharp who died in 1840.[2]

---

[1] Ch. VI.
[2] J. H. Friswell, 'Novelists' Names', *The Train*, Oct. 1856. For Michael William Sharp the painter, see *D.N.B.*

This panorama of time, place and public events relates together whatever Thackeray in his novels gives as happening in pockets of it. This is history, he seems to say; in one novel I give you one sample of the minutely peopled soil, and in another a further sample taken from the same huge landscape. He offers his wares as new pieces for that vast jigsaw that none of us can choose but work at as we inevitably come to know more of the past.

These obvious means of unification show that Thackeray planned his work to form a whole. If I now turn to means that are less obvious, it is to these obvious ones that I add them.

CHAPTER III

The Oneness of Form and Manner

As 'a work of construction' Thackeray declared *Tom Jones* to be 'quite a wonder'.[1] None of his own novels are wonders of this sort, or as much collected into themselves even as *Dombey and Son*. As an architect of plot he contrasted his powers with those of the admired Dumas:

> Alexandre Dumas describes himself, when inventing the plan of a work, as lying silent on his back for two whole days on the deck of a yacht in a Mediterranean port. At the end of the two days he arose, and called for dinner. In those two days he had built his plot. He had moulded a mighty clay, to be cast presently in perennial brass. The chapters, the characters, the incidents, the combinations were all arranged in the artist's brain ere he set a pen to paper.[2]

It was on the authority of an inspiration more diffuse than Dumas's that *The Newcomes*, for instance, was begun:

> Two years ago, walking with my children in some pleasant fields, near to Berne in Switzerland, I strayed from them into a little wood; and, coming out of it presently, told them how the story had been revealed to me somehow, which for three and twenty months the reader has been pleased to follow.[3]

And, as Professor Greig has noted, Thackeray experienced his sylvan vision very late in the day—he had already written enough of the novel for three numbers, though it is of course possible that, before publication

---

[1] *English Humourists*, 'Lecture the Fifth. Hogarth, Smollett, and Fielding'.
[2] *Roundabout Papers*, 'De Finibus'.   [3] *The Newcomes*, ch. LXXX.

began a month or so later, he made revisions.[1] The only
big novel he had the chance to provide with a perfect
shape before publication was *Esmond*, which, as I have
said, he published all at once. Even there the chance
cannot be said to have been taken. What shape *Esmond*
has is mainly the effect of the sudden marriage of
Esmond and Rachel at the very end, which throws a
net, but a loose one, round the whole story—I shall
speak of the quality of its surprise later. Here and there
in all the novels enough pattern exists to suggest that
Thackeray had it in him to have made a big intricate
unity. It was left unmade from choice, I think, even if
from easy choice. For him the novel form was a vast
ground inviting him to know it as a Cockney knows
London, with knowledge that is the result of explorations
coming to an end simply because they stop. The lack
of edged shape in his novels is not a negative thing, but
deliberate and positive, the achievement of an aspiration towards rendering the vastness of the world and the
never-endingness of time. He was at home in vastness
and never-endingness—at home in them because of an
untiring delight for taking in details, the nature and
import of which I shall consider later. One of his most
characteristic gestures is to cut a matter off with an 'etc.,
etc.'.[2] This formula he uses as an artist who spares the
reader what both know too well, not as a weakling seeking
to cover up exhaustion. Detail flows on to his page in-
cessantly. And when in addition to letting it flow, he
thinks about the implications it has for him—and he
thinks about them very often—there is no stoppage of
the detail meanwhile. When he thinks and muses over
the detail, no break is perceptible—it is merely as if he

[1] Greig, p. 174.
[2] I have noted the earlier use of this gesture by Peacock and Disraeli.

is easing his stance by transferring his weight from one leg to the other—of which more later. He needed an immense size of novel because the products of his imagination—the hundreds of people and their countless actions—were subjected to the attentions of the understanding and the emotions together. He gave the novel all his mind. Whatever the limitations of that mind when placed against George Eliot's, and perhaps Fielding's, he gave it all to his novels. So vast was his idea of the form that only the writer complete could breathe in it long enough to create it whole.

At the close of *The Newcomes* the narrator 'keeps a lingering hold of [the] hand' of the reader, loth to sever the connection, though hoping to form it again.[1] Long as are his novels, he would have preferred them longer. The times, he noted, were against any writer's employing the narrative method open to Cervantes, and which he may have envied:

> I read Don Quixote nearly through when I was away. What a vitality in those two characters! What gentlemen they both are! I wish Don Quixote was not thrashed so very often. There are sweet pastoralities through the book, and that piping of shepherds and pretty sylvan ballet which dances always round the principal figures is delightfully pleasant to me—it would kill any book now to make it so long, and introduce all those long fantastic processions interludes and the like.[2]

Meanwhile, in the midst of the nineteenth century, there was no doubt of a certain good fortune: he could reap the benefits of publishing in parts.

We do not yet know enough about the effect of that method of publishing on the shape of novels. The effect,

---

[1] Quoted below, p. 80.   [2] *Letters*, III, 304.

it is already clear, was considerable.[1] For the parts into which the novel was to fall, though they might not be fixed in number from the start, were fixed in size. Whatever the method of composing adopted by the individual novelist, his novel had to fall into parts of the right size; and, it followed, into parts coherent enough to stand on their own. A novelist like Trollope may have found the shaping of the parts unnecessarily irksome, since he wrote his novels complete before their piecemeal issue began. But it was a very different thing for Thackeray, as it was for Dickens. Thackeray wrote his novels part by part, as the printer printed them, and as the reader read them. He therefore saw the parts, most of them, before there was a whole to see; some of the parts may have been seen before the whole was even foreseen, or foreseen with any distinctness. This way of working suited him well. His genius loved a rhythm of furious effort alternating with indolent recovery, of solitude at the desk (even though the desk were in club or inn) alternating with society (particularly at the dinner-table). And this rhythm of working was made the more attainable for him by the rhythm of publishing. He could enjoy what he called 'the grumble and excitement of the yellow cover',[2] just as if he were still a journalist. Happily as a journalist, he gave his novels as much as possible of the quality he poured into *The Roundabout Papers*, that late collection of pieces contributed to *The Cornhill* by its editor, which record the hovering movements of a free, mature, homely intelligence so subtly as to seem a work of nature rather than art, so gently as

[1] In these studies, as they concern Dickens, Professor John Butt has been a pioneer. The most interesting result so far has, I think, been 'Dickens at work on *Dombey and Son*', in which he collaborated with Kathleen Tillotson (*Essays and Studies 1951*, edited by the present writer for the English Association).

[2] *Letters*, III, 251.

to seem breathing rather than speech. And he kept the process going as long as possible; no other novel published in parts, to my knowledge, reached so high a number of them as *Pendennis*, *The Newcomes*, and *The Virginians*, all of which reached twenty-four. This being so, it would be best to think of his novels as the batches of manuscript he thrust into the hands of the despairing printer's boy, and next best to think of them as they existed on the shelves of their first readers, as a mighty run of pamphlets. His genius fulfilled itself most happily in the long string of parts. Following the sentences in honour of Dumas which I quoted at the beginning of this chapter comes the account of his own way of covering ground: the imagery he uses tallies accurately with its major term:

My Pegasus wont fly, so as to let me survey the field below me. He has no wings, he is blind of one eye certainly, he is restive, stubborn, slow; crops a hedge when he ought to be galloping, or gallops when he ought to be quiet. He never will show off when I want him. Sometimes he goes at a pace which surprises me. Sometimes, when I most wish him to make the running, the brute turns restive, and I am obliged to let him take his own time. I wonder do other novel-writers experience this fatalism? They *must* go a certain way, in spite of themselves.[1]

Essentially a novelist of a thousand brilliant spurts, it is probable that no vast work would have come from him at all if the system of publishing in parts, whether separately or in magazines, had not allowed him to write in lengths timed beyond dispute by the public clock. And so it is also probable that having got the rhythm of the huge job going, he need not have changed from one novel to another where he did. As it was, there was as little closing down of the regular fountain as

[1] *Roundabout Papers*, 'De Finibus'.

possible. Why should there be? The reservoir tapped one fortnight was fed by kindly rains the other. There was little waiting about for ideas: he found them ready formed during the act of finishing the novel, or the piece of novel, on hand.[1] The ideas for *The Newcomes* were shaping while he was still working on *Esmond*[2]—a pro-

[1] When, for instance, he had almost finished *Vanity Fair*, the letter of a chance correspondent prompted him to sketch a sequel to some parts of it; he sat down on the spot, it seems, and spun off a whole lot more. Not much of this except the general idea was used to round off the last number of the novel—in transcribing the letter I limit myself to what concerns Becky:

Mrs. Rawdon Crawley, whom I saw last week, and whom I informed of your...desire to have her portrait, was good enough to permit me to copy a little drawing made of her "in happier days," she said with a sigh, by Smee, the Royal Academician.

Mrs. Crawley now lives in a small but very pretty little house in Belgravia, and is conspicuous for her numerous charities, which always get into the newspapers, and her unaffected piety. Many of the most exalted and spotless of her own sex visit her, and are of opinion that she is a *most injured woman*. There is no *sort of truth* in the stories regarding Mrs. Crawley and the late Lord Steyne. The licentious character of that nobleman alone gave rise to reports from which, alas! the most spotless life and reputation cannot always defend themselves. The present Sir Rawdon Crawley (who succeeded his late uncle, Sir Pitt, 1832; Sir Pitt died on the passing of the Reform Bill) does not see his mother, and his undutifulness is a cause of the deepest grief to that admirable lady. "If it were not for *higher things*", she says, how could she have borne up against the world's calumny, a wicked husband's cruelty and falseness, and the thanklessness (sharper than a serpent's tooth) of an adored child? But she has been preserved, mercifully preserved, to bear all these griefs, and awaits her reward *elsewhere*. The italics are Mrs. Crawley's own.

She took the style and title of Lady Crawley for some time after Sir Pitt's death in 1832; but it turned out that Colonel Crawley, Governor of Coventry Island, had died of fever three months before his brother, whereupon Mrs. Rawdon was obliged to lay down the title which she had prematurely assumed.

The late Jos. Sedley, Esq., of the Bengal Civil Service, left her two lakhs of rupees, on the interest of which the widow lives in the practices of piety and benevolence before mentioned. She has lost what little good looks she once possessed, and wears false hair and teeth (the latter give her rather a ghastly look when she smiles), and—for a pious woman—is the best-crinolined lady in Knightsbridge district...

P.S. 2.—The India mail just arrived announces the utter ruin of the Union Bank of Calcutta, in which all Mrs. Crawley's money was. Will Fate never cease to persecute that suffering saint?' (*Letters*, II, 375 ff.; cf. the italics with those on pp. 26 f. below.)

[2] See *The Works of...Thackeray with Biographical Introductions by his Daughter, Anne Ritchie*, 13 vols., 1898-9, VIII, xxii.

cess of which the vision in the little wood near Berne was a culminating incident. This kind of overlap was the more practicable because the mood of his fiction, even where the matter was as different as it ever was with him, remained constant. Examine, for example, the evidence of the first paragraph of 'De Finibus', which we cannot but take as literal autobiography:

When Swift was in love with Stella, and despatching her a letter from London thrice a month by the Irish packet, you may remember how he would begin letter No. XXIII., we will say, on the very day XXII. had been sent away, stealing out of the coffee-house or the assembly so as to be able to prattle with his dear; "never letting go her kind hand, as it were",[1] as some commentator or other has said in speaking of the Dean and his amour. When Mr. Johnson, walking to Dodsley's, and touching the posts in Pall Mall as he walked, forgot to pat the head of one of them, he went back and imposed his hands on it,—impelled I know not by what superstition. I have this I hope not dangerous mania too. As soon as a piece of work is out of hand, and before going to sleep, I like to begin another: it may be to write only half a dozen lines: but that is something towards Number the Next. The printer's boy has not yet reached Green Arbour Court with his copy. Those people who were alive half an hour since, Pendennis, Clive Newcome, and (what do you call him? what was the name of the last hero? I remember now!) Philip Firmin have hardly drunk their glass of wine, and the mammas have only this minute got their children's cloaks on, and have been bowed out of my premises—and here I come back to the study again: *tamen usque recurro.*

And after fobbing off the readers who wish he were a different sort of novelist, he reverts to 'my original subject' with:

What an odd, pleasant, humorous, melancholy feeling it is to sit in the study, alone and quiet, now all these people are

[1] Cf. the ending of *The Newcomes*, quoted below pp. 79 f.

gone who have been boarding and lodging with me for twenty months! They have interrupted my rest: they have plagued me at all sorts of minutes: they have thrust themselves upon me when I was ill, or wished to be idle, and I have growled out a "Be hanged to you, can't you leave me alone now?" Once or twice they have prevented my going out to dinner. Many and many a time they have prevented my coming home, because I knew they were there waiting in the study, and a plague take them! and I have left home and family, and gone to dine at the Club, and told nobody where I went. They have bored me, those people. They have plagued me at all sorts of uncomfortable hours. They have made such a disturbance in my mind and house, that sometimes I have hardly known what was going on in my family, and scarcely have heard what my neighbour said to me. They are gone at last; and you would expect me to be at ease? Far from it. I should almost be glad if Woolcomb would walk in and talk to me; or Twysden reappear, take his place in that chair opposite me, and begin one of his tremendous stories.

Not begin a new story so much as continue an old— 'I like continuations', he declared in his 'Proposals for a Continuation of "Ivanhoe"'. 'I can't but see [*The Newcomes*]', he said, as 'a repetition of past performances'.[1] Of *Philip*, his last major work, he observed that

I can repeat old things in a pleasant way, but I have nothing fresh to say.[2]

In a sense—a crude flippant sense—he had nothing fresh to say, except perhaps certain things in *Esmond* and *Denis Duval*, after *Vanity Fair*, even after *The Book of Snobs*. And with his characteristic self-criticism went a vivid praise of the fertility of Dickens—his fertility for inventing with the utmost variety. If we take his self-criticism too seriously we shall misunderstand him, on

[1] *Letters*, III, 287.   [2] *Letters*, IV, 242 n.

this occasion as on others. There were several good reasons, some of which I have already given, for his keeping to the one field. There was no sense of thinness for William Caldwell Roscoe, his first great substantial critic,[1] when he noted that '*Vanity Fair* is the name, not of one, but of all Mr. Thackeray's books';[2] Roscoe noted also that 'his imagination [was] one which does not naturally conceive in separate wholes...'.[3] This being so, it is partly by accident that he did not melt several vast novels into one. 'You gentlemen', says Colonel Newcome,

"You gentlemen who write books, Mr. Pendennis, and stop at the third volume, know very well that the real story often begins afterwards".[4]

And towards the close of the book, Thackeray says:

We are ending our history, and yet poor Clive is but beginning the world.[5]

It is more regretful than accurate. The real story in a novel of Thackeray does not wait till after the novel is ended; but because he saw the careers of his personages as going on *pari passu* with the continuing of time, he would have liked to follow their courses even further than he did. If his times had allowed or, to put it

[1] Throughout my book I have drawn on W. C. Roscoe's long essay on Thackeray. A word of introduction is called for—Roscoe is quite unknown today, though his biographer, R. H. Hutton, rightly estimated his 'claims to some permanent, if modest, place in English literature' and rightly believed that 'Finer and subtler criticisms the present day has nowhere produced' (Roscoe, I, ix, cvi), praise which in effect was corroborated by Walter Bagehot (ibid., I, cxxii). Roscoe was one of that group of brilliant young men sufficiently indicated by the names I have just mentioned, who were among the first to benefit by the newly founded University College in Gower Street. His life was brief, running only from 1823 to 1858. The forty-page essay 'W. M. Thackeray, Artist and Moralist' was published originally in 1856, and therefore did not take account of *The Virginians*, *Philip*, *Lovel the Widower*, or the rest of the later writings.

[2] II, 281.   [3] II, 308.
[4] *The Newcomes*, ch. XXIII.   [5] Ch. LXXIV.

differently, if there had been more readers like the Brownings and Ruskin, or like Tennyson—

What I dislike is beginning a new novel. I should like to have a novel to read in a million volumes, to last me my life[1]

—with enough encouragement of this kind Thackeray might have given us a smaller number of even bigger novels.

If so, not much of what went into the six big novels would have gone unexpressed. As it is, his achievement is essentially what once did exist, the array of a hundred parts on the shelf. Those parts visibly had this larger, if looser, unity, suggesting with a sweep of saffron that the novels are to be read as one immense saga.

2

Instead of design Thackeray's novels give us continuity. This virtue was not claimed for them by their author, who seldom claimed any virtue for them—one of the pleasant things about him is the low value he placed on himself or anything of his. Far from claiming continuity, he imputed a stoppage to his novels at some point during their career for the reader. Whenever he made occasion to show someone dozing over a novel, that novel was one of his own. Brown the elder, displaying the amenities of the club to Brown the younger, finds a member unconscious:

What a calm and pleasant seclusion the library presents after the bawl and bustle of the newspaper-room! There is never anybody here. English gentlemen get up such a prodigious quantity of knowledge in their early life, that they leave off reading soon after they begin to shave, or never look at anything but a newspaper. How pleasant this

[1] Allingham, p. 293.

room is,—isn't it? with its sober draperies, and long calm lines of peaceful volumes—nothing to interrupt the quiet— only the melody of Horner's nose as he lies asleep upon one of the sofas. What is he reading? Hah! *Pendennis*, No. VII— hum, let us pass on.[1]

Or there is this from that late essay which begins its joke in the Ciceronian title 'De Finibus':

After a day's work (in which I have been depicting, let us say, the agonies of Louisa on parting with the Captain, or the atrocious behaviour of the wicked Marquis to Lady Emily) I march to the Club, proposing to improve my mind and keep myself "posted up", as the Americans phrase it, with the literature of the day. And what happens? Given, a walk after luncheon, a pleasing book, and a most comfortable arm-chair by the fire, and you know the rest. A doze ensues. Pleasing book drops suddenly, is picked up once with an air of some confusion, is laid presently softly in lap: head falls on comfortable arm-chair cushion: eyes close: soft nasal music is heard. Am I telling Club secrets? Of afternoons, after lunch, I say, scores of sensible fogies have a doze. Perhaps I have fallen asleep over that very book to which "Finis" has just been written. "And if the writer sleeps, what happens to the readers?" says Jones, coming down upon me with his lightning wit. What? You *did* sleep over it? And a very good thing too.

In the imputation of somniferousness to his novels Thackeray is telling us something important about them. He believes they should be enjoyable. Sometimes their enjoyableness is so exciting as to keep us awake, breathlessly or delightedly, as that of Dumas's did Thackeray:

I...began to read Monte Christo at six one morning and never stopped till eleven at night.[2]

---

[1] *Mr. Brown's Letters to his Nephew*, 'Mr. Brown the Elder takes Mr. Brown the Younger to a Club', I. Number VII of *Pendennis* consists of chs. XXIV–XXVI, racy chapters in which Pen begins his infatuation for Blanche Amory. [2] *Letters*, III, 304.

Let us by all means have as many novels as possible of the Dumas kind. The boy that Thackeray found absorbed in one of them earned the same epithet, 'sensible', as the fogy who dozed over one of Thackeray's:

it was a NOVEL that you were reading, you lazy, not very clean, good-for-nothing, sensible boy! It was D'Artagnan locking up General Monk in a box, or almost succeeding in keeping Charles the First's head on. It was the prisoner of the Château d'If cutting himself out of the sack fifty feet under water (I mention the novels I like best myself—novels without love or talking, or any of that sort of nonsense, but containing plenty of fighting, escaping, robbery, and rescuing)—cutting himself out of the sack, and swimming to the Island of Montecristo. O Dumas! O thou brave, kind, gallant old Alexandre! I hereby offer thee homage....[1]

But he goes on to bless his own novels for the unexpected reason that readers may owe one of them a sound and blissful doze, and if so, 'a very good thing too'. This recklessly humble way of talking is of course a proof of his awareness of his power: only a great novelist whom a mature reader does *not* sleep over—except in post-prandial circumstances to which even a thriller by Wilkie Collins would capitulate—can afford to impute to his work any soporiferousness and flagging.

In claiming continuity for his novels I am not thinking first of those qualities in a story which make most strongly for wakefulness. I do not propose to prove that his plots, though lacking design, have the power of making us read on to see 'what happens'. That they have this primary and necessary source of continuity I take for granted, reserving till later some remarks on their merits of probability, without which the readers Thackeray looked for would not have persisted in

[1] *Roundabout Papers*, 'On a Lazy Idle Boy'.

reading. Here I am speaking rather of pace and un-brokenness of pace, qualities within the reach of writings other than narrative.

That his novels achieve this more intellectual sort of continuity there is much evidence. Critics who admire them and critics who, speaking roundly, do not, agree in being aware of it, and, because they differ in what they name as continuing, witness to a continuity strongly flowing: together the separate streams make a river. Because of this I need not group my witnesses; a chronological order will do. A reviewer in *Fraser's* noted that in *Vanity Fair*

the narrative flows on with surprising quietness, considering the periodical form of publication for which it was written, and which ordinarily demands an "effect" of some sort at each monthly fall of the curtain.[1]

Praising a number of the same novel—the fifteenth, chapters LI–LIII—Charlotte Brontë wrote:

Forcible, exciting in its force, still more impressive than exciting, carrying on the interest of the narrative in a flow, deep, full, resistless, it is still quiet—as quiet as reflection, as quiet as memory....[2]

A few years later Roscoe, speaking of the novels in general, noted that Thackeray

tells you page after page of ordinary incident with the fresh-ness of a perennial spring.[3]

In 1861, the twenty-seven-year-old George du Maurier recommended *Vanity Fair* to his fiancée with

I should like you to read that Book of Books over again, as carefully as I have just done,

---

[1] Sept. 1848, p. 322.
[2] *The Brontës*, II, 201; letter of 29 March 1848.   [3] II, 271.

adding, 'and if you don't finish it a wiser woman than you began, I'll be demnitioned'.[1] A year later he read it again, unflaggingly down to its small details:

read Vanity Fair till 1 o'clock. Of all the magnificent works! It's as fine as the bible, perfect wit and wisdom in every line....[2]

Like du Maurier, Henry James bore witness to continuity, since the minutiae he praised come thick and fast:

There is no writer of whom one bears better being reminded, none from whom any chance quotation, to whom any chance allusion or reference, is more unfailingly delectable. Pick out something at hazard from Thackeray, and ten to one it is a prize.[3]

William Crary Brownell, one of the best critics America has produced, and she has produced many good ones, knew that

Thackerayans read " Philip "—or even " Lovel the Widower " —without finding a dull page in it...partly, no doubt, out of mere momentum. But every one cannot be a Thackerayan, and for others the interest of " Philip " now and then flags, probably.[4]

My next three witnesses dislike what is continuing—the chronological order adopted for convenience is telling us something of the course of Thackeray's reputation. Quiller-Couch wrote:

I dare to say that [his] gift of loose, informal, preaching was Thackeray's bane *as a novelist*. The ease with which it came to him, and the public's readiness to accept it, just tempted him to slouch along.[5]

---

[1] *The Young George du Maurier, a Selection of his Letters, 1860–67*, ed. Daphne du Maurier, 1951, p. 71.   [2] Ibid. p. 174.
[3] Review of *Thackerayana* in *The Nation*, New York, 9 Dec. 1875, p. 376.   [4] P. 14.
[5] *Charles Dickens and other Victorians*, 1925, p. 147.

Then there is Mr Edmund Wilson, who has amusingly compared the commentary in Thackeray's novels to the spilth of a leaking tap.[1] And, finally, Dr Leavis, who gets from Thackeray the meagre rewards of a mere 'going on and on'.[2]

'Mere momentum', a 'going on and on'—for 'mere' I suggest we read 'sheer', and I can claim the lectoral persistence of Dr Leavis as propitious—either the reader stops or he proceeds, and if he proceeds he is impelled forward with power, the inertia of an unwilling novel-reader being that of an unwilling donkey. But there is enough glad testimony to Thackeray's continuity without resorting to coercion, and testimony, too, from various angles.

3

It is because Thackeray placed a high value on continuousness that, here and there in the novels, he hit on certain methods of writing, some of which are more characteristic of later novelists than of his predecessors. I propose to distinguish two or three of them, mainly by the means of a display of passages.

First, his representation of the consciousness of his personages as lazily taking in whatever offers and going on doing so for some time. I shall show later that Thackeray in general is not greatly concerned with the mind itself, whether occupied lazily or vigorously, whether conscious or half-conscious. All the more remarkable, then, that he writes at times like a novelist for whom the stream of consciousness is of first importance. Here are some instances. First, of the method

[1] *Classics and Commercials*, 1951, p. 262.
[2] *The Great Tradition*, 1948, p. 21. I look into his paragraph on Thackeray in Appendix II, pp. 288 ff. below.

used casually, for the sake merely of raising a laugh at the odd way our minds effect their transitions from idea to idea:

"You were saying, Philip, that you love to recognise the merits of all men whom you see," says gentle Agnes, "and I believe you do".

"Yes!" cries Phil, tossing about the fair locks. "I think I do. Thank heaven, I do. I know fellows who can do many things better than I do—everything better than I do."

"Oh, Philip!" sighs the lady.

"But I don't hate 'em for it."

"You never hated any one, sir. You are too brave! Can you fancy Philip hating any one, mamma?"

Mamma is writing, "Mr. and Mrs. Talbot Twysden request the honour of Admiral and Mrs. Davis Locker's company at dinner on Thursday the so-and-so." "Philip what?" says mamma, looking up from her card. "Philip hating any one! Philip eating any one! Philip! we have a little dinner on the 24th. We shall ask your father to dine. We must not have too many of the family. Come in afterwards, please."[1]

In the following piece the method is used to indicate the irrepressibility of a narrow moral judgment: the heat of Mrs Hobson's indignation is partly conveyed by the vehement unsignalled intrusion of scraps of her direct speech into an indirect account of her thoughts and a direct account of the author's:

The breaking of the engagement with the Marquis of Farintosh was known in Bryanstone Square; and you may be sure interpreted by Mrs. Hobson in the light the most disadvantageous to Ethel Newcome. A young nobleman— with grief and pain Ethel's aunt must own the fact—a young man of notoriously dissipated habits but of great wealth and rank, had been pursued by the unhappy Lady Kew— Mrs. Hobson would *not* say by her *niece*, that were *too*

[1] *Philip*, ch. IX.

dreadful—had been pursued, and followed, and hunted down in the most notorious manner, and finally made to propose! Let Ethel's *conduct* and *punishment* be a warning to my dearest girls, and let them bless *Heaven* they have parents who are not worldly! After all the trouble and pains, Mrs. Hobson did not say *disgrace*, the Marquis takes *the very first pretext* to break off the match, and leaves the unfortunate girl for ever![1]

Or there is this—one of the most brilliant passages in Thackeray: Clive is listening to Barnes's lecture, and Ethel, the girl he ought to have married, is in the audience:

Of course she knew that Clive was present. She was aware of him as she entered the Hall; saw him at the very first moment; saw nothing but him I daresay, though her eyes were shut and her head was turned now towards her mother, and now bent down on the little niece's golden curls. And the past and its dear histories, and youth and its hopes and passions, and tones and looks for ever echoing in the heart, and present in the memory—these, no doubt, poor Clive saw and heard as he looked across the great gulf of time, and parting, and grief, and beheld the woman he had loved for many years. There she sits; the same, but changed: as gone from him as if she were dead; departed indeed into another sphere, and entered into a kind of death. If there is no love more in yonder heart, it is but a corpse unburied. Strew round it the flowers of youth. Wash it with tears of passion. Wrap it and envelop it with fond devotion. Break heart, and fling yourself on the bier, and kiss her cold lips and press her hand! It falls back dead on the cold breast again. The beautiful lips have never a blush or a smile. Cover them and lay them in the ground, and so take thy hat-band off, good friend, and go to thy business. Do you suppose you are the only man who has had to attend such a funeral? You will find some men smiling and at work the day after. Some come to the grave now and

[1] *The Newcomes*, ch. LXI. Cf. Becky Sharp's italics, p. 16 *n.* 1 above.

again out of the world, and say a brief prayer, and a "God bless her!" With some men, she gone, and her viduous mansion your heart to let, her successor, the new occupant, poking in all the drawers, and corners, and cupboards of the tenement, finds her miniature and some of her dusty old letters hidden away somewhere, and says—Was this the face he admired so? Why, allowing even for the painter's flattery, it is quite ordinary, and the eyes certainly do not look straight. Are these the letters you thought so charming? Well, upon my word, I never read anything more common-place in my life. See, here's a line half blotted out. O, I suppose she was crying then—some of her tears, idle tears. . . . Hark, there is Barnes Newcome's eloquence still plapping on like water from a cistern—and our thoughts, where have they wandered? far away from the lecture—as far away as Clive's almost. And now the fountain ceases to trickle; the mouth from which issued that cool and limpid flux ceases to smile; the figure is seen to bow and retire; a buzz, a hum, a whisper, a scuffle, a meeting of bonnets and wagging of feathers and rustling of silks ensues. Thank you! delightful I am sure! I really was quite overcome; Excellent; *So* much obliged, are rapid phrases heard amongst the polite on the platform. While down below, yaw! quite enough of *that*. Mary Jane cover your throat up, and don't kitch cold, and don't push *me*, please Sir. Arry! Coom along and av a pint a ale, &c., are the remarks heard, or perhaps not heard, by Clive Newcome, as he watches at the private entrance of the Athenaeum, where Sir Barnes's carriage is waiting with its flaming lamps, and domestics in state liveries. One of them comes out of the building bearing the little girl in his arms, and lays her in the carriage. Then Sir Barnes, and Lady Ann, and the Mayor; then Ethel issues forth, and as she passes under the lamps, beholds Clive's face as pale and sad as her own.[1]

It is in *Lovel the Widower*, however, that we get the most extended account of the mind's dealing with its

[1] *The Newcomes*, ch. LXVI.

experience while that experience is flowing into it; the subtlety of the account may be read in the shifting tenses of the verbs: Mr Batchelor, the supposed narrator, is recounting his acts and thoughts:

I did not cut any part of myself with my razor. I shaved quite calmly. I went to the family at breakfast. My impression is I was sarcastic and witty. I smiled most kindly at Miss Prior when she came in. Nobody could have seen from my outward behaviour that anything was wrong within. I was an apple. Could you inspect the worm at my core! No, no. Somebody, I think old Baker, complimented me on my good looks. I was a smiling lake. Could you see on my placid surface, amongst my sheeny water-lilies, that a corpse was lying under my cool depths? "A bit of devilled chicken?" "No, thank you. By the way, Lovel, I think I must go to town to-day." "You'll come back to dinner, of course?" "Well—no". "Oh, stuff! You promised me to-day and to-morrow. Robinson, Brown and Jones are coming to-morrow, and you must be here to meet them." Thus we prattle on. I answer, I smile, I say, "Yes, if you please, another cup," or, "Be so good as to hand the muffin", or what not. But I am dead. I feel as if I am under ground, and buried. Life, and tea, and clatter, and muffins are going on, of course; and daisies spring, and the sun shines on the grass whilst I am under it. Ah, dear me! it's very cruel: it's very, very lonely: it's very odd! I don't belong to the world any more. I have done with it. I am shelved away. But my spirit returns and flitters through the world, which it has no longer anything to do with: and my ghost, as it were, comes and smiles at my own tombstone. Here lies Charles Batchelor, the Unloved One. Oh! alone, alone, alone! Why, Fate! didst ordain that I should be companionless? Tell me where the Wandering Jew is, that I may go and sit with him. Is there any place at a lighthouse vacant?[1]

[1] The chapter of *Lovel the Widower* from which this passage is taken appeared in No. 6 of *The Cornhill*; four months earlier, in No. 2, Thackeray had printed an anonymous article, 'Life among the Lighthouses', which he may have expected to give additional point to this sally.

Who knows where is the Island of Juan Fernandez? Engage
me a ship and take me there at once. Mr. R. Crusoe,
I think? My dear Robinson, have the kindness to hand me
over your goatskin cap, breeches, and umbrella. Go home,
and leave *me* here. Would you know who is the solitariest
man on earth? That man am I. Was that cutlet which I ate
at breakfast anon, was that lamb which frisked on the mead
last week (beyond yon wall where the unconscious cucumber
lay basking which was to form his sauce)—I say, was that
lamb made so tender, that I might eat him? And my heart,
then? Poor heart! wert thou so softly constituted only that
women might stab thee? So I am a Muff, am I? And she
will always wear a lock of his "dear hair", will she? Ha!
ha! The men on the omnibus looked askance as they saw
me laugh. They thought it was from Hanwell, not Putney,
I was escaping. Escape? Who can escape? I went into
London. I went to the Clubs. Jawkins, of course, was there;
and my impression is that he talked as usual. I took another
omnibus, and went back to Putney. "I will go back and
revisit my grave", I thought. It is said that ghosts loiter
about their former haunts a good deal when they are first
dead; flit wistfully among their old friends and companions,
and I daresay, expect to hear a plenty of conversation and
friendly tearful remark about themselves. But suppose they
return, and find nobody talking of them at all? Or suppose,
Hamlet (Père, and Royal Dane) comes back and finds
Claudius and Gertrude very comfortable over a piece of cold
meat, or what not? Is the late gentleman's present position as
a ghost a very pleasant one? Crow, Cocks! Quick, Sun-dawn!
Open, Trap-door! *Allons*: it's best to pop underground
again. So I am a Muff, am I? What a curious thing that
walk up the hill to the house was! What a different place
Shrublands was yesterday to what it is to-day! Has the sun
lost its light, and the flowers their bloom, and the joke its
sparkle, and the dish its savour? Why, bless my soul! what is
Lizzy herself—only an ordinary woman—freckled certainly
—incorrigibly dull, and without a scintillation of humour;
and you mean to say, Charles Batchelor, that your heart

30

once beat about *that* woman? Under the intercepted letter of that cold assassin, my heart had fallen down dead, irretrievably dead. I remember, *à propos* of the occasion of my first death, that perpetrated by Glorvina—on my second visit to Dublin—with what a strange sensation I walked under some trees in the Phoenix Park beneath which it had been my custom to meet my False One Number 1. There were the trees—there were the birds singing—there was the bench on which we used to sit—the same, but how different! The trees had a different foliage, exquisite amaranthine; the birds sang a song paradisaical; the bench was a bank of roses and fresh flowers, which young Love twined in fragrant chaplets around the statue of Glorvina. Roses and fresh flowers? Rheumatisms and flannel-waistcoats, you silly old man! Foliage and Song? O namby-pamby driveller! A statue?—a doll, thou twaddling old dullard!—a doll with carmine cheeks, and a heart stuffed with bran——I say, on the night preceding that ride to and from Putney, I had undergone death—in that omnibus I had been carried over to t'other side of the Stygian Shore. I returned but as a passionless ghost, remembering my life-days, but not feeling any more. Love was dead, Elizabeth! Why, the doctor came, and partook freely of lunch, and I was not angry. Yesterday I called him names, and hated him, and was jealous of him. To-day I felt no rivalship; and no envy at his success; and no desire to supplant him. No—I swear—not the slightest wish to make Elizabeth mine if she would. I might have cared for her yesterday—yesterday I had a heart. Psha! my good sir or madam. You sit by me at dinner. Perhaps you are handsome, and use your eyes. Ogle away. Don't balk yourself, pray. But if you fancy I care a threepenny-piece about you—or for your eyes—or for your bonny brown hair—or for your sentimental remarks, sidelong warbled—or for your praise to (not of) my face— or for your satire behind my back—ah me!—how mistaken you are! *Peine perdue, ma chère dame!* The digestive organs are still in good working order—but the heart? *Caret.*[1]

---

[1] *Lovel the Widower,* ch. VI.

These passages indicate that the continuity of Thackeray's novels sprang from deeply within his nature. They indicate how well he himself was aware of the streamingness of experience. Not surprisingly, for he was one of those for whom narrative is as natural as the flow of the blood. Narrative pervades his writings. Even his thinking as it works in passages of commentary, both in and out of the novels, is a sort of narrative; it is closer to the narrative in his novels than to, say, the essays of Bacon.

4

Another method contributes to the sort of continuity I am remarking, the method of delaying the completion of what is to be said of a thing. Here are three compact instances, the first Mr Batchelor's, speaking to Miss Prior, the girl all the men in *Lovel the Widower* lose their hearts to:

"Let me see your eyes. Why do you wear spectacles? You never wore them in Beak Street", I say. You see I was very fond of the child. She had wound herself around me in a thousand fond ways. Owing to a certain Person's conduct my heart may be a ruin—a Persepolis, sir—a perfect Tadmor. But what then? May not a traveller rest under its shattered columns? May not an Arab maid repose there till the morning dawns and the caravan passes on? Yes, my heart is a Palmyra, and once a queen inhabited me (O Zenobia! Zenobia! to think thou shouldst have been led away captive by an O'D[owde]!) Now I am alone, alone in the solitary wilderness. Nevertheless, if a stranger comes to me I have a spring for his weary feet, I will give him the shelter of my shade. Rest thy cheek awhile, young maiden, on my marble—then go thy ways, and leave me.[1]

[1] Ch. II.

The stroke 'my marble' is kept till we had almost, but not quite, forgotten the image of the ruin. Similarly the stroke 'excavate' in this passage:

In letter No. 2, the first two pages are closely written in Clive's hand-writing, describing his pursuits and studies, and giving amusing details of the life at Baden, and the company whom he met there—narrating his *rencontre* with their Paris friend, M. de Florac, and the arrival of the Duchesse d'Ivry, ...whose titles the Vicomte will probably inherit. Not a word about Florac's gambling propensities are mentioned in the letter; but Clive honestly confesses that he has staked five napoleons, doubled them, quadrupled them, won ever so much, lost it all back again, and come away from the table with his original five pounds in his pocket—proposing never to play any more. "Ethel", he concludes, "is looking over my shoulder. She thinks me such a delightful creature that she is never easy without me. She bids me to say that I am the best of sons and cousins, and am, in a word, a darling du...." The rest of this important word is not given, but *goose* is added in the female hand. In the faded ink, on the yellow paper that may have crossed and recrossed oceans, that has lain locked in chests for years, and buried under piles of family archives, while your friends have been dying and your head has grown white—who has not disinterred mementoes like these—from which the past smiles at you so sadly, shimmering out of Hades an instant but to sink back again into the cold shades, perhaps with a faint, faint sound as of a remembered tone—a ghostly echo of a once familiar laughter? I was looking of late at a wall in the Naples' museum, whereon a boy of Herculaneum eighteen hundred years ago had scratched with a nail the figure of a soldier. I could fancy the child turning round and smiling on me after having done his etching. Which of us that is thirty years old has not had his Pompeii? Deep under ashes lies the Life of Youth,—the careless Sport, the Pleasure and Passion, the darling Joy. You open an old letter-box and look at your own childish scrawls, or your mother's letters to you when you were at school; and excavate your heart. O me for the day when the whole city shall be bare and the chambers unroofed—and every cranny visible to the Light above, from the Forum to the Lupanar![1]

In my third instance a delayed image completes the description of the baby:

Milman Street is such a quiet little street that our friends had not carpeted it in the usual way; and three days after her temporary absence, as Nurse Brandon sits by her patient's bed, powdering the back of a small pink infant that makes believe to swim upon her apron, a rattle of wheels is heard in the quiet street—of four wheels, of one horse, of a jingling carriage, which stops before Philip's door. "It's the trap", says Nurse Brandon, delighted. "It must be those kind Ringwoods", says Mrs. Philip. "But stop, Brandon. Did not they, did not we?—oh, how kind of them!" She was trying to recal the past. Past and present for days had been strangely mingled in her fevered brain. "Hush, my dear! you are to be kep' quite still," says the nurse—and then proceeded to finish the polishing and powdering of the pink frog on her lap.[2]

These are handy instances of a method which Thackeray practises often enough to keep us on the watch, expectancy improving our sense of the continuity.

5

Another method contributing to the continuity is that of a recurrent conciseness of phrasing. Though he is sometimes thought of as a babbler, he is, when he so wishes, a master of economy. We reserve that encomium for writers who can convey much in amount briefly, much in complexity simply. By nature Thackeray writes lightly and flowingly. Sometimes the content of the writing is itself light. When weighty, he still writes

[1] *The Newcomes*, ch. XXVIII.   [2] *Philip*, ch. XLI.

lightly. And when complex or obscure, he still writes simply: he can fix with a pin what in other hands requires gimlets and screws. Instances are everywhere: after Pen's first sight of the Fotheringay 'the curtain fell upon him like a pall';[1] Becky, having made her calculations, feels that if Rawdon does happen to be killed at Waterloo, she can 'look her [widow's] weeds steadily in the face';[2] after the ball Lord Kew 'proceeded to cover up old Lady Kew';[3] Clive, at the party, 'is looking with all his might into the eyes of Miss Sherrick';[4] Major Pendennis receives from the hand of Lady Clavering 'a brief wrench of recognition';[5] Mr Ringwood gives Philip 'almost the whole of one finger to shake';[6] the cheeks of Charlotte 'flung out' for Philip 'their blushes of welcome'.[7]

One of the reasons why we read on, and so discover the long continuity of Thackeray, is that such pungent simplicities soon come to be expected. Without them much of the complex material of the novels could not have been expressed without obstructing the flow.

6

And so to the last of these occasional agencies making for continuity, the last and the most persistently recurrent—Thackeray's characteristic imagery.

Imagery is a matter that we of the twentieth century can touch more surely than could most of our predecessors. We have grown so sensitive to it that images stare at us from the page. All to the good—with the obvious reservation that we must not allow sensitiveness in that quarter to impair our sensitiveness in others.

---

[1] *Pendennis*, ch. IV. [2] *Vanity Fair*, ch. XXXII.
[3] *The Newcomes*, ch. XXXIII. [4] Ibid. ch. XXIII.
[5] *Pendennis*, ch. XXXVI. [6] *Philip*, ch. XL.
[7] Ibid. ch. XX.

3-2

My claim that his imagery solidifies the Thackerayan unity is founded on its tending to fall into systems, two in number—that according to provenance and that according to repetition. Thackeray tends to take his images from a limited number of matters, principal among them being his own comfortable urban house, particularly perhaps its kitchen and dining-room. I cite instances haphazardly. In *From Cornhill to Cairo* the lips of a 'coal black' negress are 'the size of sausages'.[1] In *The Book of Snobs* the size of a Chinese slipper is that of 'a salt-cruet'[2] and of a cameo that of a muffin.[3] In *The Virginians* Lady Maria is described by Henry's mother as 'a great, gawky, carrotty creature with a foot like a pair of bellows'.[4] Later at one point she 'looks as pale as a table-cloth'.[5] After a fight, young Denis Duval's 'black eye is as big as an omelette'.[6] On another embarrassing occasion his 'poor mother sate boiling red like a lobster fresh out of the pot'.[7] Going to London for the first time the boy's 'portmanteau', over which he fusses importantly, 'was about as large as a good-sized apple-pie'.[8] When Morgiana is working up for her debut on the operatic stage, we hear of campaigns prepared for winning over the press and are given this beautiful sentence: 'Artists cannot be advertised like Macassar oil or blacking, and they want it to the full as much.'[9] In *Vanity Fair* we hear of an old aunt with 'a front of light coffee-coloured hair'.[10] Lady Kew's face is 'as grim and yellow as her brass knocker'.[11] A typical father has a 'bow-window of a waist-coat'.[12] In the same novel the sky is 'the hue of brown paper', and the

[1] Ch. xv.
[2] Ch. iv.
[3] Ch. xv.
[4] Ch. xvi.
[5] Ch. lvi.
[6] Ch. xv.
[7] Ch. iii.
[8] *Denis Duval*, ch. v.
[9] *The Ravenswing*, ch. viii.
[10] Ch. ix.
[11] *The Newcomes*, ch. xliv.
[12] Ch. xvii.

General 'as soft as mutton'. In *Lovel the Widower* Lady Baker 'turn[ed] me a shoulder as cold as that lamb which I offered to carve for the family'.[1] Later we hear that 'Her heart was pincushioned with [the] filial crimes' of her son.[2] Thackeray often behaves as Pen did at the ball, who

was delighted with his mischief. The two prettiest girls in the room were quarrelling about him. He flattered himself he had punished Miss Laura. He leaned in a dandified air, with his elbow over the wall, and talked to Blanche: he quizzed unmercifully all the men in the room—the heavy dragoons in their tight jackets—the country dandies in their queer attire—the strange toilettes of the ladies. One seemed to have a bird's nest in her head; another had six pounds of grapes in her hair, beside her false pearls. "It's a *coiffure* of almonds and raisins", said Pen, "and might be served up for dessert." In a word, he was exceedingly satirical and amusing.[3]

Thackeray would have laughed heartily over Mr Wilson's simile of the leaking tap. Had not Clive himself employed almost the same image for describing the eloquence of Barnes—his lecture 'still plapping on like water from a cistern'?[4] The images provide further instances of his economy. You know more about lips than their size when they are compared to sausages, and if a cameo is as big as a muffin it is also coloured and configurated like one.

The images, forceful in themselves, have additional force in that they recur. If you are sensitive to imagery —unduly sensitive perhaps—Thackeray's novels will be dominated for you by a set of recurring symbols. It is partly by their means that he expresses his philosophy.

[1] Ch. III.
[2] Ch. IV. Thackeray invented the nonce-word 'pin-cushioned' (= pierced as a pincushion with pins): see *O.E.D.*
[3] Ch. XXVI.   [4] See above, p. 28.

They include the following—again I list them in haphazard order, as suggesting their irregular occurrence: the animals of Æsop; the mermaid, symbolizing the illicit seductions of the flesh (Thackeray drew a mermaid in the not-very-lurid initial letters of two chapters in *Pendennis* and a better one as headpiece to his Preface); the Turkish marriage market; Babylon; theatres, especially lighted scenes on the popular stage, or scenes from which the lights are being extinguished (how many authors have copied these effects of his); the good Samaritan (which recurs often in *The Virginians* and which forms the spine of *Philip*—Thackeray also sketches it in as the subject of the picture hanging on the wall in the room in which Dobbin has his last interview with Jos Sedley while Becky is ensconced behind the curtain); things out of *The Arabian Nights, The Rape of the Lock* and *Othello*; the sun (of which later); the idea of Vanity Fair (the supposed date of the action of *Esmond* is not too early to miss a reference);[1] and the many references to persons and images first met in classical poets and historians. These latter are not the trove of a deep scholar—it has been noted how unconvincing is the supposed classical learning of Philip's father. But the classics familiar to schoolboys are all the better for a novelist, who would be foolish to rely for his powerful effects on images which, being esoteric, are for most of us devoid of associations. How often in Thackeray—and, I add, how freshly—crop up the *atra cura* seated behind the horseman, or, less often, the *amare aliquid* mingled with the cup of pleasure. How often does his glance dive into antiquity in order to characterize a heroine—Fanny Bolton is the 'poor little Ariadne of Shepherd's Inn';[2] or it may be a Lady Maria

---

[1] Bk III, ch. vi.   [2] *Pendennis*, ch. LXIV.

who receives the comparison; Beatrix, spoken of in the midst of a campaign, is 'this Helen'.[1] Or the commentary will throw out the following:

Lais, quite moral, and very neatly, primly, and straitly laced;—Phryne, not the least dishevelled, but with a fixature for her hair, and the best stays, fastened by mamma;—your High Church or Evangelical Aspasia...[2]

Or in *Vanity Fair* comes this of 'Madame Rawdon':

So our little wanderer went about setting up her tent in various cities of Europe, as restless as Ulysses or Bampfylde Moore Carew.[3]

These are some that I have noted. The reader is aware of their recurrence because Thackeray is not an author given to colour of this kind, and also because when they come they blaze. Here is one of the passages drawing on the mermaid:

I defy any one to say that our Becky, who has certainly some vices, has not been presented to the public in a perfectly genteel and inoffensive manner. In describing this syren, singing and smiling, coaxing and cajoling, the author, with modest pride, asks his readers all round, has he once forgotten the laws of politeness, and showed the monster's hideous tail above water? No! Those who like may peep down under waves that are pretty transparent, and see it writhing and twirling, diabolically hideous and slimy, flapping amongst bones, or curling round corpses; but above the water-line, I ask, has not everything been proper, agreeable, and decorous, and has any the most squeamish immoralist in Vanity Fair a right to cry fie? When, however, the syren disappears and dives below, down among the dead men, the water of course grows turbid over her, and it is labour lost to look into it ever so curiously. They look pretty enough when they sit upon a rock, twanging their

[1] *Esmond*, bk II, ch. XII. [2] *Philip*, ch. IX.
[3] Ch. LXIV.

39

harps and combing their hair, and sing, and beckon to you to come and hold the looking-glass; but when they sink into their native element, depend on it those mermaids are about no good, and we had best not examine the fiendish marine cannibals, revelling and feasting on their wretched pickled victims. And so, when Becky is out of the way, be sure that she is not particularly well employed, and that the less that is said about her doings is in fact the better.[1]

And here a fierce gorgeous version of the marriage market theme from *Philip*, supposedly the book of a tired writer:

What is love, young heart? It is two thousand a year, at the very lowest computation; and with the present rise in wages and house-rent, that calculation can't last very long. Love? Attachment? Look at Frank Maythorn, with his vernal blushes, his leafy whiskers, his sunshiny, laughing face, and all the birds of spring carolling in his jolly voice; and old General Pinwood hobbling in on his cork leg, with his stars and orders, and leering round the room from under his painted eyebrows. Will my modest nymph go to Maythorn, or to yonder leering Satyr, who totters towards her in his white and rouge? Nonsense. She gives her garland to the old man, to be sure. He is ten times as rich as the young one. And so they went on in Arcadia itself, *really*. Not in that namby-pamby ballet and idyll world, where they tripped up to each other in rhythm, and talked hexameters; but in the real, downright, no-mistake country—Arcadia—where Tityrus, fluting to Amaryllis in the shade, had his pipe very soon put out when Meliboeus (the great grazier) performed on his melodious, exquisite, irresistible cow-horn; and where Daphne's mother dressed her up with ribbons and drove her to market, and sold her, and swapped her, and bartered her like any other lamb in the fair. This one has been trotted to the market so long now that she knows the way herself. Her baa has been heard for—do not let us count how many seasons. She has nibbled out of countless hands; frisked in

[1] *Vanity Fair*, ch. LXIV.

many thousand dances; come quite harmless away from goodness knows how many wolves. Ah! ye lambs and raddled innocents of our Arcadia! Ah, old *Ewe*! Is it of your ladyship this fable is narrated? I say it is as old as Cadmus, and man- and mutton-kind.[1]

7

Of the images that recur, the group that does so most often is the epic. Thackeray the novelist is as conscious of the most august of literary forms as Fielding was. His reasons, however, for echoing Homer and Virgil are more subtle and numerous than those of his predecessor. For Fielding the epic offered crutches for a novelist and the chance of a few literary larks. When he called *Joseph Andrews* a comic epic in prose, he meant that he wanted to write a narrative more like the *Odyssey* than any narrative of Defoe or Richardson. If Scott's novels had existed, or Jane Austen's, he might have forgotten the epic in the enjoyment of the novel form now at last sufficiently evolved. As far as imagery went he would have been loth to forgo the fun of things like this:

> As when a hungry tigress, who long has traversed the woods in fruitless search, sees within the reach of her claws a lamb, she prepares to leap on her prey; or as a voracious pike, of immense size, surveys through the liquid element a roach or gudgeon, which cannot escape her jaws, opens them wide to swallow the little fish; so did Mrs. Slipslop prepare to lay her violent amorous hands on the poor Joseph, when luckily her mistress's bell rung, and delivered the intended martyr from her clutches.[2]

But amusing as these things were, they are now mainly amusing to schoolboys—other readers can see that the epic simile lies obvious to the paw of the parodist. Some

[1] Ch. ix.   [2] *Joseph Andrews*, bk I, ch. vi (ad fin.).

of Thackeray's own echoes of epic and epical literature
are tricks little better. For instance, among his jokes is
that of writing short bursts of blank verse like the verse
of heroic plays, which he prints as prose in the manner
of the translation of Homer done early in the eighteenth
century by Broome, Ozell and Oldisworth:

"Marry, good dame", Philip's companion said to the old
beldam, "this goodly gentleman hath a right of entrance to
yonder castle, which, I trow, ye wot not of. Heard ye never
tell of one Philip Ringwood, slain at Busaco's glorious fi—"
"Hold your tongue, and don't chaff her, Pen", growled
Firmin.
"Nay, and she knows not Philip Ringwood's grandson",
the other wag continued, in a softened tone. "This will
convince her of our right to enter. Canst recognize this
image of your queen?"[1]

Thackeray, of course, is not proud of that. It is merely
an instance of his being true to a schoolboyishness in Pen.
Usually, however, his epic references are touched or
inflamed with his genius. Instead of the epic battle
there is this slaughter after a dinner party:

as Harry uttered the exclamation, his dear cousin flung a
wine-bottle at Mr. Warrington's head, who bobbed just in
time, so that the missile flew across the room, and broke
against the wainscot opposite, breaking the face of a
pictured ancestor of the Esmond family, and then itself
against the wall, whence it spirted a pint of good port wine
over the Chaplain's face and flowered wig. "Great heavens,
gentlemen, I pray you to be quiet," cried the parson,
dripping with gore.[2]

Or more subtly:

One bottle speedily yielded up the ghost, another shed
more than half its blood, before the two topers had been
much more than half an hour together....[3]

[1] *Philip*, ch. XLII.   [2] *The Virginians*, ch. XL.   [3] *Pendennis*, ch. XVI.

The epic formula that makes the hero taller than his men is applied with a difference:

Jack Belsize from his height and strength was fitted to be not only an officer but actually a private in his...gallant regiment....[1]

The formula of scouring the plain is applied with 'scouring' taken literally:

If Anatole, the boy who scoured the plain at the Hôtel Poussin, with his *plumet* in his jacket-pocket, and his slippers soled with scrubbing brushes, saw the embrace between Philip and his good friend, I believe, in his experience at that hotel, he never witnessed a transaction more honourable, generous, and blameless.[2]

Instead of the ambrosial cloud that wraps a celestial we get this of a fight between two footmen, one of whom has been offending the other by insolently wearing a cap:

But he said no more, for little Bedford jumped some two feet from the ground, and knocked the cap off, so that a cloud of ambrosial powder filled the room with violet odours.[3]

Dolichoskion, 'casting a long shadow', is the Homeric epithet for spears; this is how it crops up in *Pendennis*:

One of the leaves of the hall door was opened, and John— one of the largest of his race—was leaning against the door pillar, with his ambrosial hair powdered, his legs crossed; beautiful, silk-stockinged; in his hand his cane, gold-headed, dolichoskion.[4]

With which we might compare in *The Rape of the Lock* such phrases as 'Propt on their bodkin spears, the sylphs....'

[1] *The Newcomes*, ch. xxix.   [2] *Philip*, ch. xxv.
[3] *Lovel the Widower*, ch. v.   [4] Ch. xxxvi.

From some of these excerpts it will be seen that
Thackeray's use of the epic resembles that of the mock-
heroic Pope in other respects also. For Thackeray has
some of the poetic quality of epic. It is a long way from
Fielding's hungry tigress and pike of enormous size to
the bottle's yielding up the ghost, or to violet odours, or
to this cry:

Great Heaven! what passion, jealousy, grief, despair, were
tearing and trying all these hearts, that but for fate might
have been happy?[1]

And when Thackeray sends his melancholy young men
to wander by the much-sounding sea, the Homeric
touch is tender.[2]

Often it is a device of the narrative method of epic
that is called in—that rather than any epic point or
image. I am here counting it among the epic images—
it is at least brief and pungent as images are, and carries
an epic reference even though one more musical than
pictorial. Often what we recall in reading Thackeray is
that epic device of a calm, staring, but tender, objectivity in narrative. Here are two sentences from *Vanity
Fair*:

No more firing was heard at Brussels—the pursuit rolled
miles away. The darkness came down on the field and city,
and Amelia was praying for George, who was lying on his
face, dead, with a bullet through his heart.[3]

So there came one morning and sunrise, when all the
world got up and set about its various works and pleasures,
with the exception of Old John Sedley, who was not to fight
with fortune, or to hope or scheme any more: but to go and
take up a quiet and utterly unknown residence in a church-
yard at Brompton by the side of his old wife.[4]

[1] *The Newcomes*, ch. LXXIX.
[2] *Pendennis*, ch. V; *The Newcomes*, ch. XLII.
[3] Ch. XXXII.   [4] Ch. LXI.

And even the close of *Rebecca and Rowena*, a 'Christmas Book', partly farcical:

That [Rebecca] and Ivanhoe were married follows of course; for Rowena's promise extorted from him was, that he would never wed a Jewess, and a better Christian than Rebecca now was never said her Catechism. Married I am sure they were, and adopted little Cedric; but I don't think they had any other children, or were subsequently very boisterously happy. Of some sort of happiness melancholy is a characteristic, and I think these were a solemn pair, and died rather early.

Narration by means of 'And...And...And', a means towards the level style often used by Virgil and by the Authorized Version, ends here with an echo from Genesis:

"Dear Lady Baker! how that red does become your ladyship." In fact, Lady B. sailed in at this juncture, arrayed in ribbons of scarlet; with many brooches, bangles, and other gimcracks ornamenting her plenteous person. And now her ladyship having arrived, Bedford announced that dinner was served, and Lovel gave his mother-in-law an arm, whilst I offered mine to Mrs. Bonnington to lead her to the adjoining dining-room. And the pacable kind soul speedily made peace with me. And we ate and drank of Lovel's best. And Lady Baker told us her celebrated anecdote of George the Fourth's compliment to her late dear husband, Sir Popham, when his Majesty visited Ireland. Mrs. Prior and her basket were gone when we repaired to the drawing-room: having been hunting all day, the hungry mother had returned with her prey to her wide-mouthed birdikins. Elizabeth looked very pale and handsome, reading at her lamp. And whist and the little tray finished the second day at Shrublands.[1]

And in this account of the death by duel of the Count of Saverne the 'And...And...' ends with an echo from

[1] *Lovel the Widower*, ch. III. 'Sir Popham' is misprinted by dittography 'Sir George' in the first edition (*The Cornhill*, I, 339).

45

drama, the 'dramatic' climaxes of novels, and Carlyle's *French Revolution*:

He had only a few pieces in his purse, and, "Tenez", says he, "this watch. Should anything befal me, I desire it may be given to the little boy who saved my—that is, her child." And the voice of M. le Comte broke as he said these words, and the tears ran over his fingers. And the seaman wept too, as he told the story to me years after, nor were some of mine wanting, I think, for that poor heart-broken, wretched man, writhing in helpless agony, as the hungry sand drank his blood. Assuredly, the guilt of that blood was on thy head, Francis de la Motte.[1]

8

It is perhaps allowable to call by the name 'device' the use made by Homer and Virgil of the movement of the sun through the sky. On one level of significance it is merely the movement of hands on a clock-face, but on another the movement of man's brief life and business against the larger movement of the heavens. *The Rape of the Lock*—Thackeray knew the poem well—had made use of this contrast for sharpening its irony—when man's life-and-business was merely that of foolish fashionable contemporaries its briefness lacked even the dignity of the brief life of the ancient heroes. Pope's method became that of Thackeray—as it had become that of Carlyle. See for instance the account of Major Pendennis after a night of splendid entertainment:

As the party went down the great staircase of Gaunt House, the morning had risen stark and clear over the black trees of the square; the skies were tinged with pink; and the cheeks of some of the people at the ball,—ah, how ghastly they looked! That admirable and devoted Major above all,

[1] *Denis Duval*, ch. IV.

—who had been for hours by Lady Clavering's side, ministering to her and feeding her body with everything that was nice, and her ear with everything that was sweet and flattering,—oh! what an object he was! The rings round his eyes were of the colour of bistre; those orbs themselves were like the plovers' eggs whereof Lady Clavering and Blanche had each tasted; the wrinkles in his old face were furrowed in deep gashes; and a silver stubble, like an elderly morning dew, was glittering on his chin, and alongside the dyed whiskers, now limp and out of curl.[1]

Perhaps that brilliant bit is a little overdone in its ferocity. More characteristic, because less painted up, is this:

The windows of the dining-room were opened to let in the fresh air, and afforded to the passers-by in the street a pleasant or, perhaps, tantalising view of six gentlemen in white waistcoats, with a quantity of decanters and a variety of fruits before them—little boys, as they passed and jumped up at the area-railings, and took a peep, said to one another, "Mi hi, Jim, shouldn't you like to be there, and have a cut of that there pine-apple?"—the horses and carriages of the nobility and gentry passed by, conveying them to Belgravian toilets: the policeman, with clamping feet, patrolled up and down before the mansion: the shades of evening began to fall: the gasman came and lighted the lamps before Sir Francis's door: the butler entered the dining-room, and illuminated the antique gothic chandelier over the antique carved oak dining-table: so that from outside the house you looked inwards upon a night scene of feasting and wax candles; and from within you beheld a vision of a calm summer evening, and the wall of St. James's Park, and the sky above, in which a star or two was just beginning to twinkle.[2]

The contrast between the day of the modern man of fashion and that of the old heroes, touched on sporadi-

[1] *Pendennis*, ch. XLV.   [2] Ibid. ch. XXXVIII.

cally in the other novels, seems part of the design of *The Virginians*. From many instances I select these:

In this easy manner the Sabbath day passed. The evening was beautiful, and there was talk of adjourning to a cool tankard and a game of whist in a summer-house; but the company voted to sit indoors, the ladies declaring they thought the aspect of three honours in their hand, and some good court cards, more beautiful than the loveliest scene of nature; and so the sun went behind the elms, and still they were at their cards; and the rooks came home cawing their even song, and they never stirred except to change partners; and the chapel clock tolled hour after hour unheeded, so delightfully were they spent over the pasteboard; and the moon and stars came out; and it was nine o'clock, and the groom of the chambers announced that supper was ready.[1]

And:

Cousin Maria made her appearance, attended by a couple of gardener's boys bearing baskets of flowers, with which it was proposed to decorate Madame de Bernstein's drawing-room against the arrival of her ladyship's company. Three footmen in livery, gorgeously laced with worsted, set out twice as many card-tables. A major-domo in black and a bag, with fine laced ruffles, and looking as if he ought to have a sword by his side, followed the lacqueys bearing fasces of wax-candles, which he placed, a pair on each card-table, and in the silver sconces on the wainscoted wall that was now gilt with the slanting rays of the sun, as was the prospect of the green common beyond, with its rocks and clumps of trees and houses twinkling in the sunshine.[2]

These recurrent images, epical and the rest, help to unify the fiction. In Shakespeare's tragedies the imagery of each play is a separate system serving the end of that particular play. Thackeray's imagery is more like that of the history plays: it binds together a great series.

[1] Ch. xv.　　　　[2] Ch. xxv.

9

I have said that design—by which I mean, of course, strict design—is absent from Thackeray's novels. The effect of a strict design is to keep as much as possible of the whole of a work in the conscious mind of the reader, so that as he reads on he becomes aware of the work as a two-dimensional thing, from point to point of which there is an interconnection, by lines as it were. A design becomes stricter as there are more of these points of interconnection.[1] In a novel of Thackeray's they are few, and some of them connect with points in other novels. Among them are to be included the means I have been noting as tributaries to the continuity. The result of these intercommunications is not design in any strictness, especially when the points lie in different novels: the lines are slack and casual, as though Thackeray was not averse from availing himself of what offered this way, though not anxious with a Fielding-like concern. What recurs—the prizes Henry James found wherever he dipped—strikes the reader rather as country houses do as he rattles across the counties in a railway train, Palladian façades mildly asserting themselves across the fields, one rather like the next which succeeds at an interval. Little more can be said for them than that they please for a moment and fade as the train pushes forward. But any organization that the novels gain on this score is mainly owing to their continuity sliding at something like a uniform rate over the whole of the writings: we never forget—for reasons which I shall go into later—that the means of our gliding along so steadily is true Thackerayan rolling

[1] I have tried elsewhere to determine the limits of the reader's stretch of consciousness while experiencing a piece of writing: see *Criticism and the Nineteenth Century*, 1951, pp. 23 ff.

stock. The main effect of his narrative method is an effect of the one-dimensional, the arrow-flighted or the serpentine.

10

The most powerful of the agents making for continuity is, of course, his style, and it is particularly powerful because, unlike the style of Dickens and Henry James, it remained constant, or as near so as matters, throughout Thackeray's career.[1]

His long novels might well have lacked this particular means of unity, since a number of authors are announced on their title-pages. Two, *Vanity Fair* and *Pendennis*, are given out as written by Thackeray himself; one, *The Virginians*, as written by himself drawing on, even sometimes transcribing, documents of the previous century; two, *The Newcomes* and *Philip*, as written by Arthur Pendennis; one as written by a person living in the late seventeenth and early eighteenth centuries, *The History of Henry Esmond, Esq. A Colonel in the service of Her Majesty Q. Anne. Written by himself*; one, *Denis Duval*, as written by a person born in 1763. But pretence or no pretence, the happy prose remains constant, or almost so.[2] As far as concerns *The Newcomes* and *Philip*, Thackeray made no effort whatever to write like Pendennis—that is, like any second contemporary person. More effort was needed when he elected to write for Esmond. He called the result his 'dismal imitation of the old style'.[3] But his feats belie this further instance of his habitual self-disparagement. In *Esmond* he felt sure enough of his skill in eighteenth-century prose to forge a paper of

---

[1] Frederic Harrison has some interesting pages in praise of the constant excellence of Thackeray's style throughout the quarter century of his career in *Studies in Early Victorian Literature*, 1895, pp. 108 ff.

[2] For the exception see below, pp. 53 f. and 110 f.

[3] *Letters*, III, 286.

The Spectator of Steele and Addison—as in *The Virginians* to forge a letter from Horace Walpole.[1] What his effort amounted to in the main was the dimming of the sparkle of his normal prose, the restriction of his vocabulary, almost perfectly achieved, to that available to a writer of the early eighteenth century, his catching the trick of using ''Tis' and 'of' as much as possible, his giving a number of sentences a balance around a middle point. Perhaps in *Esmond* he tuned his style to a particular sweetness, a shadowy Irish sweetness, as it were. He took a certain amount of care. Nevertheless his general style, in *Esmond, The Virginians*, and *Denis Duval*, does not vary much from the style in the rest of his writings. This style Henley, among many others, has tried to characterize:

His manner is the perfection of conversational writing. Graceful yet vigorous; adorably artificial yet incomparably sound; touched with modishness yet informed with distinction; easily and happily rhythmical yet full of colour and quick with malice and with meaning; instinct with urbanity and instinct with charm—it is a type of high-bred English, a climax of literary art.[2]

In this description there are faults to lay at Henley's door—'incomparably' is musical nonsense, and a worse slip is putting manner on the same plane as malice and meaning; and another, speaking of 'colour' when everything depends on the nuance. To remedy this last defect, there is Saintsbury's phrase, 'a quality at once of the opal and of the diamond'.[3] The degree of the colour is Rowlandsonian—when Rowlandson did his ink and wash drawings, his fidelity towards the gross and ugly often went with tints of the utmost delicacy.

[1] Ch. XL.
[2] *Views and Reviews: Essays in Appreciation*, 1890, p. 16.
[3] P. 186.

Apart from the faults I have suggested, Henley's description can stand. And it is in something like the same terms that we should describe a great deal of eighteenth-century prose. Thackeray was much a writer of that time himself, both by choice and training. He had read widely and happily in its literature as a whole. He was bred at Cambridge where, as at Oxford, the style of Addison had flowered into a vivid conversational speech which remains vivid in the informal prose of Newman and the constant prose of Thackeray and Arnold. Arnold was able to say, 'Johnson...wrote a prose decidedly modern...in spite of superficial differences, the style of our own day';[1] in him and in Addison 'we have got our prose'.[2] For Thackeray it was more than 'indispensable'; it released the innate eighteenth-century genius in him the more comfortably. The imitated prose of *Esmond* melts into that of the rest of the novels, and could have been read, say, by Goldsmith, without an undue sense of the unfamiliar.

This style, which was won for the eighteenth century by the seventeenth, was not won for the convenience of the tellers of stories, but by chance it was a style beautifully apt for their purposes. Its level progress flowed unhampered, and encouraged the continuity necessary for recording the course of normal occurrences or experience. As Thackeray practised it, it flowed rapidly, dimpled here and there by a fine Latin polysyllable. Henley's description misses something of the current of it, but not Quiller-Couch's:

The secret [of Thackeray's style] lies, if you will follow his sentences and surrender yourselves to their run and lull and lapse, in a curious haunting music, as of a stream; a music of

[1] *The Six Chief Lives from Johnson's 'Lives of the Poets'*, ed. Matthew Arnold, 1879, p. xviii.   [2] Ibid. p. xxiii.

which scarce any other writer of English prose has quite the natural, effortless, command. You have no need to search in his best pages, or to hunt for his purple patches. It has a knack of making music even while you are judging his matter to be poor stuff; music—and frequent music—in his most casual light-running sentences.[1]

All of which is summed up in Saintsbury's perception that Thackeray 'thought in rhythm';[2] and in that most brilliant of all the images applied to it—Thackeray's English, said James Hannay, is 'pure, clear, simple in its power, and harmonious; clean, sinewy, fine and yet strong, like the legs of a racehorse'.[3]

II

An addendum is due to the description of Thackeray's style as constant. Within the flowing style are scattered islands, as it were, of a style that is the lyric version of the narrative style. I shall say more of this later when I speak of the passages of commentary, where this second style is in evidence. If his usual narrative style may be called Addison's on the wing, or a version by Schubert, as it were, of Swift's *Gulliver's Travels* or Johnson's *Rasselas*, this second style is Thackeray's defter version of a part of Carlyle's in *The French Revolution*. That work he reviewed in *The Times*, and most of the passages there quoted suggest a debt that he himself came to owe. The debt is clearer still if we look at certain passages he did not quote, such as this:

Meanwhile, the faster, O ye black-aproned Smiths, smite; with strong arm and willing heart. This man and that, all stroke from head to heel, shall thunder alternating, and ply

---

[1] *Charles Dickens and other Victorians*, 1925, p. 151.
[2] *A History of English Prose Rhythm*, 1912, p. 383.
[3] *Studies on Thackeray* [1869], p. 12.

the great forge-hammer, till stithy reel and ring again; while ever and anon, overhead, booms the alarm-cannon,— for the City has now got gunpowder. Pikes are fabricated; fifty thousand of them, in six-and-thirty hours: judge whether the Black-aproned have been idle. Dig trenches, unpave the streets, ye others, assiduous, man and maid; cram the earth in barrel-barricades, at each of them a volunteer sentry; pile the whinstones in window-sills and upper rooms. Have scalding pitch, at least boiling water ready, ye weak old women, to pour it and dash it on Royal-Allemand, with your old skinny arms: your shrill curses along with it will not be wanting!—Patrols of the newborn National Guard, bearing torches, scour the streets, all that night; which otherwise are vacant, yet illuminated in every window by order. Strange-looking: like some naphtha-lighted City of the Dead, with here and there a flight of perturbed Ghosts.[1]

From this turn to such a passage as that quoted above from *The Newcomes*, where Clive is day-dreaming under the lecture of Barnes while Thackeray, as it were, plays soft string music.[2]

Scattered with an archipelago of such passages, Thackeray's style is constant as the sea. The contribution made by the normal style towards the unification of his novels, and indeed of his writings as a whole, is only equalled by the contribution made by his personal character as an author. To the discussion of this I now proceed. The exploration of it will take up the rest of my book, even such matters as narrative art being closely related to it.

[1] *The French Revolution*, bk v, ch. v.
[2] See above, pp. 27 f.

CHAPTER IV

The Content of the Authorial 'I'

At the outset I spoke of the foundation of all the writings in the individual mind of the author. We speak of the 'Shakespearian'; if it did not exist palpably, there would be no evidence, or merely external shreds of it, for the Shakespeare apocrypha. If we do not speak of the 'Blackmorian' or the 'Dixonian', that is merely because, though the unity achieved by the works of Sir Richard Blackmore and R. W. Dixon is recognizable, not many people are interested in recognizing it. Literature, throughout its length and breadth, readily receives the impress of each of its makers, and that this is so is no less mysterious for having as an alternative something impossible. But several kinds of literature— and these the kinds we place highest—will not admit the expression of any aspect of personal identity other than this aesthetic aspect, this complexion, as it were, of the medium used in just that way for the expression of just that matter. If an author wishes to express his own thoughts or sentiments as his own, he must write in the forms I have elsewhere called 'prose of thinking' —write a disquisition, an article, the kind of essay written, say, by Matthew Arnold. In other forms of literature the authorial 'I' is a fiction. The name that Lamb gave the essayist was an anagram of 'a lie', and the very attraction of the Elian sort of essay has been the holiday it offered from the actual self, even though the vacational frisks were played on the edges of that self. It is the form which allowed Thackeray, for instance, writing *as* 'Mr. Roundabout' and writing *of* the

notorious Dodd, to write *as* Dodd and use the words
'my wife, Mrs. Dodd', suddenly and without signal and
as if it would surprise nobody.[1] If the Elian essay is not
the place for the actual self, it is not the place for
opinions that are part of that self. Even if the writer of
this sort of essay does express opinions held by him as
an historical person, the reader as an historical person
does not accept them as such, unless he is convinced, by
evidence outside the essay, that the form has slipped for
the nonce into prose of thinking. If these conditions are
binding on the Elian essay, how much more strictly on the
novel. Speaking his ideas with an attached 'I' that does
not belong to one of the personages, a novelist cannot
present us with them as his own.

2

With the content of this 'I' Thackeray showed some
concern. I have already noted that as an historical
person he did not take full responsibility for the author-
ship of three of the long novels and of *Denis Duval*. In
The Newcomes, the one of the trio that came first in time,
he reduced his responsibility as low as he could. Em-
barking on that novel, he told a friend that

Mr. Pendennis is to be the writer of his friend's memoirs and
by the help of this little mask.... I shall be able to talk
more at ease than in my own person.[2]

Soon afterwards another correspondent was informed
that

Mr. Pendennis is the author of the book, and he has taken
a great weight off my mind, for under that mask and acting,
as it were, I can afford to say and think many things that
I couldn't venture on in my own person, now that it is a
person, and I know the public are staring at it.[3]

[1] *The Roundabout Papers*, 'On a Medal of George the Fourth'.
[2] *Letters*, III, 297 f.   [3] *Letters*, IV, 436.

Pendennis-in-the-first-person was designed, therefore, to rule out the necessity for such appeals as the following in *Vanity Fair*:

And, as we bring our characters forward, I will ask leave, as a man and a brother, not only to introduce them, but occasionally to step down from the platform, and talk about them: if they are good and kindly, to love them and shake them by the hand: if they are silly, to laugh at them confidentially in the reader's sleeve: if they are wicked and heartless, to abuse them in the strongest terms which politeness admits of.

Otherwise you might fancy it was I who was sneering at the practice of devotion, which Miss Sharp finds so ridiculous; that it was I who laughed good humouredly at the reeling old Silenus of a baronet—whereas the laughter comes from one who has no reverence except for prosperity, and no eye for anything beyond success. Such people there are living and flourishing in the world—Faithless, Hopeless, Charityless: let us have at them, dear friends, with might and main. Some there are, and very successful too, mere quacks and fools: and it was to combat and expose such as those, no doubt, that Laughter was made.[1]

The phrase 'the strongest terms that politeness admits of' reminds us that Thackeray did not contemplate saying anything in his novels that would offend against the law of libel. When he did come near such an offence by drawing Lord Steyne in a way that too closely resembled the Marquis of Hertford who had died a few years earlier, it was no part of his purpose, and he withdrew the sketch from the second issue of the first edition in book form. Nor was there any risk that a story of his would be publicly burnt for blasphemy, as Anthony Froude's story, *The Nemesis of Faith*, was burned in a lecture-room of Exeter College in 1848. Nor, again, was indecency in question—a matter I shall

[1] Ch. viii.

57

touch on later.[1] It was against subtler matters that Thackeray was seeking to guard himself. But why, we ask, all this of novels? Making all this fuss over masks, was he not misjudging the plane of the mind on which we meet a novel, and making himself ridiculous by troubling to delegate powers a novelist cannot possess? In that passage from *Vanity Fair* he attempted to force an entry into the frame of his novel as an historical person, forgetting that a novel asks its reader to suspend his disbelief, and that the obliging reader is at a loss if the obliged author fails to honour the other side of the bargain. To attempt to stop the voice of the narrator for another is to risk throwing the reader's good will to the winds. That good will, where Thackeray and *Vanity Fair* are concerned, remains good only by the reader's wilful misunderstanding of Thackeray's suspected intention, by his refusing to take the 'I' as denoting anyone but the story-teller. As far as the novels went the only place for the written remarks of Thackeray as Thackeray was prose of thinking—was the preface, availed of in *Pendennis*, and the footnote, availed of in the first edition in book form of *Philip* where 'W.M.T.' is the signature appended to a note explaining a point about the new matter of anaesthetics.[2]

It is true that Thackeray was forgetting the eternal laws of literature, but it is also true that he had reason: at that time those laws were being forgotten right and left. Evidence of the confusion exists everywhere in the book reviews of the time. It is discussed in Arnold's famous preface of 1853. I propose, however, to illustrate it from the note supplied by Sydney Dobell for the second edition of his *Balder. Part the First*. That poetic drama, which was never completed, was first published

[1] Below, pp. 123 ff. [2] III, 163: ch. xxxvi.

in 1852, the year in which Thackeray published *Esmond*. Its reception drew from the author a statement which in 1854 he fixed to the unsold copies and so gave them the specious dignity of a second edition. 'I understand', he says in this Prefatory Note,

that the public press have described my hero to be egoistic, self-contained, and sophistical, imperfect in morality, and destitute of recognised religion, mistaken in his estimate of his own powers and productions, and sacrificing to visionary hopes and dreamy distant philanthropies the blessing that lay in his embrace, and 'the duty which was nearest'.

And he goes on:

This is precisely the impression which I wished the readers of this volume to receive...

What then did he complain of? He complained of

the indecorous haste and uncharitable dogmatism with which, as I have seen and am informed, [my critics] have taken for granted that I must personally admire the character I think fit to delineate...

Dobell's critics had mistaken a poetic drama for prose of thinking, and Dobell met their criticism on the ground usually agreed to be the true one, by saying that in a poetic drama the author is not responsible as a person for the views expressed. When he proceeded to say that far from intending to recommend the character of his Balder he was offering it as a warning, the conclusion was inescapable: the only unambiguous written medium for ideas is prose of thinking.

For Thackeray there was also a complication inherent in the particular version of the novel form which he was using. All but one of his long novels, as I have said, were first published section by section. This form of publication could not but make an author interesting as a man. He could not but appear to his readers as a superior sort of family tradesman whose monthly parcels were welcome enough to suggest that the sender was accessible as a man.

The laws of literature were being ignored, and authors were suffering accordingly. For Thackeray, as for Dobell and Arnold, it was subtler matters than blasphemy and the like that were at stake. For the mid-nineteenth century was one of those recurrent periods when people are urged by the Zeitgeist to make up their minds on as many matters as possible. It was a time of intellectual warfare, when vague notions became ideas, and ideas beliefs. Becoming beliefs, they attached themselves to people, and so joined the other beliefs, religious in the stricter or broader sense, which were having a decisive effect on practice, making people change professions they had taken up 'without thinking' or at a time when thinking was not so binding on practice, making people withdraw from the membership of public institutions, making them leave one church for another or for none at all, making them quarrel with close friends, marry this person rather than that, even not marry at all. This being so, readers felt themselves trifled with when ideas warm enough to be believed in were expressed by writers who assumed a literary per-mission not to believe in them.

Many were the ideas that Thackeray did not care to believe in! As I shall note later on, he was not greatly interested in ideas, let alone in believing in them. But just because his novels closely resembled actual life, they abounded in occasions which showed or reminded a reader where he himself stood—say, as a religious or political person—which might or might not be where it seemed that Thackeray was standing. Not being him-self a person for whom ideas on these matters ever could have much sharpness he was less willing to have ideas attached to him by readers who did not scruple to attach them. He could not forget, let us say, the embarrassment that Charlotte Brontë had caused him: the clash between them had amounted to an 'incident'. In the second edition of *Jane Eyre*, published in January 1848, she had declared

> Conventionality is not morality. Self-righteousness is not religion. To attack the first is not to assail the last. To pluck the mask from the face of the Pharisee, is not to lift an impious hand to the Crown of Thorns;[1]

and so proceeded to its particular application, which I reproduce shorn of its Biblical references:

> There is a man in our own days whose words are not framed to tickle delicate ears: who, to my thinking, comes before the great ones of society [like an Old Testament figure]; and who speaks truth as deep, with a power as prophet-like and as vital—a mien as dauntless and as daring. Is the satirist of "Vanity Fair" admired in high places? I cannot tell; but I think if some of those amongst whom he hurls the Greek fire of his sarcasm, and over whom he flashes the levin-brand of his denunciation, were to take his warnings in time [it would be well].
>
> Why have I alluded to this man? I have alluded to him, reader, because I think I see in him an intellect profounder and more unique than his contemporaries have yet recognised; because I regard him as the first social regenerator of the day—as the very master of that working corps who would restore to rectitude the warped system of things; because I think no commentator on his writings has yet found the comparison that suits him, the terms which rightly characterize his talent. They say he is like Fielding[2]: they talk of his wit, humour, comic powers. He resembles Fielding as an eagle does a vulture: Fielding could stoop on carrion, but Thackeray never does. His wit is bright, his

---

[1] Pp. viii f.   [2] As *The Sun* on p. 210 below.

humour attractive, but both bear the same relation, to his serious genius that the mere lambent sheet-lightning playing under the edge of the summer-cloud, does to the electric death-spark hid in its womb. Finally; I have alluded to Mr. Thackeray, because to him—if he will accept the tribute of a total stranger—I have dedicated this second edition of "JANE EYRE".

CURRER BELL[1]

Dec. 21*st*, 1847.

With the deserved praise Thackeray must have been pleased, but also much embarrassed by the undeserved. He was no prophet, no public reformer. And when Charlotte Brontë met him she felt the inevitable chill. As Mr Gordon Ray has put it:

When she at last met Thackeray in December, 1849, she was puzzled to find that he was not after all "terribly in earnest against the falsehood and follies of the world". Indeed, she failed altogether to comprehend either his ambivalent outlook on London society, which, though he might satirize, he could not do without, or his thoroughly practical view of literature, induced by a dozen years of writing for his living. Thackeray, who despaired of presenting his ideas in a light that would win her sympathy, took refuge in persiflage.[2]

Thackeray's fear at bottom was a fear of being dragged as a person into practical affairs. To make Pendennis the fictional narrator of Thackeray's fiction was a means of retreating into what the most earnest or the least literary readers must see as nearer to inaccessibility. On the other hand he knew he must not retreat too far. He wanted to continue to 'say and think many things', some of which 'I couldn't venture on in my own person' in prose of thinking, but which in a novel he could 'afford to say and think' more safely now that the 'I' of the commentary was demonstrably Pendennis. Or

---

[1] *Jane Eyre*, 1848, I, viii ff.   [2] *Letters*, I, xciii f.

Thackeray as drawn by Richard Doyle (Brit. Mus., undated).

Above: Thackeray's 'self-portrait' used as tail-piece for Number III of
    Vanity Fair.
Below: Thackeray's design on the wrapper of the parts of *Vanity Fair*.

rather, to revert, more safely *still*. For the mask he donned so deliberately as the narrator of *The Newcomes* fitted over a mask already in place. In any event, however, times being what they were, the more masks the better. In his relief at inventing the offices of Pendennis, Thackeray overlooked the mask he had designed and worn as the author of *Vanity Fair*. In chapter VIII, which fell in the third number, he referred to 'the moralist, who is holding forth on the cover [and who] professes to wear neither gown nor bands, but only the very same long-eared livery in which his congregation is arrayed'. This picture, he assured his readers, was 'an accurate portrait of your humble servant'. As tail-piece to the chapter that followed he sketched another 'portrait'. (These 'portraits' are reproduced opposite.) The tail-piece is a fair specimen of the way Thackeray drew his face for the amusement of friends and the readers of those many books which he enlivened with self-portraits. It is as recognizably 'like' Thackeray as the picture of the clown on the cover is not; but of course it is not a portrait but a caricature. If that was the face behind the mask, no mask was necessary. Moreover, in the text of *Vanity Fair* he had made ample provision for essential anonymity by a series of mystifications. In chapter VI, which gave an account of a visit to Vauxhall Gardens, those who knew nothing of his biography might take it that he was a bachelor:

Captain Dobbin had some thoughts of joining the party at supper: as, in truth, he found the Vauxhall amusement not particularly lively—but he paraded twice before the box where the now united couples were met, and nobody took any notice of him. Covers were laid for four. The mated pairs were prattling away quite happily, and Dobbin knew he was as clean forgotten as if he had never existed in this world.

"I should only be *de trop*", said the Captain, looking at them rather wistfully. "I'd best go and talk to the hermit", —and so he strolled off out of the hum of men, and noise, and clatter of the banquet, into the dark walk, at the end of which lived that well-known pasteboard Solitary. It wasn't very good fun for Dobbin—and, indeed, to be alone at Vauxhall, I have found, from my own experience, to be one of the most dismal sports ever entered into by a bachelor.

Later, in chapter IX, he seemed to be married to Julia and to have children:

What a dignity it gives an old lady, that balance at the banker's! How tenderly we look at her faults if she is a relative (and may every reader have a score of such), what a kind good-natured old creature we find her! How the junior partner of Hobbs and Dobbs leads her smiling to the carriage with the lozenge upon it, and the fat wheezy coachman! How, when she comes to pay us a visit, we generally find an opportunity to let our friends know her station in the world! We say (and with perfect truth) I wish I had Miss MacWhirter's signature to a cheque for five thousand pounds. She wouldn't miss it, says your wife. She is my aunt, say you, in an easy careless way, when your friend asks if Miss MacWhirter is any relative? Your wife is perpetually sending her little testimonies of affection, your little girls work endless worsted baskets, cushions, and footstools for her. What a good fire there is in her room when she comes to pay you a visit, although your wife laces her stays without one! The house during her stay assumes a festive, neat, warm, jovial, snug appearance not visible at other seasons. You yourself, dear sir, forget to go to sleep after dinner, and find yourself all of a sudden (though you invariably lose) very fond of a rubber. What good dinners you have—game every day, Malmsey-Madeira, and no end of fish from London. Even the servants in the kitchen share in the general prosperity; and, somehow, during the stay of Miss MacWhirter's fat coachman, the beer is grown much stronger, and the consumption of tea and sugar in the

nursery (where her maid takes her meals) is not regarded in
the least. Is it so, or is it not so? I appeal to the middle
classes. Ah, gracious powers! I wish you would send me an
old aunt—a maiden aunt—an aunt with a lozenge on her
carriage, and a front of light coffee-coloured hair—how my
children should work workbags for her, and my Julia and
I would make her comfortable! Sweet—sweet vision!
Foolish—foolish dream!

'We...you...I.' As a member of 'we' and 'you' the
author has a rich aunt, as 'I' he has not. Are Julia and
the children, we wonder, as much part and parcel of the
sweet vision as the aunt? Clearly there was no firm fact
here for any hunter after the private life of Thackeray,
and excuses in plenty for him to ride off on. It is Elia,
from whom Thackeray learned much, who prophetically
defined his 'mixed perspectives', to use Pater's phrase:

> Here is a young and courtly Mandarin, handing tea to a
> lady from a salver—two miles off. See how distance seems
> to set off respect! And here the same lady, or another—for
> likeness is identity on tea-cups—is stepping into a little fairy
> boat, moored on the hither side of this calm garden river,
> with a dainty mincing foot, which in a right angle of
> incidence (as angles go in our world) must infallibly land
> her in the midst of a flowery mead—a furlong off on the
> other side of the same strange stream![1]

When in other books than *Vanity Fair* the author speaks
on this same matter, it is to suggest that he hides the
propria persona as much as not. In the book for which he
was at pains to provide himself with a mask, he remarked
that

> If the secret history of books could be written, and the
> author's private thoughts and meanings noted down along-
> side of his story, how many insipid volumes would become
> interesting, and dull tales excite the reader![2]

---

[1] 'Old China.'   [2] *Pendennis*, ch. XLI.

The history, we note, is, and remains, secret history. On another occasion there is the same firm grasp of the eternal distinctions:

Whilst I am talking, for instance, in this easy chatty way, what right have you, my good sir, to know what is really passing in my mind? It may be that I am racked with gout, or that my eldest son has just sent me in a thousand pounds' worth of college-bills, or that I am writhing under an attack of the Stoke Pogis Sentinel, which has just been sent me under cover, or that there is a dreadfully scrappy dinner, the evident remains of a party to which I *didn't* invite you, and yet I conceal my agony, I wear a merry smile....[1]

3

The same distinctions, I think, rule the more wholly narrative autobiography in the novels. Some of the action they contain, we now know, was suggested by the actions of Thackeray, boy, youth and man. We might expect this of any novelist, let alone a novelist voluminous and unromantic as Thackeray. But in using autobiographical material no doubt he made the same sort of reservations he caused Pen to make:

There was not the slightest doubt then that this document contained a great deal of Pen's personal experiences, and that "Leaves from the life-book of Walter Lorraine" would never have been written but for Arthur Pendennis's own private griefs, passions, and follies. As we have become acquainted with these in the first volume of his biography, it will not be necessary to make large extracts from the novel of "Walter Lorraine", in which the young gentleman had depicted such of them as he thought were likely to interest the reader, or were suitable for the purposes of his story.[2]

Even if Thackeray, like Pen, drew on a great deal of his personal experiences, no doubt he also depicted what he

---

[1] *The Virginians*, ch. LVI.   [2] *Pendennis*, ch. XLI.

took in accordance with principles external to them, 'the purposes of the story'. Those purposes are slighted if his critics and biographers assume that they allowed or imposed an incompleteness of abstraction, that Thackeray knew his job so little as to intrude into a story confessions that were too overt and displays of a too private emotion. The question has exercised recent writers on Thackeray, and I shall speak of them at length later.[1] At best the novels are dangerous ground for his biographers. The last word, airily and warningly oracular, must remain that of Thackeray's Mr Batchelor:

> though it is all true, there is not a word of truth in it.[2]

There is also another principle which ought to deter the critics and biographers who peer into the novels for autobiography. Thackeray is an author who writes for the common reader. The common reader does not find it difficult to stay inside the novels, which include, when the novels are Thackeray's, the 'showman' on the edge of his stage. The reader of this sort looks on whatever he is given of autobiography (so claimed by biographers) and philosophy (for which Thackeray had some tremors) in the light that plays over the fiction as a whole. He does not give a thought to the author, in proportion as the narrative and the commentary are good. Nor can the author, knowing when he is well off, want him to. Such is the attitude of the common reader, and it is that attitude which the critic should himself preserve, however finely he investigates it.

So far as the philosophy in the novels goes, that critic[3] was mistaken who alleged that readers of the novels are frequently disturbed by the broken-nosed intrusions of the man. If any face intrudes, it is that of the 'mask' of

---

[1] See Appendix 1 below, pp. 273 ff.   [2] *Lovel the Widower*, ch. 1.
[3] I cannot recall his identity.

the narrator and moralist. When a voice issues from that mask, it is the voice of the story-teller which has been sounding since the first of all stories. And being that, is it not indeed as much the voice of the reader himself? So Thackeray hoped and believed. On one occasion, for confirmation of a point, the author calls on the reader to 'Lay down this page, and think...'.[1] On another he interposes:

Any man or woman with a pennyworth of brains, or the like precious amount of personal experience, or who has read a novel before, must, when Harry pulled out those faded vegetables [the rose and its leaves given him by Lady Maria] just now, have gone off into a digression of his own, as the writer confesses for himself he was diverging whilst he has been writing the last brace of paragraphs. If he sees a pair of lovers whispering in a garden alley or the embrasure of a window, or a pair of glances shot across the room from Jenny to the artless Jessamy, he falls to musing on former days when, &c. &c. These things follow each other by a general law, which is not as old as the hills, to be sure, but as old as the people who walk up and down them. When, I say, a lad pulls a bunch of amputated and now decomposing greens from his breast and falls to kissing it, what is the use of saying much more? As well tell the market-gardener's name from whom the slip-rose was bought—the waterings, clippings, trimmings, manurings, the plant has undergone—as tell how Harry Warrington came by it. *Rose, elle a vécu la vie des roses*, has been trimmed, has been watered, has been potted, has been sticked, has been cut, worn, given away, transferred to yonder boy's pocket-book and bosom, according to the laws and fate appertaining to roses.

And how came Maria to give it to Harry? And how did he come to want it and to prize it so passionately when he got the bit of rubbish? Is not one story as stale as the other?

[1] *The Virginians*, ch. XXII.

Are not they all alike? What is the use, I say, of telling them over and over? Harry values that rose because Maria has ogled him in the old way; because she has happened to meet him in the garden in the old way; because he has taken her hand in the old way; because they have whispered to one another behind the old curtain (the gaping old rag, as if everybody could not peep through it!); because, in this delicious weather, they have happened to be early risers and go into the park; because dear Goody Jenkins in the village happened to have a bad knee, and my Lady Maria went to read to her, and give her calves'-foot jelly, and because somebody, of course, must carry the basket. Whole chapters might have been written to chronicle all these circumstances, but à quoi bon? The incidents of life, and love-making especially, I believe to resemble each other so much, that I am surprised, gentlemen and ladies, you read novels any more. Psha! Of course that rose in young Harry's pocket-book had grown, and had budded, and had bloomed, and was now rotting, like other roses. I suppose you will want me to say that the young fool kissed it next? Of course he kissed it. What were lips made for, pray, but for smiling and simpering and (possibly) humbugging, and kissing, and opening to receive mutton-chops, cigars, and so forth? I cannot write this part of the story of our Virginians, because Harry did not dare to write it himself to anybody at home, because, if he wrote any letters to Maria (which, of course, he did, as they were in the same house, and might meet each other as much as they liked), they were destroyed; because he afterwards chose to be very silent about the story, and we can't have it from her Ladyship, who never told the truth about anything. But cui bono? I say again. What is the good of telling the story? My gentle reader, take your story: take mine. To-morrow it shall be Miss Fanny's, who is just walking away with her doll to the school-room and the governess (poor victim! she has a version of it in her desk): and next day it shall be Baby's, who is bawling out on the stairs for his bottle.[1]

[1] *The Virginians*, ch. xviii.

Thackeray knows that what he is saying is universal truth, 'a general law'. To the voice of the narrator 'every bosom', as Dr Johnson would say, 'returns an echo'.

In Thackeray's novels there is much of the 'I' not belonging to any of his personages. We might fix the distinction between it and Thackeray himself by using a phrase which occurs in the preface to *Pendennis* and calling it 'the person writing', or, more simply, the author. But, however we name it, its content is one of the most palpable things in our literature. Stronger than Fielding's, its tender manly force is as pervasive as the more womanish force of Sterne; and it is more directly vocal than Henry James's. It is an agency of unification more powerful even than any of the rest.

When I write 'Thackeray' in the pages that follow it will mean the authorial person unless it clearly means the man.

CHAPTER V

The Author's Conduct of His Commentary

In most of the novels the 'person writing' is present most noticeably in what I can provisionally call their passages of commentary.

Thackeray has been severely blamed for these. The charge that their matter is poor stuff, that they offend when judged as if they were pieces of essay or sermon, I shall meet in my last chapter. Here I wish to defend them against the charge that they intrude. When this issue is raised, we touch the very hub of the novels. The critic who likes Thackeray's novels must show that they are great without having their commentary shorn away; indeed he must show that they are greater because of their commentary. Unless he can maintain that, his praise of Thackeray might as well cease.

Defending Thackeray on this score, I start with the objections raised by Mr Lubbock. His classic book, *The Craft of Fiction*, has some good things to say about those novels of Thackeray which it touches on. But on one occasion crucial for my purpose Thackeray is seen askew. At a point in his argument Mr Lubbock brings him in to contrast him with Flaubert. Perhaps if Mr Lubbock had been using his powers to write of Thackeray alone he might have been—he might have become—fairer to him; it is a law of criticism, however numerous the exceptions to it, that one can see truly only what one sees in and for itself; that a contrast seized on as handy, though perhaps not so certainly a comparison, usually depends for its existence on the falsification of the minor term. He is noting that since *Madame Bovary* is not herself subtle enough to tell all that Flaubert wants telling about her, her maker faces the

dilemma that appears in any story, wherever the matter to be represented is the experience of a simple soul or a dull intelligence. If it is the experience and the actual taste of it that is to be imparted, the story must be viewed as the poor creature saw it; and yet the poor creature cannot tell the story in full. A shift of the vision is necessary. [In *Madame Bovary* the] author's wit...must supply what is wanting.[1]

And Flaubert is praised for managing the transition 'without awkwardness': he

is not the kind of story-teller who will leave it undisguised; he will not begin by "going behind" Emma, giving her view, and then openly, confessedly, revert to his own character and use his own standards. There is nothing more disconcerting in a novel than to *see* the writer changing his part in this way—throwing off the character into which he has been projecting himself and taking a new stand outside and away from the story.[2]

And so, by contrast, to Thackeray:

Perhaps it is only Thackeray, among the great, who seems to find a positively wilful pleasure in damaging his own story by open maltreatment of this kind; there are times when Thackeray will even boast of his own independence, insisting in so many words on his freedom to say what he pleases about his men and women and to make them behave as he will. ...When one has lived *into* the experience of somebody in the story and received the full sense of it, to be wrenched out of the story and stationed at a distance is a shock that needs to be softened or muffled in some fashion. Otherwise it may weaken whatever was true and valid in the experience; for here is a new view of it, external and

[1] Percy Lubbock, *The Craft of Fiction*, ed. 1929, p. 87.
[2] Ibid.

detached, and another mind at work, the author's—and that sense of having shared the life of the person in the story seems suddenly unreal.[1]

To rectify the misconception of Thackeray in this passage I must examine his narrative method as a whole. For this course I shall need Mr Lubbock's help, borrowing two of his terms—'panorama' and 'scene'— and also his distinction between the narrator who knows everything and the narrator who chooses not to.

To take first what Mr Lubbock says of those 'familiar resources of a story-teller, which everybody uses as a matter of course':

Sometimes [Flaubert] seems to be describing what he has seen himself, places and people he has known, conversations he may have overheard; I do not mean that he is literally retailing an experience of his own, but that he writes as though he were.... His object is to place the scene before us, so that we may take it in like a picture gradually unrolled or a drama enacted. But then again the method presently changes. There comes a juncture at which, for some reason, it is necessary for us to know more than we could have made out by simply looking and listening. Flaubert, the author of the story, must intervene with his superior knowledge. Perhaps it is something in the past of the people who have been moving and talking on the scene; you cannot rightly understand this incident or this talk, the author implies, unless you know—what I now proceed to tell you.[2]

So far there is not necessarily a distinction that matters very much. A scene supposed to exist in the past may be observed as wholly from outside as a scene supposed to exist in the present. Nor even when Mr Lubbock continues with his alternative:

Or it may be that he—who naturally knows everything, even the inmost, unexpressed thought of the characters—

---

[1] Ibid. pp. 87 ff.   [2] Op. cit. p. 65.

wishes us to share the mind of Bovary or of Emma, not to wait only on their words and actions....[1]

These familiar methods, rightly claimed as 'fundamental' in their 'differences', do not offer a ready means of dividing novelists into kinds because they are used by every novelist—or were until recently. It is only when we measure the amount they are used that they serve for differentiation. The question to ask of a novelist is which method does he favour *in the main*—to be free of the minds of his characters or to stand outside them? Does he prefer the role of god or man? Does he often assume omniscience, or mainly confine himself to using his wits as when observing his fellow creatures in actual life? Does he prefer, so to speak, the role of biographer and historian to that of dramatist?

In all Thackeray's novels some of the divine freedom is taken. Inevitably in *Esmond* and *Denis Duval*, which are presented as autobiographies. Writing about themselves, their supposed authors have no choice but to know, as we say, their own minds. In the other novels freedom is taken occasionally, but when so is not always taken, as by most other novelists, as a matter of course. Sometimes there is even a trace of fuss. On two occasions in *Vanity Fair* and on one in *Philip* we are reminded that novelists have the privilege of knowing everything;[2] in *Pendennis* a joke is added to the claim:

novelists are supposed to know everything, even the secrets of female hearts, which the owners themselves do not perhaps know...[3]

Or the writer will signalize unspoken thoughts as 'secret' thoughts; or, as in *The Newcomes*, frankly admit

[1] Op. cit. p. 65.
[2] *Vanity Fair*, chs. III and XXXIII; *Philip*, ch. X.   [3] Ch. XXIII.

that 'we are not in the young lady's secrets';[1] or, as in
Philip, he will say 'I think he was glad';[2] or sometimes
unspoken thoughts will be put in inverted commas as if
they were overheard monologue; or there is a special
justification—when we get a long string of them from
Becky it is rather because, being in the country and so
not having an audience she cares to talk to, she talks to
herself. Thackeray feels he is taking a liberty.

That liberty he takes against the grain. Much can be
read into the famous sentence that closes *Vanity Fair*:

Come children, let us shut up the box and the puppets, for
our play is played out.

Does Thackeray, we ask, see himself as the showman of
a known story—of such a story as that of Punch and
Judy—or is he the showman who invents his story, like
the novelist who at the end of Scott's essay on Bage, is
compared to 'the master of a puppet show, [who] has
his drama under his absolute authority'? Thackeray is
both the one and the other. He has invented his story,
but pretends to have been given it. The opening chapter
of *Vanity Fair* is called 'Before the Curtain', which does
not say where the responsibility for 'the present story'
lies—an uncertainty removed, however, by the first
sentence of chapter I:

While the present century was in its teens, and on one
sun-shiny morning in June, there drove up to the great iron
gate of Miss Pinkerton's academy for young ladies, on
Chiswick Mall, a large family coach....

The story is given out unmistakably as history, as merely
a further piece of the history everybody is already
familiar with. *The Newcomes* opens with a chapter called

---

[1] Ch. xxvii.   [2] Ch. xxxvii.

'The Overture', and again we are left in doubt until the opening of the story proper, when we find we are again to be given an extension of the familiar past. It is as a historian dealing with material existing externally that he wishes to pass off his novelist self and his stuff of the imagination. The eighth part of *The Newcomes*—what we know as chapter XXIV—opens as follows:

This narrative, as the judicious reader no doubt is aware, is written maturely and at ease, long after the voyage is over, whereof it recounts the adventures and perils; the winds adverse and favourable; the storms, shoals, shipwrecks, islands, and so forth, which Clive Newcome met in his early journey in life. In such a history events follow each other without necessarily having a connection with one another. One ship crosses another ship, and after a visit from one captain to his comrade, they sail away each on his course. The Clive Newcome meets a vessel which makes signals that she is short of bread and water; and after supplying her, our captain leaves her to see her no more. One or two of the vessels with which we commenced the voyage together, part company in a gale, and founder miserably; others, after being wofully battered in the tempest, make port; or are cast upon surprising islands where all sorts of unlooked-for prosperity awaits the lucky crew. Also, no doubt, the writer of the book, into whose hands Clive Newcome's logs have been put, and who is charged with the duty of making two octavo volumes out of his friend's story; dresses up the narrative in his own way; utters his own remarks in place of Newcome's; makes fanciful descriptions of individuals and incidents with which he never could have been personally acquainted; and commits blunders, which the critics will discover. A great number of the descriptions in "Cook's Voyages", for instance, were notoriously invented by Dr. Hawkesworth, who "did" the book: so in the present volumes, where dialogues are written down, which the reporter could by no possibility have heard, and where motives are detected which the persons actuated by them certainly never confided to the writer, the public must once for all be warned that the author's individual fancy very likely supplies much of the narrative; and that he forms it as best he may, out of stray papers, conversations reported to him, and his knowledge, right or wrong, of the characters of the persons engaged. And, as is the case with the most orthodox histories, the writer's own guesses or conjectures are printed in exactly the same type as the most ascertained patent facts. I fancy, for my part, that the speeches attributed to Clive, the Colonel, and the rest, are as authentic as the orations in Sallust or Livy, and only implore the truth-loving public to believe that incidents here told, and which passed very probably without witnesses, were either confided to me subsequently as compiler of this biography, or are of such a nature that they must have happened from what we know happened after. For example, when you read such words as QVE ROMANVS on a battered Roman stone, your profound antiquarian knowledge enables you to assert that SENATVS POPVLVS was also inscribed there at some time or other. You take a mutilated statue of Mars, Bacchus, Apollo, or Virorum, and you pop him on a wanting hand, an absent foot, or a nose, which time or barbarians have defaced. You tell your tales as you can, and state the facts as you think they must have been. In this manner, Mr. James (historiographer to her Majesty), Titus Livius, Professor Alison, Robinson Crusoe, and all historians proceeded. Blunders there must be in the best of these narratives, and more asserted than they can possibly know or vouch for.

And so in *The Virginians* and *Philip*. Granted that everything took place in the imagination, Thackeray was averse from creating more than the historian finds. What the historian finds is records, and, if he is present on the scene itself, what the senses take in. Those are the limits Thackeray preferred. He invented the invisible and inaudible as rarely as possible. Even where, in the first chapter of *The Virginians*, he is claiming *carte blanche*, he gives himself out as drawing on it only for sights and sounds:

I have drawn the figures as I fancied they were; set down conversations as I think I might have heard them...

A little earlier in the same introductory chapter he speaks of his two 'Virginians'—the colonel in scarlet and the general in blue and buff—as having

lived just on the verge of that Old World from which we are drifting away so swiftly. They were familiar with many varieties of men and fortune. Their lot brought them into contact with personages of whom we read only in books, who seem alive, as I read in the Virginians' letters regarding them, whose voices I almost fancy I hear, as I read the yellow pages....

Preferring the historian's conditions, he would not have been surprised to find an historian proper choosing to stand in his shoes:

what matters most in history is not what happened, but what people said about it when it was happening—about it, and round about it, because, after all, very little of any man's time is spent in talking about the things that get into the history books. But it is the little, unnoticed, things that make up "the endowment of the age" and so in the long run settle whether history shall move this way or that. Hence follows the rule which I always try to observe: "Go on reading till you can hear people talking".[1]

When he smiled at historians as writers whose material is often more imaginary than they think, it was a way not of placing them among novelists but himself among historians.

[1] G. M. Young, *Last Essays*, 1950, p. 9.

78

Because Thackeray is a self-styled historian, I do not think Mr Lubbock should have troubled to charge him with

even boast[ing] of his own independence, insisting in so many words on his freedom to say what he pleases about his men and women and to make them behave as he will.[1]

No doubt he has in mind the closing paragraph of *The Newcomes*:

What about Sir Barnes Newcome ultimately? My impression is that he is married again, and it is my fervent hope that his present wife bullies him. Mrs. Mackenzie cannot have the face to keep that money which Clive paid over to her, beyond her lifetime; and will certainly leave it and her savings to little Tommy. I should not be surprised if Madame de Montcontour left a smart legacy to the Pendennis' children; and Lord Kew stood godfather in case—in case Mr. and Mrs. Clive wanted such an article. But have they any children? I, for my part, should like her best without, and entirely devoted to little Tommy. But for you, dear friend, it is as you like. You may settle your fable-land in your own fashion. Anything you like happens in fable-land. Wicked folks die apropos (for instance, that death of Lady Kew was most artful, for if she had not died, don't you see that Ethel would have married Lord Farintosh the next week?)—annoying folks are got out of the way; the poor are rewarded—the upstarts are set down in fable-land, —the frog bursts with wicked rage, the fox is caught in his trap, the lamb is rescued from the wolf, and so forth, just in the nick of time. And the poet of fable-land rewards and punishes absolutely. He splendidly deals out bags of sovereigns, which won't buy anything; belabours wicked backs with awful blows, which do not hurt: endows heroines with preternatural beauty, and creates heroes, who, if ugly sometimes, yet possess a thousand good qualities, and usually end by being immensely rich; makes the hero and

[1] Op. cit. p. 88.

79

heroine happy at last, and happy ever after. Ah, happy, harmless fable-land, where these things are! Friendly reader! may you and the author meet there on some future day! He hopes so; as he yet keeps a lingering hold of your hand, and bids you farewell with a kind heart.

Even here, we note, Thackeray is speaking mainly of the fable-lands of others—readers and poets.

A passage relevant to this matter occurs in 'The Art of Fiction', in which Henry James rounded on Trollope for doing what Mr Lubbock charges to Thackeray:

the novel is history. That is the only general description (which does it justice) that we may give of the novel. But history also is allowed to represent life; it is not, any more than painting, expected to apologize. The subject-matter of fiction is stored up likewise in documents and records, and if it will not give itself away, as they say in California, it must speak with assurance, with the tone of the historian. Certain accomplished novelists have a habit of giving themselves away which must often bring tears to the eyes of people who take their fiction seriously. I was lately struck, in reading over many pages of Anthony Trollope, with his want of discretion in this particular. In a digression, a parenthesis or an aside, he concedes to the reader that he and this trusting friend are only 'making believe'. He admits that the events he narrates have not really happened, and that he can give his narrative any turn the reader may like best. Such a betrayal of a sacred office seems to me, I confess, a terrible crime; it is what I mean by the attitude of apology, and it shocks me every whit as much in Trollope as it would have shocked me in Gibbon or Macaulay. It implies that the novelist is less occupied in looking for the truth (the truth, of course I mean, that he assumes, the premises that we must grant him, whatever they may be) than the historian, and in doing so it deprives him at a stroke of all his standing-room. To represent and illustrate the past, the actions of men, is the task of either writer, and the only difference that I can see is, in proportion as he succeeds, to the honour of the novelist, consisting as it does in his having more difficulty in collecting his evidence, which is so far from being purely literary. It seems to me to give him a great character, the fact that he has at once so much in common with the philosopher and the painter; this double analogy is a magnificent heritage.

Here James is writing as if with Thackeray's pen. To listen to Thackeray you would not think him one of the world's great inventors of stories. He succeeded so well in his pretence that, as Mr Forsythe has said of *The History of Henry Esmond*, his

air of the utmost veracity...deceive[s] the average reader into believing that [what he writes] is history indeed.[1]

Thackeray would have reckoned it the best of compliments. Some of his personages—the Pretender, Benjamin Franklin, George Washington—were given to him by history books; what he did with them after taking them is 'another story'. But he made no distinction between them and the rest—the personages of which the materials lay permanently scattered over life for all the world to see, but which had lain neglected till he gathered them out of his memory—everybody's memory —into just those clusters. He asks us to take his Becky Sharp as we take his Queen Anne. He created from scratch most of the personages he imagined, but pretended merely to imagine persons already created for him. In *Pendennis* he remarked:

Sir Roger and Mr. Spectator are as real to us now as the two doctors [Johnson and Goldsmith] and the boozy[2] and faithful Scotchman. The poetical figures live in our memory just as much as the real personages....[3]

[1] R. S. Forsythe, *A Noble Rake: The Life of Charles, Fourth Lord Mohun, Being a Study in the Historical Background of Thackeray's 'Henry Esmond'*, Cambridge, Mass., 1928, p. viii.
[2] A pun on 'Bozzy'=Boswell.　　　[3] Ch. XLIX.

The observation would continue to stand if we supplanted Sir Roger and Mr Spectator with invented personages of Thackeray. He availed himself of an ambiguity which on one occasion a pupil of Becky had found useful:

[Rebecca] and Miss Rose thus read together many delightful French and English works, among which may be mentioned those of the learned Dr. Smollett, of the ingenious Mr. Henry Fielding, of the graceful and fantastic Monsieur Crébillon the younger, whom our immortal poet Gray so much admired, and of the universal Monsieur de Voltaire. Once, when Mr. Crawley asked what the young people were reading, the governess replied "Smollett". "Oh, Smollett," said Mr. Crawley, quite satisfied. "His history is more dull, but by no means so dangerous as that of Mr. Hume. It is history you are reading?" "Yes," said Miss Rose; without, however, adding that it was the history of Mr. Humphrey Clinker.[1]

2

This consideration of drama, novel and history brings us to Mr Lubbock's terms, 'panorama' and 'scene'. Both terms he illustrates from *Vanity Fair*. It is as a scene that he takes Thackeray's presentation of the incident that marks the major crisis in Becky's fortunes. Hitherto we have had 'panorama'—

we have been listening to Thackeray, on the whole, while he talked about Becky—talked with such extraordinary brilliance that he evoked her in all her ways and made us see her with his eyes; but now it is time to see her with our own....[2]

We misunderstand Thackeray's method, however, unless we see that Mr Lubbock exaggerates the extent of the shift. He errs in describing the 'scene' as 'strictly

[1] *Vanity Fair*, ch. x.   [2] Op. cit. p. 100.

dramatic'. That no scene in Thackeray ever is, except, of course, those few tête-à-tête conversations, which, for economy's sake and with a glance at the contemporary stage, he prints as drama. With that exception, the presenter of the scene is always seen performing the act of presenting it, treating it as if it were also panorama. To look more closely at Mr Lubbock's instance, and to begin with the setting: Rawdon, we are told,

walked home rapidly. It was nine o'clock at night. He ran across the streets, and the great squares of Vanity Fair, and at length came up breathless opposite his own house. He started back and fell against the railings, trembling as he looked up. The drawing-room windows were blazing with light. She had said that she was in bed and ill. He stood there for some time, the light from the rooms on his pale face.[1]

So far this preliminary is panorama, with one moment's recourse by the author to omniscience: we are given the inside of Rawdon's mind in 'She had said that she was in bed and ill'. Apart from this one sentence—and even that evinces knowledge of an external fact, what Becky had written in her letter, not knowledge of thought —we discern Rawdon's mind only on the evidence of our eyes: which is plentiful evidence—witness 'rapidly . . . across. . . at length. . . breathless. . . started. . . fell. . . trembling. . . for some time. . . pale'. But even in this passage, Thackeray is more than a pair of eyes—more, however, not because he enters the minds of his personages, but because he gives us his own. If it is Rawdon who is observed to run across the streets and squares, it is 'the person writing' who calls the squares 'great', for 'great' is ironic and Rawdon is in no mood for literary

[1] *Vanity Fair*, ch. LIII.

refinements. Nor in any mood for the periphrasis, painful as it is, of 'the wretched woman':

Rawdon opened the door and went in. A little table with a dinner was laid out—and wine and plate. Steyne was hanging over the sofa on which Becky sate. The wretched woman was in a brilliant full toilette.

In the scene that follows we have aural experience added to ocular—words are spoken and we hear them. But at this point, too, we get something more. The 'person writing' not only sees and hears but comments. When Rawdon has flung Lord Steyne to the ground, we are told not only what might have been seen by any sharp-eyed onlooker, that Rebecca 'stood there trembling before him' but also what could only have been seen by eyes sharpened on the flint of a mind's power of insight, that 'she admired her husband, strong, brave, victorious'. And it is 'the person writing' who adds the remote, cool, Homeric touch, a touch also of the mock-heroic such as Thackeray often added to his narrative:

[Rawdon] tore the diamond ornament out of her breast, and flung it at Lord Steyne. It cut him on his bald forehead. Steyne wore the scar to his dying day.

And if Thackeray intended an echo of the phrase 'wore the star', that is another ironic touch added from outside the scene.

Thackeray has scenes by the hundred. I do not give much weight to Mr Lubbock's remark that he jibbed at big ones. It may happen once or twice in *Vanity Fair*. But on the whole his novels are a string of scenes of all sizes. With his aspiration to hear his persons speak, how could it be otherwise? But even in a scene Thackeray is panoramic also, and he distances the picture and conversations by his own commentary on them.

3

I am not yet concerned with what I think Thackeray's reasons for keeping as near the method of the historian as he could, but of course he would not have allowed himself to choose it if he had not valued its golden opportunities as a medium for fictional narrative. In particular he valued the status it gave to the thing seen, a status even superior to that of the thing heard. Thackeray was not interested in rendering any visible object for its own sake. Even as a maker of drawings he was always using the scene to convey his sense of the human. In his travel books of necessity there is description of place, but it is all done gaily as if in letters home, or in conversation with a friend, and always with an eye to what is amusingly or interestingly human. In his novels his gift for rendering visible things is used almost solely to the advantage of his personages or his philosophy—I shall have more to say of this later. His eye is not that of a child: it is sharp for the thing that tells character or emotion, as sharp for this purpose as the eye of Chaucer, Shakespeare or Pope. When he made notes for his fiction, some of them took the form of drawings. No novelist gets straighter and deeper into the mind, but it is by staying on the flesh.

Take as an instance his reading of the eyes of his personages. For Bacon eyes were 'that part' of the face 'which doth most show the spirit and life of a person';[1] for Hume they were 'the great Index of the Mind'.[2] Such an index Thackeray found them. The 'opal eyes' of young Woolcomb, the rich mulatto who attracts Agnes away from Philip, remind us of his racial blood,

[1] Quoted René Wellek, *The Rise of Literary History*, p. 13.
[2] Quoted the Twickenham edition of Pope, II, 336.

but also suggest the strangeness, for an English girl, of his physical attractiveness, his wealth and his moral instability.[1] The green eyes of Becky Sharp match something vivid in the mind. Blanche Amory's mind is read in her glances:

"Sing me one of the old songs after dinner, will you", said Pen, with an imploring voice.

"Shall I sing you an English song, after dinner," asked the Sylphide, turning to Mr. Foker. "I will, if you will promise to come up soon": and she gave him a perfect broadside of her eyes.[2]

Two chapters later:

she gave [Pen] the full benefit of her eyes,—both of the fond appealing glance into his own, and of the modest look downwards towards the carpet, which showed off her dark eyelids and long fringed lashes.[3]

(The eyelids of Major Pendennis, we remember, are 'wrinkled'.) On the other hand Laura lays on Warrington 'a look full of tender brightness'.[4] That which Rachel gave Esmond was 'stately', and on another occasion her eyes are 'fine'.[5] Mrs Lambert 'look[s] at her husband with her very best eyes'.[6] At the party Mr Sherrick directs 'savage winks' to nudge his wife.[7] And there are the eyes of Dr Firmin, set in what a face:

that smile of Firmin's was a very queer contortion of the handsome features. As you came up to him, he would draw his lips over his teeth, causing his jaws to wrinkle (or dimple if you will) on either side. Meanwhile his eyes looked out from his face, quite melancholy and independent of the little transaction in which the mouth was engaged. Lips said, "I am a gentleman of fine manners and fascinating

---

[1] *Philip*, ch. VIII.   [2] *Pendennis*, ch. XXXVIII.
[3] Ibid. ch. XL.   [4] Ibid. ch. LIV.
[5] Bk I, ch. IX.   [6] *The Virginians*, ch. XXI.
[7] *The Newcomes*, ch. XXIII.

address, and I am supposed to be happy to see you. How do you do?" Dreary, sad, as into a great blank desert, looked the dark eyes. I *do* know one or two, but only one or two faces of men, when oppressed with care, which can yet smile *all over*.[1]

Thackeray's personages, even when no more than seen, have a good deal of inside to them. It was an incomplete verdict that Charlotte Brontë passed on Jane Austen:

Her business is not half so much with the human heart as with the human eyes, mouth, hands and feet...[2]

To complete it one must add that these outward things declare the inner. For Thackeray, if not for Jane Austen, even Charlotte Brontë's last unfair item can be retained. I shall come to note the significant feet of the Fotheringay.[3] And what could be more devastatingly expressive than the feet of Miss Baughton?

Mrs. Gandish, Colonel Topham, Major M'Cracken are announced, and then, in diamonds, feathers and splendour Lady Baughton and Miss Baughton, who are going to the Queen's ball, and Sir Curry Baughton, not quite in his deputy-lieutenant's uniform as yet, looking very shy in a pair of blue trousers, with a glittering stripe of silver down the seams. Clive looks with wonder and delight at these ravishing ladies, rustling in fresh brocades, with feathers, diamonds, and every magnificence. Aunt Ann has not her court-dress on as yet; and Aunt Maria blushes as she beholds the newcomers, having thought fit to attire herself in a high dress, with a Quaker-like simplicity, and a pair of gloves more than ordinarily dingy. The pretty little foot she has, it is true, and sticks it out from habit; but what is Mrs. Newcome's foot compared with that sweet little chaussure which Miss Baughton exhibits and withdraws? The shiny white

[1] *Philip*, ch. III.   [2] *The Brontës*, III, 99.
[3] See below, p. 139.

87

satin slipper, the pink stocking which ever and anon peeps from the rustling folds of her robe, and timidly retires into its covert—that foot, light as it is, crushes Mrs. Newcome.[1]

It is therefore in a special sense that we understand Roscoe's criticism that Thackeray

never penetrates into the interior, secret, *real* life that every man leads in isolation from his fellows....[2]

We must take this to mean that Thackeray seldom concerned himself with the history moment-by-moment of the interior life, with the object Wordsworth discerned when he spoke of 'tracing...passion through many of its more subtle windings'.[3] Windings have been traced very much during the last hundred years. They were largely ignored by Thackeray. The unseen and the unheard which did interest him was the nature of what was winding, and the figure it cut at certain readable points on its career—a career which, as I shall show, he saw as circular.

4

There are sometimes special opportunities open to an author who is not so entangled in the minds of his personages as to fail to see that, on some occasions, their depths are best revealed by an addition made to the account of things external—by a rendering of the suddenly new value the scene has acquired as if by the external assistance of the pathetic fallacy. Towards the close of *The Newcomes* we get this account of the contentious household of which Clive is the supposed head:

A little voice is heard crying over-head—and giving a kind of gasp, the wretched father stops in some indifferent speech he was trying to make—"I can't help myself", he groans out; "my poor wife is so ill, she can't attend to the child. Mrs. Mackenzie manages the house for me—and—

[1] *The Newcomes*, ch. XIX.   [2] II, 266.
[3] The 1800 Preface to *The Lyrical Ballads*.

here! Tommy, Tommy! Papa's coming!" Tommy has been crying again, and flinging open the studio door, Clive calls out, and dashes up-stairs.

I hear scuffling, stamping, loud voices, poor Tommy's scared little pipe—Clive's fierce objurgations, and the Campaigner's voice barking out—"Do, sir, do! with my child suffering in the next room. Behave like a brute to me, do. He shall not go out. He shall not have the hat"—"He shall"—"Ah—ah!" A scream is heard. It is Clive tearing a child's hat out of the Campaigner's hands, with which, and a flushed face, he presently rushes down-stairs, bearing little Tommy on his shoulder.

"You see what I am come to, Pen," he says with a heart-broken voice, trying, with hands all of a tremble, to tie the hat on the boy's head. He laughs bitterly at the ill-success of his endeavours. "Oh, you silly papa!" laughs Tommy, too.

The door is flung open, and the red-faced Campaigner appears. Her face is mottled with wrath, her bandeaux of hair are disarranged upon her forehead, the ornaments of her cap, cheap, and dirty, and numerous, only give her a wilder appearance. She is in a large and dingy wrapper, very different from the lady who had presented herself a few months back to my wife—how different from the smiling Mrs. Mackenzie of old days!

"He shall *not* go out of a winter day, sir," she breaks out. "I have his mother's orders, whom you are *killing*. Mr. Pendennis!" She starts, perceiving me for the first time, and her breast heaves, and she prepares for combat, and looks at me over her shoulder.

"You and his father are the best judges upon this point, ma'am," says Mr. Pendennis, with a bow.

"The child is delicate, sir," cries Mrs. Mackenzie; "and this winter—".

And so to this:

"Enough of this", says Clive, with a stamp, and passes through her guard with Tommy, and we descend the stairs, and at length are in the free street.[1]

[1] Ch. LXXV.

When the house, which is the Englishman's castle, is no longer free, the street, ordinarily a public and so a controlled place, has freedom thrust upon it. We learn of the relief for the minds of the escaped by means of a change discerned in the quality of the scene.

Another instance. When Philip is coming to the end of his stormy courtship of Charlotte, some of his opposers are ready to show their goodwill. This is how the narrator words the sudden ending of the tension:

And Philip says, when in this his agony of grief and doubt he found a friendly hand put out to him, he himself was so exceedingly moved that he was compelled to fly out of the company of the old men, into the night, where the rain was pouring—the gentle rain.[1]

I suggest that a novelist chary, on any pretext, of settling down in the minds of his personages is the readier to make use of such powerful means of expressing those minds. I have called it the historian's method, but at places like these it deserves to be called that of the epic poet. And such places are common in the novels of Thackeray.

5

These things being so, then the passages of commentary are nearer the stuff of the action than Mr Lubbock sees, and his difficulty is proportionately less:

When one has lived *into* the experience of somebody in the story and received the full sense of it, to be wrenched out of the story and stationed at a distance is a shock that needs to be softened and muffled in some fashion.[2]

Is Mr Lubbock quite clear about what it is in the novels that we 'live into'? Live deeply into something we do—

---

[1] *Philip*, ch. xxvii.   [2] Op. cit. p. 88.

Trollope, in a passage I shall quote later,[1] speaks of Thackeray's 'touching the innermost core of his subject' —but not into personages pure and simple. Rather it is into personages presented, mused over and judged. Thus from *pure* personage to *pure* commentary no transition is possible, and so no wrench. The transitions, which are therefore smooth, are from narrative with criticism to criticism with narrative. If, while reading Thackeray, we look into the composition of our experience, we find that a portion of it, even when the narration is at its purest, is experience of commentary. Thackeray is the critic, not merely of certain things, but of everything he invents. So habitual to him is his historian's method that we ought to be surprised when he gives us the invisible and unreadable thoughts of his characters—not the other way round, when he gives us his own. He is a critic constantly. Sometimes a critical idea runs hand in hand with the narrative for a long stretch. *Philip*, as I have said, is built about the story of the good Samaritan, as if it were an enormous illustration of it, the full title of the novel reading: *The Adventures of Philip on his Way through the World*; *shewing who robbed him, who helped him, and who passed him by.* Chapter xxxi of *The Virginians* is equally and constantly about the stages of inebriation[2] and the stages by which the Rev. Mr Sampson learned exactly how things stood between Henry and Lady Maria. The action in one of the chapters of *Vanity Fair* is subsumed under the heading 'How to live well on nothing a-year'. And so on. Sometimes, on the other hand, the criticism exists in dropped single words. Thackeray has a score of

---

[1] See below, p. 127.
[2] Thackeray had already distinguished those of 'the merriment of the three-bottle point' to 'the sickly stupidity of the seventh' in *Catherine* ('Chapter the Last').

critical epithets that recur constantly—'little', 'great', 'poor' (often with 'little'), 'dingy', 'old', 'absurd', 'dismal', 'simpering', 'smirking', 'darling', 'sacred'. These words throw a net of the same one thread over the length and breadth of his work. They are, as it were, the tiny footprints of his philosophy implanted as he moves from one passage of moral disquisition, of philosophy, to another. Each offers its small recurrent criticism of the life he has invented, and of life itself.

There is also the criticism conveyed by single words that do not recur. Towards the end of *The Newcomes* we have the little scene in which the mother-in-law— Mrs Mackenzie, the 'old campaigner'—protects her daughter from what she thinks Clive's cruelty:

Behind that "situation" [Rosey is pregnant] the widow shielded herself. She clung to her adored child, and from that bulwark discharged abuse and satire at Clive and his father. He could not rout her out of her position. Having had the advantage on the first two or three days, on the four last he was beaten, and lost ground in each action. Rosey found that in her situation she could not part from her darling mamma. The Campaigner for her part averred that she might be reduced to beggary—that she might be robbed of her last farthing and swindled and cheated—that she might see her daughter's fortune flung away by unprincipled adventurers, and her blessed child left without even the comforts of life—but desert her in such a situation, she never would—no, never! Was not dear Rosa's health already impaired by the various shocks which she had undergone? Did she not require every comfort, every attendance? Monster! ask the doctor! She would stay with her darling child in spite of insult and rudeness and vulgarity. (Rosa's father was a king's officer, not a company's officer, thank God!) She would stay as long at least as Rosa's situation continued, at Boulogne, if not in London, but with her child. They might refuse to send her money, having robbed her of all her own, but she would pawn her gown off her back for her child. Whimpers from Rosey—cries of "Mamma, mamma, compose yourself,"—convulsive sobs—clenched knuckles— flashing eyes—embraces rapidly clutched—laughs—stamps —snorts—from the dishevelled Campaigner—grinding teeth —livid fury and repeated breakages of the third commandment by Clive—I can fancy the whole scene. He returned to London without his wife, and when she came she brought Mrs. Mackenzie with her.[1]

'Clutched' conveys judgment as well as sense impression. In *Esmond* the 'nymph on the opera-machine quaver[s] out her last song';[2] in *Pendennis* Blanche 'shook out a little song';[3] and in *Philip* we 'quaver out *Peccavimus*'.[4] Though these words are not recurrent, they clearly fall into a system (which, by the way, Thackeray passed on to Henry James). They are words conveying criticism as certainly as the words that recur. They convey criticism of one and the same kind, distant yet tender, that of the author who can speak of his personages as puppets, who can write arresting words such as 'and the little flame of life is popped out'.[5]

Not all these single words bear the same amount of criticism. They shade off from a word like 'sacred', which is wholly criticism, to a word like 'clutched', which, as I have said, is part criticism and part transcript of sense impression. Often the criticism does not exist in the words on the plane they pretend to be occupying, but is supplied by the reader, who sees them to occupy another also: they look innocent as they lie on the page of the writer; as they enter the mind of the reader the *double entendre* creates itself. Instances come everywhere. I shall mention later the stroke of genius

---

[1] Ch. LXXIV. [2] Bk III, ch. IV.
[3] Ch. XXII. [4] Ch. XXVII.
[5] *The Roundabout Papers*, 'Autour de mon Chapeau'.

by which the religious Becky is made to write hymns—
anything to be in the limelight, even in church. Or
there is the Rev. Charles Honeyman reproving
Pendennis:

"Satire! satire! Mr. Pendennis", says the divine, holding
up a reproving finger of lavender kid, "beware of a wicked
wit!"[1]

Or this piece of dialogue (the 'he' is the same
Honeyman):

"He can't make less than a thousand a year out of his
chapel.... A thousand a year, besides the rent of the wine-
vaults below the chapel."

"Don't, Charles!" says his wife, with a solemn look.
"Don't ridicule things in that way."

..."I wonder if [the tenants of the vaults are the people]
with whom Kew and Jack Belsize had that ugly row?"

"What ugly row?—don't say ugly row. It is not a nice
word to hear the children use. Go on, my darlings. What
was the dispute of Lord Kew and Mr. Belsize...?"[2]

Again, in the same book, Barnes delivers two lectures as
part of his campaign for getting into Parliament:

"What do you think your darling, Sir Barnes Newcome
Newcome, has been doing during the recess?" cries Warrington. "I had a letter, this morning, from my liberal and
punctual employer, Thomas Potts, Esquire, of the 'Newcome Independent', who states, in language scarcely
respectful, that Sir Barnes Newcome Newcome is trying to
come the religious dodge, as Mr. Potts calls it. He professes
to be stricken down by grief on account of late family circumstances; wears black, and puts on the most piteous
aspect, and asks ministers of various denominations to tea
with him; and the last announcement is the most stupendous
of all. Stop, I have it in my great coat;" and, ringing the
bell, George orders a servant to bring him a newspaper from

[1] *The Newcomes*, ch. XIX.   [2] *The Newcomes*, ch. XI.

94

his great-coat pocket. "Here it is, actually in print," Warrington continues, and reads to us. "'Newcome Athenaeum. 1. for the benefit of the Newcome Orphan Children's Home, and 2. for the benefit of the Newcome Soup Association, without distinction of denomination. Sir Barnes Newcome Newcome, Bart., proposes to give two lectures, on Friday the 23rd, and Friday the 30th, instant. No. 1, The Poetry of Childhood; Doctor Watts, Mrs. Barbauld, Jane Taylor. No. 2, The Poetry of Womanhood, and the Affections; Mrs. Hemans, L.E.L. Threepence will be charged at the doors, which will go to the use of the above two admirable Societies'. Potts wants me to go down and hear him. He has an eye to business. He has had a quarrel with Sir Barnes, and wants me to go down and hear him, and smash him, he kindly says. Let us go down, Clive. You shall draw your cousin as you have drawn his villainous little mug a hundred times before; and I will do the smashing part, and we will have some fun out of the transaction."[1]

This piece of the story begins with the explicit criticism of him delivered by his opponents, but nobody comments on Barnes's choice of subject for his lectures. The choice nevertheless is judged, as it were privately between themselves, by writer and reader, both of whom are well aware of Barnes's deficiencies as husband and father.

In Thackeray's novels, then, criticism that is implicit exists as plentifully—indeed, much more plentifully, for it is almost everywhere—as criticism that is explicit. We may prefer the implicit; the compliment it pays us is pleasing, and, being pleased, we place a higher value on what we ourselves have found, our esteem for the author benefiting accordingly. But the degrees of our pleasure do not affect the nature of what produces it. If the writer does the showing or the reader the finding, what is shown

---

[1] *The Newcomes*, ch. LXV.

or found is alike criticism. There is no break, then, even if there is a step, from single words of criticism to passages of it, or from implicit commentary to explicit. His philosophy exists in two modes, one to be looked at for itself, as it were a silver luminousness in the sky; and the other to be seen, less detached in its effects, in the transfigurement it produces on what lies under its mild or searching rays. If we 'live into' the personages of the novels (and we do), we do not shake off the philosophy in the process of penetration. Threads which do not break attach us to the criticism we may think we have left outside. And the threads twitch constantly.

From this it is merely a step to the defence of the commentary when it becomes a sermon. If the commentary arises out of the constant manner in which everything is seen by the person writing, it arises also, as I have said, out of the constant manner in which everything is seen by the reader. On some occasions, the author tells us he speaks for the reader, expressing for him what is latent in his mind. Usually there is no need of that assurance. And so there is no break, but again at most a step, when commentary becomes homily. 'This book', says the 'person writing' of *The Newcomes*, 'is not a sermon, except where it cannot help itself, and the speaker pursuing the destiny of his narrative finds such a homily before him'.[1] This remark makes as strong a claim as possible for the integrity of the novels—the person writing does not say 'except where I cannot help myself'. The criticism directed at the story is so vigorous and assured, at least from the time of *Vanity Fair* onwards, that, as well as to speak with and for the reader, it dares to direct itself *at* the reader. By virtue of the length of time that both of them have been hobnobbing

[1] Ch. xxxviii.

96

together, the liberties that cannot but be taken by any preacher can be taken as agreed by the reader preached at by Thackeray. Addressing himself to the conscience of the reader as well as to his intellect, the writer has taken all necessary pains to remind him that his conscience exists, and that it is ready to be appealed to. Moral questions have been put, all with foregone but painful answers, the reader having no option but to supply them.

6

Having seen how universal in the narrative of Thackeray is his philosophy, we can see, too, how universal in the passages of philosophy is narrative. Inside the passages of philosophy we are still seeing actions as well as receiving thoughts. Even when they are homilies, they resemble the homilies that are packed with story. In *The Virginians* Thackeray mentions Law's *Serious Call to a Devout and Holy Life*. To many of our great writers that book has seemed as good a religious book as exists outside the Bible. And half of it is story, personage, 'character'. So with Thackeray's passages of commentary. They are always half narrative, drawing on the same human stuff as the narrative draws on. I have said already that the passages of musing carry as much detail as the passages of narrative. Their detail is usually narrative detail. And many of Thackeray's passages of commentary melt into the particular narrative stuff of the novels they contribute to. Look, for instance, at this passage from *The Newcomes* which deals with family prayers in the house of Sir Brian; criticism conveyed by different means jostles with picture and with story:

Some four or five weeks after the quasi reconciliation between Clive and his kinsman, the chief part of Sir Brian Newcome's family were assembled at the breakfast-table together, where the meal was taken in common, and at the early hour of eight (unless the senator was kept too late in the House of Commons overnight): and Lady Ann and her nursery were now returned to London again, little Alfred being perfectly set up by a month of Brighton air. It was a Thursday morning; on which day of the week, it has been said the *Newcome Independent* and the *Newcome Sentinel* both made their appearance upon the baronet's table. The household from above and from below; the maids and foot-men from the basement; the nurses, children, and governesses from the attics; all poured into the room at the sound of a certain bell.

I do not sneer at the purpose for which, at that chiming eight o'clock bell, the household is called together. The urns are hissing, the plate is shining; the father of the house standing up, reads from a gilt book for three or four minutes in a measured cadence. The members of the family are around the table in an attitude of decent reverence, the younger children whisper responses at their mother's knees; the governess worships a little apart; the maids and the large footmen are in a cluster before their chairs, the upper servants performing their devotion on the other side of the side-board; the nurse whisks about the unconscious last-born and tosses it up and down during the ceremony. I do not sneer at that—at the act at which all these people are assembled—it is at the rest of the day I marvel; at the rest of the day, and what it brings. At the very instant when the voice has ceased speaking and the gilded book is shut, the world begins again, and for the next twenty-three hours and fifty-seven minutes, all that household is given up to it. The servile squad rises up and marches away to its basement, whence, should it happen to be a gala day, those tall gentlemen at present attired in Oxford mixture, will issue forth with flour plastered on their heads, yellow coats, pink breeches, sky-blue waistcoats, silver lace, buckles in their shoes, black silk bags on their backs, and I don't know what insane emblems of servility and absurd bedizenments of folly. Their very manner of speaking to what we call their masters and mistresses will be a like monstrous masquerade. You know no more of that race which inhabits the basement floor, than of the men and brethren of Timbuctoo, to whom some among us send missionaries. If you met some of your servants in the streets (I respectfully suppose for a moment that the reader is a person of high fashion and a great establishment), you would not know their faces. You might sleep under the same roof for half a century, and know nothing about them. If they were ill, you would not visit them, though you would send them an apothecary and of course order that they lacked for nothing. You are not unkind, you are not worse than your neighbours. Nay, perhaps if you did go into the kitchen, or to take the tea in the servants' hall, you would do little good, and only bore the folks assembled there. But so it is. With those fellow Christians who have just been saying Amen to your prayers, you have scarcely the community of Charity. They come, you don't know whence; they think and talk you don't know what; they die, and you don't care, or *vice versâ*. They answer the bell for prayers as they answer the bell for coals: for exactly three minutes in the day you all kneel together on one carpet—and, the desires and petitions of the servants and masters over, the rite called family worship is ended.

Exeunt servants, save those two who warm the newspaper, adminster the muffins, and serve out the tea. Sir Brian reads his letters, and chumps his dry toast. Ethel whispers to her mother, she thinks Eliza is looking very ill. Lady Ann asks, which is Eliza? Is it the woman that was ill before they left town? If she is ill, Mrs. Trotter had better send her away. Mrs. Trotter is only a great deal too good-natured. She is always keeping people who are ill. Then her Ladyship begins to read the *Morning Post*, and glances over the names of the persons who were present at Baroness Bosco's ball, and Mrs. Toddle Tompkyns's *soirée dansante* in Belgrave Square.

"Everybody was there," says Barnes, looking over from his paper.[1]

[1] Ch. xiv.

Or this from towards the end of the novel:

The Colonel accompanied Clive to the lodgings which we had found for the young artist, in a quarter not far removed from the old house in Fitzroy Square, where some happy years of his youth had been spent. When sitters came to Clive—as at first they did in some numbers, many of his early friends being anxious to do him a service—the old gentleman was extraordinarily cheered and comforted. We could see by his face that affairs were going on well at the studio. He showed us the rooms which Rosey and the boy were to occupy. He prattled to our children and their mother, who was never tired of hearing him, about his grandson. He filled up the future nursery with a hundred little knickknacks of his own contriving; and with wonderful cheap bargains, which he bought in his walks about Tottenham Court Road. He pasted a most elaborate book of prints and sketches for Boy. It was astonishing what notice Boy already took of pictures. He would have all the genius of his father. Would he had had a better grandfather than the foolish old man, who had ruined all belonging to him!

However much they like each other, men in the London world see their friends but seldom. The place is so vast that even next door is distant; the calls of business, society, pleasure, so multifarious that mere friendship can get or give but an occasional shake of the hand in the hurried moments of passage. Men must live their lives; and are per force selfish, but not unfriendly. At a great need you know where to look for your friend, and he that he is secure of you. So I went very little to Howland Street, where Clive now lived; very seldom to Lamb Court, where my dear old friend Warrington still sate in his old chambers, though our meetings were none the less cordial when they occurred, and our trust in one another always the same. Some folks say the world is heartless: he who says so either prates common-places, (the most likely and charitable suggestion) or is heartless himself, or is most singular and unfortunate in having made no friends. Many such a reasonable mortal cannot have: our nature, I think, not sufficing for that sort of polygamy. How many persons would you have to deplore your death; or whose death would you wish to deplore? Could our hearts let in such a harem of dear friendships, the mere changes and recurrences of grief and mourning would be intolerable, and tax our lives beyond their value. In a word, we carry our own burthen in the world; push and struggle along on our own affairs; are pinched by our own shoes—though heaven forbid we should not stop and forget ourselves sometimes, when a friend cries out in his distress, or we can help a poor stricken wanderer in his way. As for good women—these, my worthy reader, are different from us—the nature of these is to love, and to do kind offices, and devise untiring charities:—so, I would have you to know, that, though Mr. Pendennis was *parcus suorum cultor et infrequens*, Mrs. Laura found plenty of time to go from Westminster to Bloomsbury; and to pay visits to her Colonel and her Clive, both of whom she had got to love with all her heart again, now misfortune was on them; and both of whom returned her kindness with an affection blessing the bestower and the receiver; and making the husband proud and thankful whose wife had earned such a noble regard. What is the dearest praise of all to a man? his own—or that you should love those whom he loves? I see Laura Pendennis ever constant and tender and pure; ever ministering in her sacred office of kindness—bestowing love and followed by blessings—which would I have, think you; that priceless crown hymeneal, or the glory of a Tenth Edition?

Clive and his father had found not only a model friend in the lady above mentioned, but a perfect prize landlady in their happy lodgings.[1]

Or there is this from chapter XXVII of *The Virginians*:

The poor lady was agitated herself by the flutter and agitation which she saw in her young companion. Gracious Heaven! Could that tremor and excitement mean that she was mistaken, and that the lad was still faithful? "Give me

[1] Ch. LXXIV.

your arm, and let us take a little walk," she said, waving round a curtsey to the other two gentlemen: "my Aunt is asleep after her dinner". Harry could not but offer the arm, and press the hand that lay against his heart. Maria made another fine curtsey to Harry's bowing companions, and walked off with her prize. In her griefs, in her rages, in the pains and anguish of wrong and desertion, how a woman remembers to smile, curtsey, caress, dissemble! How resolutely they discharge the social proprieties; how they have a word, or a hand, or a kind little speech or reply for the passing acquaintance who crosses unknowing the path of the tragedy, drops a light airy remark or two (happy self-satisfied rogue!), and passes on. He passes on, and thinks that woman was rather pleased with what I said. "That joke I made was rather neat. I do really think Lady Maria looks rather favourably at me, and she's a dev'lish fine woman, begad she is!" O you wiseacre! Such was Jack Morris's observation and case as he walked away leaning on the arm of his noble friend, and thinking the whole Society of the Wells was looking at him. He had made some exquisite remarks about a particular run of cards at Lady Flushington's the night before, and Lady Maria had replied graciously and neatly, and so away went Jack perfectly happy.

The absurd creature! I declare we know nothing of anybody (but *that* for my part I know better and better every day). You enter smiling to see your new acquaintance, Mrs. A. and her charming family. You make your bow in the elegant drawingroom of Mr. and Mrs. B? I tell you that in your course through life you are for ever putting your great clumsy foot upon the mute invisible wounds of bleeding tragedies. Mrs. B.'s closets for what you know are stuffed with skeletons. Look there under the sofa-cushion. Is that merely Missy's doll, or is it the limb of a stifled Cupid peeping out? What do you suppose are those ashes smouldering in the grate?—Very likely a suttee has been offered up there just before you came in: a faithful heart has been burned out upon a callous corpse, and you are looking on the *cineri doloso*. You see B. and his wife receiving their company before dinner. Gracious powers! Do you know that that bouquet which she wears is a signal to Captain C., and that he will find a note under the little bronze Shakespear on the mantelpiece in the study? And with all this you go up and say some uncommonly neat thing (as you fancy) to Mrs. B. about the weather (clever dog!), or about Lady E.'s last party (fashionable buck!), or about the dear children in the nursery (insinuating rogue!). Heaven and earth, my good Sir, how can you tell that B. is not going to pitch all the children out of the nursery window this very night, or that his lady has not made an arrangement for leaving them, and running off with the Captain? How do you know that those footmen are not disguised bailiffs?—that yonder large-looking Butler (really a skeleton) is not the pawnbroker's man? and that there are not skeleton rotis and entrées under every one of the covers? Look at their feet peeping from under the tablecloth. Mind how you stretch out your own lovely little slippers, Madam, lest you knock over a rib or two. Remark the Death's-head moths fluttering among the flowers. See, the pale winding-sheets gleaming in the wax-candles! I know it is an old story, and especially that this preacher has yelled vanitas vanitatum five hundred times before. I can't help always falling upon it, and cry out with particular loudness and wailing, and become especially melancholy, when I see a dead love tied to a live love. Ha! I look up from my desk, across the street: and there come in Mr. and Mrs. D. from their walk in Kensington Gardens. How she hangs on him! how jolly and happy he looks, as the children frisk round! My poor dear benighted Mrs. D., there is a Regent's Park as well as a Kensington Gardens in the world. Go in, fond wretch! Smilingly lay before him what you know he likes for dinner. Show him the children's copies and the reports of their masters. Go with Missy to the piano, and play your artless duet together; and fancy you are happy!

"There go Harry and Maria taking their evening walk on the common, away from the village which is waking up from its after-dinner siesta, and where the people are beginning to stir and the music to play. With the music Maria knows Madame de Bernstein will waken: with the candles she must be back to the tea-table and the cards. Never mind. Here is a minute. It may be my love is dead, but here is a minute to kneel over the grave and pray by it. He certainly was not thinking about her: he was startled and did not even know her. He was laughing and talking with Jack Morris and my Lord March. He is twenty years younger than she. Never mind. To-day is to-day in which we are all equal. This moment is ours. Come, let us walk a little way over the heath, Harry. She will go, though she feels a deadly assurance that he will tell her all is over between them, and that he loves the dark-haired girl at Oakhurst.

The passages of commentary stream with the life of the book. The flowing continuity is not broken by them.

Take finally as an instance of the intimate and obliging connection of story and commentary the following passage, which is a very ordinary sample of the narrative of *The Virginians*. Lord Castlewood has been retailing to Madame de Bernstein the occasion when Harry, now known as the second son and given out as penniless, repeats his generous offer to stand by his engagement to the ageing Lady Maria who rejects him with feelings very mixed:

"You should have heard her take leave of him!" [explains Lord Castlewood]. "*C'était touchant, ma parole d'honneur!* I cried. Before George, I could not help myself. The young fellow with muddy stockings, and his hair about his eyes, flings himself amongst us when we were at dinner; makes his offer to Molly in a very frank and noble manner, and in good language, too; and she replies. Begad it put me in mind of Mrs. Woffington in the new Scotch play, that Lord Bute's man has wrote—Douglas—what d'ye call it? She clings round the lad; she bids him adieu in heart-rending accents. She steps out of the room in a stately despair—no more chocolate, thank you. If she had made a *mauvais pas* no one could retire from it with more dignity. 'Twas a masterly retreat after a defeat. We were starved out of our position, but we retired with all the honours of war."

"Molly won't die of the disappointment!" said my lord's aunt, sipping her cup.

My lord snarled a grin, and showed his yellow teeth. "He, he!" he said, "she hath once or twice before had the malady very severely, and recovered perfectly. It don't kill, as your ladyship knows, at Molly's age."

Then the first comment:

How should her ladyship know? She did not marry Doctor Tusher until she was advanced in life. She did not become Madame de Bernstein until still later. Old Dido, a poet remarks, was not ignorant of misfortune, and hence learned to have compassion on the wretched.

Then the second comment:

People in the little world, as I have been told, quarrel and fight, and go on abusing each other, and are not reconciled for ever so long. But people in the great world are surely wiser in their generation. They have differences; they cease seeing each other. They make it up and come together again, and no questions are asked. A stray prodigal, or a stray puppy-dog is thus brought in under the benefit of an amnesty, though you know he has been away in ugly company. For six months past, ever since the Castlewoods and Madame de Bernstein had been battling for possession of poor Harry Warrington, these two branches of the Esmond family had remained apart. Now, the question being settled, they were free to meet again, as though no difference ever had separated them: and Madame de Bernstein drove in her great coach to Lady Castlewood's rout, and the Esmond ladies appeared smiling at Madame de Bernstein's drums, and loved each other just as much as they previously had done.

But on this follows:

"So, sir, I hear you have acted like a hard-hearted monster about your poor brother Harry!" says the Baroness, delighted, and menacing George with her stick.

"I acted but upon your ladyship's hint, and desired to see whether it was for himself or his reputed money that his kinsfolk wanted to have him," replies George, turning rather red.

The commentary, that is, serves the purpose of changing the scene. Not only is there a new scene but we are in the midst of it without any heralding or scene-setting, and without any jar, the commentary serving as the painted curtain dropped and lifted in the theatre.

This scene proceeds for a score of lines, George and Madame de Bernstein exchanging remarks. Then:

"But it is a knight of old, it is a Bayard, it is the grand-father come to life!"

The scene we find has changed again, by other means but equally without our knowing, since that tripartite exclamation is followed by

cried Madame de Bernstein to her attendant, as she was retiring for the night.

And that by another:

And that evening, when the lads left her, it was to poor Harry she gave the two fingers, and to George the rouged cheek, who blushed for his part, almost as deep as that often-dyed rose, at such a mark of his old kinswoman's favour.

The mention of Harry prepares for what follows. I quote the sequel at length because it shows how effortlessly Thackeray turns the great wheel of the writing, in and out of story (itself touched with commentary) and com-mentary (itself half story). If there is a leaking tap, as

Mr Wilson thinks, it is one that drips with kindly oil; by its aid the machinery works with smoothness, ease and silence:

Although Harry Warrington was the least envious of men, and did honour to his brother as in all respects his chief, guide, and superior, yet no wonder a certain feeling of humiliation and disappointment oppressed the young man after his deposition from his eminence as Fortunate Youth and heir to boundless Virginian territories. Our friends at Kensington might promise and vow that they would love him all the better after his fall; Harry made a low bow and professed himself very thankful; but he could not help perceiving, when he went with his brother to the state entertainment with which my Lord Castlewood regaled his new-found kinsman, that George was all in all to his cousins: had all the talk, compliments, and *petits soins* for himself, whilst of Harry no one took any notice save poor Maria, who followed him with wistful looks, pursued him with eyes conveying dismal reproaches, and, as it were, blamed him because she had left him. "Ah!" the eyes seemed to say, "'tis mighty well of you, Harry, to have accepted the freedom which I gave you; but I had no intention, sir, that you should be so pleased at being let off." She gave him up, but yet she did not quite forgive him for taking her at her word. She would not have him, and yet she would. O, my young friends, how delightful is the beginning of a love-business, and how undignified, sometimes, the end!...

This is what Harry Warrington, no doubt, felt when he went to Kensington and encountered the melancholy reproachful eyes of his cousin. Yes! it is a foolish position to be in; but it is also melancholy to look into a house you have once lived in, and see black casements and emptiness where once shone the fires of welcome. Melancholy? Yes; but, ha! how bitter, how melancholy, how absurd to look up as you pass sentimentally by No. 13, and see somebody else grinning out of window, and evidently on the best terms with the landlady. I always feel hurt, even at an inn which I frequent, if I see other folks' trunks and boots at the doors of the rooms which were once mine. Have those boots lolled on the sofa which once I reclined on? I kick you from before me, you muddy, vulgar highlows!

So considering that his period of occupation was over, and Maria's rooms, if not given up to a new tenant, were, at any rate, to let, Harry did not feel very easy in his cousin's company, nor she possibly in his. He found either that he had nothing to say to her, or that what she had to say to him was rather dull and common-place, and that the red lip of a white-necked pipe of Virginia was decidedly more agreeable to him now than Maria's softest accents and most melancholy *moue*. When George went to Kensington, then, Harry did not care much about going, and pleaded other engagements.[1]

7

There is an aesthetic virtue in the commentary when we consider the passages of it in their place in the novels. When Clive Newcome had looked at the Venus of Milo he paid it this lyrical homage in a letter to Pendennis:

"Next morning the governor had letters to deliver after breakfast; and left me at the Louvre door. I shall come and live here I think. I feel as if I never want to go away. I had not been ten minutes in the place before I fell in love with the most beautiful creature the world has ever seen. She was standing silent and majestic in the centre of one of the rooms of the statue gallery; and the very first glimpse of her struck one breathless with the sense of her beauty. I could not see the colour of her eyes and hair exactly, but the latter is light, and the eyes I should think are grey. Her complexion is of a beautiful warm marble tinge. She is not a clever woman, evidently; I do not think she laughs or talks much—she seems too lazy to do more than smile. She is only beautiful. This divine creature has lost an arm which has been cut off at the shoulder, but she looks none the less lovely for the accident. She may be some two-and-thirty years old; and she was born about

[1] Ch. LVII.

two thousand years ago. Her name is the Venus of Milo.
O, Victrix! O, lucky Paris! (I don't mean this present
Lutetia, but Priam's son.) How could he give the apple
to any else but this enslaver,—this joy of gods and men?
at whose benign presence the flowers spring up, and the
smiling ocean sparkles, and the soft skies beam with serene
light! I wish we might sacrifice. I would bring a spotless kid, snowy-coated, and a pair of doves, and a jar of
honey—yea, honey from Morel's in Piccadilly, thyme-
flavoured, narbonian, and we would acknowledge the
Sovereign Loveliness, and adjure the Divine Aphrodite.
Did you ever see my pretty young cousin, Miss Newcome,
Sir Brian's daughter? She has a great look of the huntress
Diana. It is sometimes too proud and too cold for me. The
blare of those horns is too shrill, and the rapid pursuit
through bush and bramble too daring. O, thou generous
Venus! O, thou beautiful bountiful calm! At thy soft feet
let me kneel—on cushions of Tyrian purple. Don't show
this to Warrington, please: I never thought when I began
that Pegasus was going to run away with me.

"I wish I had read Greek a little more at school: it's too
late at my age; I shall be nineteen soon, and have got my
own business; but when we return I think I shall try and
read it with Cribs. What have I been doing, spending six
months over a picture of Sepoys and Dragoons cutting each
other's throats? Art ought not to be a fever. It ought to be
a calm; not a screaming bull-fight or a battle of gladiators,
but a temple for placid contemplation, wrapt worship,
stately rhythmic ceremony, and music solemn and tender.
I shall take down my Snyders' and Rubens' when I get
home; and turn quietist. To think I have spent weeks in
depicting bony Life Guardsmen delivering cut one, or
Saint George, and painting black beggars off a crossing!"[1]

Matthew Arnold, characterizing the same sort of effect,
was to speak of its 'calm' and 'cheerfulness',[2] which
Pater, encouraged by other of Arnold's writings,

[1] *The Newcomes*, ch. XXII.
[2] The Preface to the *Poems* of 1853, § 1.

modified into 'blitheness and repose'.[1] It would have been rather Pater's phrase that Thackeray would have subscribed to. His books have blitheness and their abundant repose is partly owing to their commentary, which suggests a cool timelessness overarching the happy, the fierce, the indolent flow of the narrative.

8

Is there not also a further aesthetic value in the commentary? In the eighteenth century aestheticians considered variety a merit in a work of art. Some of the things I have said of Thackeray's novels have drawn attention away from his variety. His uniformity is of more importance, but within that overarching virtue some variety does exist. From the sorts of variety provided by the commentary I shall revert to one I have already noted. The commentary provides for a certain variety in the style. Think for a moment of Dickens's novels. They have different styles by the hundred. And this range is possible because Dickens is not—to put it briefly—an historian. His creatures are bits of human beings wonderfully exaggerated and coloured. Thackeray gives us people of the world speaking—so it seems—as they do in the world. But he escapes the drabness of the 'realist' novel by way of the very melodiousness of his writing, but also by way of the orchestration of what I may call his odes and psalms. The motto for this might come from *The Roundabout Papers* where in the essay 'On some late great victories' he cries, as it were metrically:

Bang, ye gongs! and drummers, drub the thundering skins!

Seldom do we get from Thackeray outbursts of noise so loud, but the nearest to brass and drums, so far as the

[1] *The Renaissance*, 1873, p. 201.

novels go, is in the commentary. 'Bang, ye gongs...'
is not only motto, but formula: often the outbursts, like
those of the admired Carlyle, are imperative and apos-
trophic. Debarred by the chosen laws of his narrative
from giving any of his personages the theatre rhetoric of,
say, an Edith Dombey, he gives us a version of it in the
commentary, a level and quieter version that relieves the
general style without breaking or disturbing it. Often his
morality is expressed with the gusto that Dickens put
into the description of his personages.

9

It is in the passages of commentary that we get the most
obvious ties binding Thackeray's long novels to his
shorter works. His Browns, Joneses and Smiths and his
names of places and clubs figure in the shorter works
and in the novels. Much could be learned of his
interests from a study of these unobtrusive figureheads.
The *Thackeray Dictionary* lists eighteen Browns and one
Browne; twenty-seven Joneses and 'the celebrated Fon-
tarabian Statuesque' figuring at 'the Wells', who gives
herself out as 'Jonesini'; and twenty-two Smiths. They
are all representative of social groups, indeed of the
same; perhaps they are the same individual plumply
allegorical. Given the time and opportunity Thackeray
could supply details about them (or him) by the
hundred, as when he devotes sixteen pages to one
Thomas Brown who addresses letters of good advice to
his nephew Bob (another of the recurring persons).
Meanwhile, whether in the long run or the phrase, a
Brown, Jones or Smith does duty as a sample of his
group or of his typical self. They crop up as much in the
shorter works as in the novels; the latter, that is, belong
expressly to the same world as the former.

10

The critic of Thackeray, I have said, must stand or fall by the success of his proof that the novels would suffer from the loss of their commentary. Proposing the operation, the surgeon would be in Shylock's dilemma. Each pound or dram of flesh streams with the blood of the whole system. 'Conceive *The Newcomes*', said Brownell,

without the presence of Thackeray upon the stage—minus the view it gives us of the working of its author's mind, the glimpses of his philosophy, the touches of his feeling.[1]

Conceive it—you cannot, and, after the quotations I have made from it, I cannot believe you want to. Another remark of Brownell's runs:

Even critics who think it bad art for an author to obtrude his personality must admit that the evil is lessened in proportion to the interest of the personality so obtruded.[2]

The interest of that personality lies in every sentence of the fiction. Its interest is so strong that we are pleased to have the world of Thackeray's imagination come to us through his literary personality, as we are pleased to have, say, the scene of Gainsborough's 'Going to Market' come to us through the atmosphere of morning dusk, in which is mingled paleness, luminousness, lichenous yellow, and a sunny grey.[3] It was because in

[1] P. 17.   [2] P. 16.
[3] This account of the morning dusk I leave as I wrote it before seeing the picture (which hangs in Ken Wood House, London) in its cleaned state. As could have been foretold, some of the yellow of the morning has gone with the varnish. The dusk is now lighter than before and being less golden is not quite so appropriate for suggesting the atmosphere of Thackeray's novels. Is it known, I wonder, whether painters made allowances when mixing their colours for the varnish they intended to supply, or knew would be supplied against their will? The two states of this picture, January 1952 and April 1952, do not help us to say. Both represented morning, though different mornings.

America there is no visible atmosphere that Gertrude Stein said that there would be no great painting done there. The stories told by Thackeray have the constant advantage of a soft atmosphere; they lie, as it were, in the Indian summer of his breath, in the sheen of his candles—advertising the first of the big novels as a thing presented on a stage by its showman, he ended the list of attractions with this item:

the whole...brilliantly illuminated with the Author's own candles.[1]

If we read his novels at all, we must read every word of them. Their credentials cover the whole and are wholly sound. Their author comes of the age-old stock of story-tellers, the stock of epic poets and of all novelists before and of his time, who liked both to tell a story and show their literary selves in the act of interpreting it. For the readers of their own first day the novels had a further strong recommendation. Writing in one great popular form (the novel), Thackeray contrived to write also in the other great popular form (the sermon). To-day sermons are scarcely as much valued as they were. But we are still interested in a criticism of life, and this Thackeray's novels provide in other forms than that of homily. No other form gives us more of life than the novel. No other form therefore invites so much criticism of life. The first of his *Roundabout Papers* happens to praise Dumas; the second happens to mention as the author's bedside books, Montaigne's Essays and Howell's *Familiar Letters*. If we see Thackeray as following his predecessors as well as preceding some of his successors, we shall not necessarily proscribe the running of story and musing together. The mixing is a

[1] *Vanity Fair*, 'Before the Curtain'. By 'candles' Thackeray no doubt meant his pictorial illustrations.

legitimate act, the worth of the result depending on the ingredients. In his essay 'De Finibus' he notes that

> Among the sins of commission which novel-writers not seldom perpetrate, is the sin of grandiloquence, or tall-talking, against which, for my part, I will offer up a special *libera me*. This is the sin of schoolmasters, governesses, critics, sermoners, and instructors of young or old people. Nay (for I am making a clean breast, and liberating my soul), perhaps of all the novel-spinners now extant, the present speaker is the most addicted to preaching. Does he not stop perpetually in his story and begin to preach to you? When he ought to be engaged with business, is he not for ever taking the Muse by the sleeve, and plaguing her with some of his cynical sermons? I cry *peccavi* loudly and heartily. I tell you I would like to be able to write a story which should show no egotism whatever—in which there should be no reflections, no cynicism, no vulgarity (and so forth), but an incident in every other page, a villain, a battle, a mystery in every chapter. I should like to be able to feed a reader so spicily as to leave him hungering and thirsting for more at the end of every monthly meal.[1]

Is he not here offering us a choice? Of course no one wants novels of mystery and battles and violence to bear the Thackerayan trellis of commentary. For this reason the violent career of Barry Lyndon is narrated by himself, least musing of narrators. For novels nearer to life as life is known to most of us, commentary is less redundant, and so less unwelcome.

[1] This is the limited ground on which Thackeray allowed praise for the serial thrillers of Eugène Sue: see 'Thieves' Literature of France'.

CHAPTER VI

The Author's Truthfulness of Personage and Action

The 'person writing', whose presence is felt everywhere in the novels, is a person interested in being truthful—that is the first thing, and almost the last, to say about his authorial character.

When *Pendennis* appeared in book form he wrote a preface for it. A preface being prose of thinking, he spoke *in propria persona*; and so to his biographer. But prefacing a novel, he spoke not only as the author but about him; and so to a critic of his novels. That preface contains the following:

as we judge of a man's character, after long frequenting his society, not by one speech, or by one mood or opinion, or by one day's talk, but by the tenor of his general bearing and conversation; so of a writer, who delivers himself up to you perforce unreservedly, you say, Is he honest? Does he tell the truth in the main? Does he seem actuated by a desire to find out and speak it? Is he a quack, who shams sentiment, or mouths for effect? Does he seek popularity by claptraps or other arts? I can no more ignore good fortune than any other chance which has befallen me. I have found many thousands more readers than I ever looked for. I have no right to say to these, You shall not find fault with my art, or fall asleep over my pages; but I ask you to believe that this person writing strives to tell the truth. If there is not that, there is nothing.[1]

With this preface to guide him, Brownell praised Thackeray the author as 'above all a lover of truth'.[2]

---

[1] I have already thrown doubts on the advisability of describing Thackeray or any other writer as 'a writer, who delivers himself up to you perforce unreservedly'.   [2] P. 17.

How did the love of truth bear on the novels and, bearing on them without intermission, help give them their unity?

In exploring Brownell's testimonial it is obvious that we shall not be concerned with truth as an object that is mockingly, perhaps inaccessibly, abstruse. The abstract term as he used it is not more important than his concrete subject, the person writing, which limited its application to the interests proper to a novelist. Truth for a novelist is that commonplace, precious truth which carries the consent of the mass of his readers. Seeking to provide that, the only questions he need concern himself with are: Will my readers, because of what they already know for themselves about life, be disposed to accept my personages as actual people, not as, say, dream-fulfilments or ogres? Will they be disposed to approve the action of my stories as likely to fall to the lot of man? Will they sympathize with my comments on ordinary human life, and think they 'ring true'?

2

Look first at his personages. These he was interested in making seem actually alive. Personages not seeming to be alive would not have existed in a truthful relationship to men. They seemed actual persons to their creator—witness, for instance, the passage from 'De Finibus' which I have already quoted,[1] and which must be autobiographical. It was only because of his modesty that he called them his puppets. And even the word puppets may have carried a more human connotation for him than for us, who think of puppets as small doll-like things. Puppets for Thackeray may have meant the

---

[1] See above, p. 17.

pygmies we find in the drawings of the day, those of 'Phiz' and Doyle, who illustrated the original edition of *The Newcomes*, some of whose pygmies swarm in the frame of the wrapper that he designed for *Punch* in the eighteen-forties, and which, daubed with crimson, still survives. These grotesque figures are small men, not 'life-size' dolls. The last sentence of *Vanity Fair* may have been meant to set the showman at a distance from men, ironically seen as children, rather than to stand him close to dolls.

Here I must pause to praise all novelists (and playwrights) who have the power to make us accept their creatures as actual. How old-fashioned a recommendation! Nowadays there is often little patience with the belief that personages seemingly actual are a prime requisite to a novel or play, unless perhaps it is declaredly and obviously an allegory. In a paragraph which I investigate below,[1] Dr Leavis dismisses Thackeray's power in this line as if it were of no more advantage to the novels, and no more difficult to come by, than, say, the power to make a workmanlike description in a detective novel. In a novel or play as I see it, the suspension of our disbelief in that particular quarter is the basis on which we accept everything else, the basis, in a great novel or great play, supporting even towers that are 'cloud-capp'd' or 'topless'. Because Shakespeare—to think of him for a moment—gives us a great deal more than the seeming actuality of his personages is no reason for slighting what that overplus is additional to. We must not speak of him as if he were a Webster. His imagery, for instance, apart from any degree of its quality as sensuous poetry interesting in its own right, owes some of its force to the seeming actuality of the

[1] See Appendix II, pp. 288 ff. below.

personages who speak it, or has credentials thrust upon it by coming in a play of which the personages in general seem actual. If that were not so we should resent it. We have little patience with the imagery of Webster—except in isolation from the play—because he did not see first to the suspending of our disbelief in the improbability that his personages exist and act as people[1] —we may wish that this were not so but cannot help ourselves: if only, we cry, he had confined himself to writing lyrics, or solaced himself, as Browning was to, with the less exacting form of the dramatic monologue. Unless the personages are made flesh, how can they seem to be tempted as we are, how can we feel with or for them? Their seeming actuality is of more account than plot, for if they are alive they will act, and being plural, will inter-act. The trouble with the personages created by 'Savonarola' Brown was not that their creator proceeded on a wrong principle but that, never coming alive, they lacked the power Brown too readily assumed he had given them 'to work out [their] destiny'.[2] If a novelist's personages are 'alive', then—to use a term of Henry James's—a little 'push' here and there by the narrator and the story is made (I shall say more of this later). One or two pushes dealt to personages seemingly actual and you get a *nouvelle* such as 'Dennis Haggarty's Wife', which is as fine and powerful as anything in Thackeray. A hundred or two pushes and you get one of his vast novels. But the pushes fail of the desired effect unless they are dealt to personages who can feel them.

[1] Reviewing a performance of *Titus Andronicus* by the Marlowe Society of Cambridge University, a special correspondent of *The Times* (10 March 1953) made this interesting comparison: 'With all its faults, *Titus Andronicus* is a much more moving play than, say, *The Duchess of Malfi*; and even its horrors have not the sheer pointlessness of Webster's.'

[2] Max Beerbohm, *Seven Men*, ed. 1920, p. 180.

The test of Thackeray's power to bestow this sort of actuality is his personage Barry Lyndon. The autobiography Thackeray makes him write could be presented to a psychologist as a document for the study of villainy and cruelty as spirited as they are calculated. But to say this is to claim that Lyndon seems an actual person. To make the same claim another way I quote the general praise bestowed on the book by one of Thackeray's successors in the editorial chair of *The Cornhill*. Introducing a reprint of the brilliant *Second Funeral of Napoleon*, Frederick Greenwood wrote:

[In his early days Thackeray] was writing for a generation so astonishingly dull as to see no merit in *Barry Lyndon*; while we in these days wonder sometimes whether even Thackeray himself ever surpassed that little book, so wonderfully vigorous and keen.[1]

Even Thackeray himself—the vigour and keenness, in other words, are those of the author of the long novels, which carries with it the proof that, being expended in a novel and not in a piece of reporting, these powers are expended on producing personages seemingly actual. Lyndon, in short, is so credible that the reader, like many personages in the book, goes in awe of him. And also horribly admires his control, for with an instinct more common in actual life than in crime stories Lyndon knows just where to stop:

This circumstance served to unite mother [Lyndon's wife] and son [Lyndon's stepson] for a little, but their characters were too different. I believe she was too fond of me ever to allow him to be sincerely reconciled to her. As he grew up to be a man, his hatred towards me assumed an intensity quite wicked to think of (and which I promise you I returned with interest); and it was at the age of sixteen,

[1] xiii, Jan.-June 1866, p. 48.

I think, that the impudent young hang-dog, on my return from Parliament one summer, and on my proposing to cane him as usual, gave me to understand that he would submit to no further chastisement from me, and said, grinding his teeth, that he would shoot me if I laid hands on him. I looked at him; he was grown, in fact, to be a tall young man, and I gave up that necessary part of his education.[1]

Moreover, in this novel, as in *Catherine*, there are scores of other personages, some of whom, notably Lyndon's wife, are much more ordinary instances of human nature. And even Lyndon himself, though he can keep his hardness fiercely whole for a very long time, breaks down into a version of the common man on several occasions; as here:

My son, little Castle-Lyndon, was a prince; his breeding and manners, even at his early age, showed him to be worthy of the two noble families from whom he was descended, and I don't know what high hopes I had for the boy, and indulged in a thousand fond anticipations as to his future success and figure in the world. But stern Fate had determined that I should leave none of my race behind me, and ordained that I should finish my career, as I see it closing now—poor, lonely, and childless. I may have had my faults, but no man shall dare to say of me that I was not a good and tender father. I loved that boy passionately, perhaps with a blind partiality; I denied him nothing. Gladly, gladly, I swear, would I have died that his premature doom might have been averted. I think there is not a day since I lost him but his bright face and beautiful smiles look down on me out of heaven where he is, and that my heart does not yearn towards him. That sweet child was taken from me at the age of nine years, when he was full of beauty and promise; and so powerful is the hold his memory has of me that I have never been able to forget him; his little spirit haunts me of nights on my restless, solitary

[1] Ch. xviii.

pillow; many a time, in the wildest and maddest company, as the bottle is going round, and the song and laugh roaring about, I am thinking of him. I have got a lock of his soft brown hair hanging round my breast now; it will accompany me to the dishonoured pauper's grave; where soon, no doubt, Barry Lyndon's worn-out old bones will be laid.[1]

Of course there is wolfishness in it, or it wouldn't be Lyndon's; and of course the breakdown into common human emotion, being that of a cruel person, is fulsomely complete. Throughout his remarkable course Lyndon is apparently an actual man.

If so, then thousands of others in all the novels and stories together. Roscoe can speak for us:

We don't say they are life-like characters; they are mere people. We feel them to be near us, and that we may meet them any day...the Major frequents Bond Street...and it is but one step from questioning the existence of Becky's finished little house in Curzon Street to admitting the philosophy of Berkeley.[2]

To Roscoe's testimony we may add Saintsbury's:

By the time at which Thackeray wrote great part of *Vanity Fair*, and the whole of its successors, it was impossible for him to draw, in words, a character out of nature or unfurnished with life.[3]

(To fix on a year so late as 1848 is to exercise an un-Saintsburian caution.) On another occasion in his book—at the close of his chapter on *The Book of Snobs*—Saintsbury deposed as follows:

And I have *seen* Captain Shindy (long after Thackeray's death, and after he had first taken up another profession and then given that up and gone into Parliament) abusing a club waiter in his own inimitable style. It is well known that Thackeray's characters have this uncanny knack of turning up alive.[4]

[1] Ch. xix. [2] ii, 272.
[3] P. 248. [4] Pp. 148f.; cf. pp. 248f.

These testimonies coming from a first reader and a reader equidistant in time between him and ourselves indicate how the personages in novels such as Thackeray's vary the proportions of one sort of truth and another according to the point of historical time at which the reader meets them. To readers meeting the truthful personages of *Vanity Fair* or *The Newcomes* when those novels were new, they seemed actual contemporaries. If at that time they were felt to have a general humanity about them—some figment of the eternal human stuff—this would not have seemed striking. But as time goes on, the general humanity comes to count for more, and that because the contemporary manners with which at first it was decked out—ways of speaking, dressing, and so on—have grown obsolete. Later readers say 'how like ourselves' all the more pointedly because differences on the surface are now glaringly apparent. When the novels are historical in the sense that *Esmond* is, and *The Virginians*, and, less strongly, *Denis Duval*, the relation of the first readers to the personages is the same in kind as that of later readers. And because of the nature of the kind, also in degree—the kind can only exist complete: the Esmond encountered in 1852 must have seemed as distant in time as he does from 1954. Much of the action of the other novels, though not strictly and wholly contemporary, was even for its first readers near enough to bring the various responses into play. For us, who come fifty years after Saintsbury, the modifications are still more striking than for him, who followed Roscoe by fifty years. Though Becky Sharp is still about—I saw her at an evening party the other day—she no longer appears in the get-up that Thackeray denoted by 'a brilliant full toilette', and which Roscoe could picture accurately, and which Saintsbury was nearer to than we by fifty years. Her seeming actuality has survived though not its original trappings: it has survived as contemporary with succeeding times because permanent, each age bringing the trappings up to date.

3

Striving to tell the truth about his personages, Thackeray created the effect that he had told the truth complete. That he had achieved this completeness was the hope he expressed in the Preface to *Pendennis*:

Even the gentlemen of our age—this is an attempt to describe one of them, no better nor worse than most educated men—even these we cannot show as they are, with the notorious foibles and selfishness of their lives and their education. Since the author of Tom Jones was buried, no writer of fiction among us has been permitted to depict to his utmost power a MAN. We must drape him, and give him a certain conventional simper. Society will not tolerate the Natural in our Art.

This is usually taken as a confession of Thackeray's, his confession to a deficiency forced on him by the taboos of the age. In point of fact its purpose was to defend the portrait of his hero, which had more truth than some of his contemporaries could take. The Preface continues:

Many ladies have remonstrated and subscribers left me, because, in the course of the story, I described a young man resisting and affected by temptation. My object was to say, that he had the passions to feel, and the manliness and generosity to overcome them. You will not hear—it is best to know it—what moves in the real world, what passes in society, in the clubs, colleges, news'-rooms,—what is the life and talk of your sons.

And so to the crux of the matter:

A little more frankness than is customary has been attempted in this story; with no bad desire on the writer's part, it is hoped, and with no ill consequence to any reader. If truth is not always pleasant; at any rate truth is best, from whatever chair—from those whence graver writers or thinkers argue, as from that at which the story-teller sits as he concludes his labour, and bids his kind reader farewell.

This is the self-justification of one who has done an unpopular thing that he deems right and proper. He has exercised, he says, a 'little more' than the customary frankness. The amount, whatever its magnitude, is amply sufficient. His account of the frustrated affair of Pen and Fanny is a complete one: it is complete for the physiologist—Pen is 'hot and eager' and Fanny, who has 'a great deal of dangerous and rather contagious sensibility', 'toss[es] upon her mattress'[1]—and there is a wealth of material for the psychologist, moralist and social historian. If it is a frustrated passion he has to report, that it is not so much Thackeray's omission as Pen's: 'My calling', Pen acknowledges, 'is not seduction'.[2] Elsewhere in this novel there is more vice to report than Pen himself cares to provide, and Thackeray leaves us in no doubt as to its nature. More of it is provided in the other novels. When Trollope came to complain of the censorship Thackeray exercised as editor of *The Cornhill*, he had ammunition enough from Thackeray's own published work.[3] We do not feel that Thackeray is blind to the complete man, which Fielding kept in view, or that he did not use his utmost power to depict that totality, draped or simpering as he found it in the world round about him. Indeed draping and simpering add to the completeness, since hypocrisy is an addition very much to the taste of Thackeray the moralist. As to the charge brought against him by

---

[1] Chs. LIII, XLVI, XLVII. [2] Ch. XLIX.
[3] See *Letters*, IV, 206.

Professor Greig—'The truth is that he never really preferred strong meat'[1]—defence is easy: why should he? Life offers meats of all strengths, and a healthy palate likes each in its place and season. Where do we find stronger meat chewed—to run the metaphor—so unflinchingly as in 'Going to See a Man Hanged'? or in *Barry Lyndon*, from which little-known masterpiece I select two passages on the theme of marriage, a theme Thackeray comments on throughout his writings:

"Well, why not a milkmaid's daughter? My good fellow, I *was* in love in youth, as most gentlemen are, with my tutor's daughter, Helena, a bouncing girl, of course older than myself" (this made me remember my own little love passages with Nora Brady, in the days of my early life), "and do you know, sir, I heartily regret I didn't marry her? There's nothing like having a virtuous drudge at home, sir, depend upon that. It gives a zest to one's enjoyments in the world, take my word for it. No man of sense need restrict himself, or deny himself a single amusement for his wife's sake; on the contrary, if he select the animal properly, he will choose such a one as shall be no bar to his pleasure, but a comfort in his hours of annoyance. For instance, I have got the gout: who tends me? A hired valet, who robs me whenever he has the power. My wife never comes near me. What friend have I? None in the wide world. Men of the world, as you and I are, don't make friends, and we are fools for our pains. Get a friend, sir, and that friend a woman—a good household drudge, who loves you. *That* is the most precious sort of friendship, for the expense of it is all on the woman's side. The *man* needn't contribute anything. If he's a rogue, she'll vow he's an angel; if he is a brute, she will like him all the better for his ill-treatment of her. They like it, sir, these women. They are born to be our greatest comforts and conveniences; our—our moral boot-jacks, as it were; and, to men in your way of life, believe me

[1] P. 19.

such a person would be invaluable. I'm only speaking for your bodily and mental comfort's sake, mind. Why didn't I marry poor Helena Flower, the curate's daughter?"[1]

And this:

The first days of a marriage are commonly very trying; and I have known couples, who lived together like turtle-doves for the rest of their lives, peck each other's eyes out almost during the honeymoon. I did not escape the common lot; in our journey westward my Lady Lyndon chose to quarrel with me because I pulled out a pipe of tobacco (the habit of smoking which I had acquired in Germany when a soldier in Bülow's, and could never give it over), and smoked it in the carriage; and also her ladyship chose to take umbrage both at Ilminster and Andover, because in the evenings when we lay there I chose to invite the landlords of the Bell and the Lion to crack a bottle with me. Lady Lyndon was a haughty woman, and I hate pride, and I promise you that in both instances I overcame this vice in her. On the third day of our journey I had her to light my pipe-match with her own hands, and made her deliver it to me with tears in her eyes; and at the Swan Inn at Exeter I had so completely subdued her, that she asked me humbly whether I would not wish the landlady as well as the host to step up to dinner with us.[2]

From the long novels it will be enough to instance the marriage of Esmond and Rachel, which, smacking of psychological incest, offended the taste of contemporary and later readers. On the appearance of the book *The Times* mixed horror and incredulity:

So matters go on until the end of the third volume, when— hear it, reader, and believe it—Beatrix runs after the Pretender...; while Henry Esmond, the importunate and high souled, the sensitive and delicate-minded, marries his own 'dear mother'![3]

---

[1] Ch. xiii.   [2] Ch. xvii.

[3] Quoted by John E. Tilford, Jr., in his interesting article 'The "Unsavoury Plot" of "Henry Esmond"', *Nineteenth-Century Fiction*, University of California Press, vi, ii, Sept. 1951, p. 123.

To which I oppose the testimony of Trollope in the obituary he wrote as editor of *The Cornhill*:

Esmond, of all his works, has most completely satisfied the critical tastes of those who profess themselves to read critically. For myself, I own that I regard *Esmond* as the first and finest novel in the English language. Taken as a whole, I think that it is without a peer. There is in it a completeness of historical plot, and an absence of that taint of unnatural life [i.e. of the untruthful] which blemishes, perhaps, all our other historical novels, which places it above its brethren. And, beyond this, it is replete with a tenderness which is almost divine,—a tenderness which no poetry has surpassed. Let those who doubt this go back and study again the life of Lady Castlewood. In *Esmond*, above all his works, Thackeray achieves the great triumph of touching the innermost core of his subject, without ever wounding the taste. We catch all the aroma, but the palpable body of the thing never stays with us till it palls us. Who ever wrote of love with more delicacy than Thackeray has written in *Esmond*? May I quote one passage of three or four lines? Who is there that does not remember the meeting between Lady Castlewood and Harry Esmond after Esmond's return? "'Do you know what day it is?' she continued. 'It is the 29th December; it is your birthday! But last year we did not drink it;—no, no! My lord was cold, and my Harry was like to die; and my brain was in a fever; and we had no wine. But now,— now you are come again, bringing your sheaves with you, my dear'. She burst into a wild flood of weeping as she spoke; she laughed and sobbed on the young man's heart, crying out wildly,—'bringing your sheaves with you,— your sheaves with you!'"[1]

Trollope found no offence. We may surmise that he could not complain of a book containing many things as overwhelming as that birthday scene. As for ourselves, we have less horror of love touched with psycho-

[1] ix, Jan.–June 1864, pp. 136f.

127

logical incestuousness than had *The Times* of 1852. Saintsbury, too, had less horror, and his comment is final:

there is...nothing for it but to confess that it is very shocking—and excessively human.[1]

Thackeray's palate was healthy. It was healthier than that of some of his first readers. With other readers around him he might have exhibited the health of his palate more freely still. As it was he had sometimes to proceed by hints, often broad as daylight. By one means and another he is not prevented from telling us all we need to know of the vices of individual personages and of their set and class. I have already quoted passages about mermaids and marriage markets which must have stung the age. And there is Lord Steyne; or the completeness of this passage, which to be fair to Thackeray's many interests I must give in its entirety:

Knowing how useless regrets are, and how the indulgence of sentiment only serves to make people more miserable, Mrs. Rebecca wisely determined to give way to no vain feelings of sorrow, and bore the parting from her husband with quite a Spartan equanimity. Indeed Captain Rawdon himself was much more affected at the leave-taking than the resolute little woman to whom he bade farewell. She had mastered this rude coarse nature; and he loved and worshipped her with all his faculties of regard and admiration. In all his life he had never been so happy, as, during the past few months, his wife had made him. All former delights of turf, mess, hunting-field, and gambling-table; all previous loves and courtships of milliners, opera-dancers, and the like easy triumphs of the clumsy military Adonis, were quite insipid when compared to the lawful matrimonial pleasures which of late he had enjoyed. She had known perpetually

[1] P. 196.

how to divert him; and he had found his house and her society a thousand times more pleasant than any place or company which he had ever frequented from his childhood until now. And he cursed his past follies and extravagances, and bemoaned his vast outlying debts above all, which must remain for ever as obstacles to prevent his wife's advancement in the world. He had often groaned over these in midnight conversations with Rebecca, although as a bachelor they had never given him any disquiet. He himself was struck with this phenomenon. "Hang it", he would say (or perhaps use a still stronger expression out of his simple vocabulary), "before I was married I didn't care what bills I put my name to, and so long as Moses would wait or Levy would renew for three months, I kept on never minding. But since I'm married, except renewing of course, I give you my honour I've not touched a bit of stamped paper."

Rebecca always knew how to conjure away these moods of melancholy. "Why, my stupid love", she would say, "we have not done with your aunt yet. If she fails us, isn't there what you call the Gazette? or, stop, when your uncle Bute's life drops, I have another scheme. The living has always belonged to the younger brother, and why shouldn't you sell out and go into the Church?" The idea of this conversion set Rawdon into roars of laughter: you might have heard the explosion through the hotel at midnight, and the haw-haws of the great dragoon's voice. General Tufto heard him from his quarters on the first floor above them; and Rebecca acted the scene with great spirit, and preached Rawdon's first sermon, to the immense delight of the General at breakfast.[1]

Instances of completeness on this score are not difficult to find.

Thackeray was interested in providing completeness also on the score of psychology. To his moral interest in hypocrisy he added a more wholly scientific interest in

[1] *Vanity Fair*, ch. xxx.

exploring what used to be called 'the heart'. I have already shown how he preferred to give the results rather than the exploration itself—the results or their bodily signs. He prefers, like Fielding, to look at the face of the clock and to read the time on it, but like Richardson has made the works, though he usually keeps them hidden. But with this distinction he gives us men complete in body, mind and heart. He plumbs the mind of Pen.

If there is one item in the treatment of Pen and Fanny that is not satisfactory, it is a part of the author's attitude to it. Thackeray seems too much to condone the attitude adopted by Pen himself. He sees the weaknesses of Pen. The title-page hints that he is his own worst enemy, a hint confirmed as we read on. He is shown as too selfish. And a part of that failing makes him callous towards Fanny's feelings: there is a touch of one-sided calculation, even of the calculation of a Major Pendennis, as well as of self-denial, discomfort and 'manliness', in his resistance of temptation. This philandering callousness is too much condoned by Thackeray, as if for once in his books he failed in delicacy of complete observation, as if on this occasion—an occasion, I remind my readers, in the mid-nineteenth century—he forgot the implications of so straight a sympathy as that shown, for instance, in *The Newcomes*:

Sin in man is so light, that scarce the fine of a penny is imposed; while for woman it is so heavy, that no repentance can wash it out.[1]

He is too much with Pen and not enough with Pen and Fanny together. The reason for this is a too crude distinction common in that age between consummated and unconsummated love. He thinks Pen is too innocent of blame because Fanny is not in danger of bearing him

[1] Ch. xxviii.

an illegitimate child. He insists on Pen's 'purity', by which he means no more than his not committing any offence that society would take note of. What is not pleasing is the assumption that whatever happens on the safe side of the line is alike innocent. We should have expected Thackeray to draw the obvious distinctions— as he does in *Vanity Fair*, for instance, when Rawdon knows that if Becky is not 'guilty', 'she's as bad as guilty'.[1] A little crudity on this score shows in Thackeray's letters, where he is found writing to Sally Baxter in these words:

I have put the two letters in the fire w[hich] I wrote yesterday—two very fine long fond sentimental letters— They were too long and sentimental and fond. A pen that's so practised as mine is runs on talking and talking: I fancy the people I speak to are sitting with me; and pour out the sense and nonsense jokes and the contrary, egotisms—whatever comes upper most. And you know what was uppermost yesterday. My heart was longing and yearning after you full of love and gratitude for your welcome of me—but the words grew a little too warm. You wouldn't like me to write letters in that strain. You might tell me to write no more: and if you did I should burst out into a misanthropical rage again—Please to let me write on: and make my frank claim to have a little place in Beatrix's heart. I told my children what a place she had got in mine. I would not hide from them or from you those honest generous feelings. When the destined man comes, with a good head and a good heart fit to win such a girl, and love and guide her; then old M[r] Thackeray will make his bow and say God bless her; as the fair creature steps away from church on the bridegroom's arm.[2]

This sort of thing, not in the modern taste, Professor Greig uses to support his theory, which I discuss below, that the life of Thackeray had too much of a say in the

---

[1] Ch. LV. [2] *Letters*, III, 151.

novels of 'the person writing'. I do not see it so—I see
the culprit, when there is anything to blame, as rather
the age. At any time when sexual relations outside
marriage are frowned on by society with an almost
fanatical severity, society revenges itself by drawing the
line the law draws, drawing it between black and the
grey that shades into white, not between white and the
grey that shades into black. We think Pen's relationship
with Fanny Bolton either not culpable at all, or more
culpable than the author thinks it, whose test is too
summary. Of course Pen did not go the lengths in
'innocence' that Becky went—'I am innocent', she
cries raucously on more than one occasion.[1] My point
is that lengths are not in question when the finest
standards are invoked, standards Thackeray is usually
sensitively aware of. But whatever his attitude to a very
complicated matter, he explores the matter complete.
We even learn that, when Fanny is finally cast off, Pen
is a little hurt because she maintains a complete silence:

Very likely Arthur looked at his own letters with some
tremor; very likely, as he received them at the family table,
feeling his mother's watch upon him (though the good soul's
eye seemed fixed upon her tea-cup or her book), he expected
daily to see a little hand-writing, which he would have
known, though he had never seen it yet, and his heart beat
as he received the letters to his address. Was he more
pleased or annoyed, that, day after day, his expectations
were not realised; and was his mind relieved, that there
came no letter from Fanny? Though, no doubt, in these
matters, when Lovelace is tired of Clarissa (or the contrary),
it is best for both parties to break at once, and each, after
the failure of the attempt at union, to go his own way, and
pursue his course through life solitary; yet our self-love, or
our pity, or our sense of decency, does not like that sudden

[1] In chs. LIII and LIV.

bankruptcy. Before we announce to the world that our firm of Lovelace and Co. can't meet its engagements, we try to make compromises: we have mournful meetings of partners: we delay the putting up of the shutters, and the dreary announcement of the failure. It must come: but we pawn our jewels to keep things going a little longer. On the whole, I dare say, Pen was rather annoyed that he had no remonstrances from Fanny. What! could she part from him, and never so much as once look round? could she sink, and never once hold a little hand out, or cry, "Help, Arthur?" Well, well: they don't all go down who venture on that voyage. Some few drown when the vessel founders; but most are only ducked, and scramble to shore. And the reader's experience of A. Pendennis, Esquire, of the Upper Temple, will enable him to state whether that gentleman belonged to the class of persons who were likely to sink or to swim.[1]

4

Thackeray, then, had a programme that made for width of truthfulness when forming the personage of Pendennis. And so with the major personages in all his long novels. When on one or two earlier occasions he brandished a programme that made for narrowness, he did not let narrowness get the better of him. Two of his early novels, *Catherine* and *Barry Lyndon*, were written with a special purpose, strengthened, no doubt, by the critical policy of *Fraser's*, to which they were contributed. The occasion for them was the novels of Bulwer and Ainsworth. Thackeray announced his programme early in *Catherine*:

This being a good opportunity for closing Chapter I, we ought, perhaps, to make some apologies to the public for introducing them to characters that are so utterly worthless; as we confess all our heroes, with the exception of Mr. Bullock, to be. In this we have consulted nature and history,

[1] Ch. LV.

rather than the prevailing taste and the general manner of authors. The amusing novel of *Ernest Maltravers*, for instance, opens with a seduction; but then it is performed by people of the strictest virtue on both sides; and there is so much religion and philosophy in the heart of the seducer, so much tender innocence in the soul of the seduced, that— bless the little dears!—their very peccadilloes make one interested in them; and their naughtiness becomes quite sacred, so deliciously is it described. Now, if we *are* to be interested by rascally actions, let us have them with plain faces, and let them be performed, not by virtuous philosophers, but by rascals. Another clever class of novelists adopt the contrary system, and create interest by making their rascals perform virtuous actions. Against these popular plans we here solemnly appeal. We say, let your rogues in novels act like rogues, and your honest men like honest men; don't let us have any juggling and thimble-rigging with virtue and vice, so that, at the end of three volumes, the bewildered reader shall not know which is which; don't let us find ourselves kindling at the generous qualities of thieves, and sympathizing with the rascalities of noble hearts. For our own part, we know what the public likes, and have chosen rogues for our characters, and have taken a story from the *Newgate Calendar*, which we hope to follow out to edification. Among the rogues, at least, we will have nothing that shall be mistaken for virtues. And if the British public (after calling for three or four editions) shall give up, not only our rascals, but the rascals of all other authors, we shall be content,—we shall apply to government for a pension, and think that our duty is done.

This run of thoughts, various, subtle and vigorous, is a good sample of the light-weight onslaught Thackeray directs against novels, and also plays, that recommend sordid vice by showing it acted by persons with cultured minds. But when he exclaims that rogues must be kept rogues, we misunderstand him unless we recognize that his definition of a rogue keeps the rogue a member of the human race. To look at the close of chapter v is to see the humane fullness of his practice: it ends with this scene between the rogue Catherine, who is now married to John Hayes, and the rogue Corporal Brock, who till lately had been the attendant on the rogue Count Galgenstein:

"And what became of the horses?" said Mrs. Catherine to Mr. Brock, when his tale was finished.

"Rips, madam," said he; "mere rips: we sold them at Stourbridge fair, and got but thirteen guineas for the two."

"And—and—the Count, Max; where is he, Brock?" sighed she.

"Whew!" whistled Mr. Brock; "what, hankering after him still? My dear, he is off to Flanders with his regiment; and, I make no doubt, there have been twenty Countesses of Galgenstein since your time."

"I don't believe any such thing, sir," said Mrs. Catherine, starting up very angrily.

"If you did, I suppose you'd laudanum him; wouldn't you?"

"Leave the room, fellow," said the lady. But she re-collected herself speedily again; and, clasping her hands, and looking very wretched at Brock, at the ceiling, at the floor, at her husband (from whom she violently turned away her head), she began to cry piteously; to which tears the Corporal set up a gentle accompaniment of whistling, as they trickled one after another down her nose.

I don't think they were tears of repentance, but of regret for the time when she had her first love, and her fine clothes, and her white hat and blue feather. Of the two, the corporal's whistle was much more innocent than the girl's sobbing; he was a rogue, but a good-natured old fellow, when his humour was not crossed. Surely our novel-writers make a great mistake in divesting their rascals of all gentle human qualities; they have such—and the only sad point to think is, in all private concerns of life, abstract feelings, and dealings with friends, and so on, how dreadfully like a rascal is to an honest man. The man who murdered the Italian boy set him first to play with his children, whom he loved, and who doubtless deplored his loss.

Could anything have been more closely and tenderly true to Catherine's feelings than her words with Brock? —Thackeray admitted to 'a sneaking kindness' for her.[1] And yet she is a rogue—only not, in Thackeray's hands, a 'romantic' one. His programme made for the keeping apart of rogues and scented ruffles, mental or material. There is no touch of the exquisite in Catherine's mind, and if when in high, brief prosperity she sports a 'gray hat with a blue feather, and red riding-coat trimmed with silver lace',[2] she loses them with the prosperity. Whether her wrists are flounced, bare, dirty or bloody, they are those of a personage seemingly actual. His programme, then, provided for the replacement of a personage seemingly a puppet by a personage seemingly human.

As for the subsidiary personages in *Catherine*, their truthfulness can be sampled from the end of the scene immediately preceding the authorial harangue I have quoted. How persuasive, by the way, is the placing of that harangue—the reader yields to it at a touch, being still half-occupied with the great scene he has just witnessed, that of the casting off of Thomas Bullock for a more dazzling lover. Here it is:

A sudden thought brought a smile of bright satisfaction in the captain's eyes,—he mounted the horse which Tummas still held,—"*Tired*, Mrs. Catherine!" said he, "and for my sake? By Heavens, you shan't walk a step farther! No, you shall ride back with a guard of honour! Back to the village, gentlemen!—right about face! Show those fellows, corporal, how to right about face. Now, my dear, mount behind me

---

[1] *Letters*, I, 433.　　　　[2] Ch. I.

on Snowball; he's easy as a sedan. Put your dear little foot on the toe of my boot; there now,—up! jump!—hurrah!"

"*That's* not the way, captain", shouted out Thomas, still holding on the rein as the horse began to move; "thee woant goo with him, will thee, Catty?"

But Mrs. Catherine, though she turned away her head, never let go her hold round the captain's waist; and he, swearing a dreadful oath at Thomas, struck him across the face and hands with his riding-whip; and the poor fellow, who, at the first cut, still held on the rein, dropped it at the second; and, as the pair galloped off, sate down on the roadside, and fairly began to weep.

"*March*, you dog!" shouted out the corporal a minute after; and so he did: and when next he saw Mrs. Catherine she *was* the captain's lady sure enough, and wore a gray hat with a blue feather, and red riding-coat trimmed with silver lace. But Thomas was then on a bare-backed horse; which Corporal Brock was flanking round a ring, and he was so occupied looking between his horse's ears, that he had no time to cry then, and at length got the better of his attachment.

5

When the impression a personage first makes on us is favourable—which is most usual, most of the personages in the long novels being of the social class that makes itself presentable—Thackeray adds what is unfavourable; where unfavourable, he adds the favourable. It is partly because of the former process that he has been called a cynic, and of the latter that he has been called a sentimentalist.

The process works for the benefit of minor personages. Illustration is redundant—open the novels where you will and you see it in action. To illustrate its operation in major characters, I propose to take Emily Costigan and Beatrix Esmond.

To Emily we are introduced as she is acting the part

of Mrs Haller in *The Stranger* under her stage name of
'Miss Fotheringay':

" . . . hurray—bravo! here's the Fotheringay."

The pit thrilled and thumped its umbrellas; a volley of
applause was fired from the gallery: the Dragoon officers
and Foker clapped their hands furiously: you would have
thought the house was full, so loud were their plaudits. The
red face and ragged whiskers of Mr. Costigan were seen
peering from the side-scene. Pen's eyes opened wide and
bright, as Mrs. Haller entered with a downcast look, then
rallying at the sound of the applause, swept the house with
a grateful glance, and, folding her hands across her breast,
sank down in a magnificent curtsey. More applause, more
umbrellas; Pen this time, flaming with wine and enthusiasm,
clapped hands and sang "bravo" louder than all. Mrs. Haller
saw him, and everybody else, and old Mr. Bows, the little
first fiddler of the orchestra, (which was this night increased
by a detachment of the band of the Dragoons, by the kind
permission of Colonel Swallowtail), looked up from the desk
where he was perched, with his crutch beside him, and
smiled at the enthusiasm of the lad.[1]

And so to this paragraph:

Those who have only seen Miss Fotheringay in later days,
since her marriage and introduction into London life, have
little idea how beautiful a creature she was at the time when
our friend Pen first set eyes on her. . . . She was of the tallest
of women, and at her then age of six-and-twenty—for six-
and-twenty she was, though she vows she was only nineteen
—in the prime and fulness of her beauty. Her forehead was
vast, and her black hair waved over it with a natural ripple
. . . and was confined in shining and voluminous braids at
the back of a neck such as you see on the shoulders of the
Louvre Venus—that delight of gods and men. Her eyes,
when she lifted them up to gaze on you, and ere she dropped
their purple-deep fringed lids, shone with tenderness and
mystery unfathomable. Love and Genius seemed to look

[1] Ch. IV.

out from them and then retire coyly, as if ashamed to have been seen at the lattice. Who could have had such a commanding brow but a woman of high intellect? She never laughed, (indeed her teeth were not good), but a smile of endless tenderness and sweetness played round her beautiful lips, and in the dimples of her cheeks and her lovely chin. Her nose defied description in those days. Her ears were like two little pearl shells, which the earrings she wore (though the handsomest properties in the theatre) only insulted. She was dressed in long flowing robes of black, which she managed and swept to and fro with wonderful grace, and out of the folds of which you only saw her sandals occasionally; they were of rather a large size; but Pen thought them as ravishing as the slippers of Cinderella. But it was her hand and arm that this magnificent creature most excelled in, and somehow you could never see her but through them. They surrounded her. When she folded them over her bosom in resignation; when she dropped them in mute agony, or raised them in superb command; when in sportive gaiety her hands fluttered and waved before her, like—what shall we say?—like the snowy doves before the chariot of Venus—it was with these arms and hands that she beckoned, repelled, entreated, embraced, her admirers —no single one, for she was armed with her own virtue, and with her father's valour, whose sword would have leapt from its scabbard at any insult offered to his child—but the whole house; which rose to her, as the phrase was, as she curtseyed and bowed, and charmed it.

From this to the opening sentence of the next paragraph:

Thus she stood for a minute—complete and beautiful— as Pen stared at her.

But for us she is already much more complete than for Pen and so much less beautiful. For we have already been shown what she had become after the passage of years. Indeed we know of her permanent defects as to teeth, and share with Pen, who is past heeding it, the knowledge of her permanent defect as to feet. Already we, but not Pen, have heard the ominous words 'her father' and suspect them to apply to the blustering 'General', the 'Cos' who 'wore a shabby military cape with a mangy collar, and a hat cocked very much over one eye',[1] whom Pen had already met without a thought of his being related to anybody, least of all to the divine Fotheringay. 'This shabby-looking buck was—was her father',[2] is how Thackeray words for him the process of swallowing the fact. The Fotheringay is Emily Costigan. And more completing details are to follow, dropped while Pen's courtship is proceeding:

Little Bows, the house-friend of the family, was exceedingly wroth at the notion of Miss Fotheringay's marriage with a stripling seven or eight years her junior. Bows, who was a cripple, and owned that he was a little more deformed even than Bingley the manager, so that he could not appear on the stage, was a singular wild man of no small talents and humour. Attracted first by Miss Fotheringay's beauty, he began to teach her how to act. He shrieked out in his cracked voice the parts, and his pupil learned them from his lips by rote, and repeated them in her full rich tones. He indicated the attitudes, and set and moved those beautiful arms of hers. Those who remember this grand actress on the stage can recal how she used always precisely the same gestures, looks, and tones; how she stood on the same plank of the stage in the same position, rolled her eyes at the same instant and to the same degree, and wept with precisely the same heart-rending pathos and over the same pathetic syllable. And after she had come out trembling with emotion before the audience, and looking so exhausted and tearful that you fancied she would faint with sensibility, she would gather up her hair the instant she was behind the curtain, and go home to a mutton chop and a glass of brown stout; and the harrowing labours of the day over, she went to bed and snored as resolutely and as regularly as a porter.[3]

[1] Ch. III. [2] Ch. V. [3] Ch. VI.

It is from the rejected but faithful Bows that, after the announcement of Miss Fotheringay's engagement by a London theatre—an engagement quietly arranged by Major Pendennis—it is from the sympathetic Bows that we get this further summary:

[Bows] came out of his place one night, and went into the house to the box where Pen was; and he held out his hand to him, and asked him to come and walk. They walked down the street together; and sate upon Chatteris bridge in the moonlight, and talked about *Her*. "We may sit on the same bridge", said he: "we have been in the same boat for a long time. You are not the only man who has made a fool of himself about that woman. And I have less excuse than you, because I'm older and know her better. She has no more heart than the stone you are leaning on; and it or you or I might fall into the water, and never come up again, and she wouldn't care. Yes—she would care for me, because she wants me to teach her: and she wont be able to get on without me, and will be forced to send for me from London. But she wouldn't if she didn't want me. She has no heart and no head, and no sense, and no feelings, and no griefs or cares, whatever. I was going to say no pleasures—but the fact is, she does like her dinner, and she is pleased when people admire her."

"And you do?" said Pen, interested out of himself, and wondering at the crabbed homely little old man.

"It's a habit, like taking snuff, or drinking drams", said the other, "I've been taking her these five years, and can't do without her. It was I made her. If she doesn't send for me, I shall follow her: but I know she'll send for me. She wants me. Some day she'll marry, and fling me over, as I do the end of this cigar."

The little flaming spark dropped into the water below, and disappeared; and Pen, as he rode home that night, actually thought about somebody but himself.[1]

[1] Ch. xiv.

The long process of transformation of the Fotheringay into Milly has scarcely been observed by the infatuated Pen. But for the reader, for whom Pen cannot but be something of a comic figure, the completed Milly is a woman to respect. When we see her in the greatest scene of all, we admire her for several things as much beyond the apprehension of her fiery and besotted father as beyond the blinded Pen's. Thackeray has completed her portrait for anybody at liberty to see it, and seeing it, we can proceed to honour its subject by measuring her against the scale applied in real life to any human being. I limit my long quotation to the ending of the scene. Costigan has been threatening a duel with Major Pendennis because he has chosen to be deceived into believing that Pen's proposal of marriage comes from a youth who is rich:

...Miss Fotheringay, though silent in general, and by no means brilliant as a conversationist, where poetry, literature, or the fine arts were concerned, could talk freely, and with good sense, too, in her own family circle. She cannot justly be called a romantic person: nor were her literary acquirements great: she never opened a Shakespeare from the day she left the stage, nor, indeed, understood it during all the time she adorned the boards: but about a pudding, a piece of needle-work, or her own domestic affairs, she was as good a judge as could be found; and not being misled by a strong imagination or a passionate temper, was better enabled to keep her judgment cool. When, over their dinner, Costigan tried to convince himself and the company, that the Major's statement regarding Pen's finances was unworthy of credit, and a mere *ruse* upon the old hypocrite's part so as to induce them, on their side, to break off the match, Miss Milly would not, for a moment, admit the possibility of deceit on the side of the adversary: and pointed out clearly that it was her father who had deceived himself, and not poor little Pen, who had tried to take them in. As for that poor lad, she said she pitied him with all her heart. And she ate an exceedingly good dinner; to the admiration of Mr. Bows, who had a remarkable regard and contempt for this woman, during, and after which repast, the party devised upon the best means of bringing this love-matter to a close. As for Costigan, his idea of tweaking the Major's nose vanished with his supply of after-dinner whisky-and-water; and he was submissive to his daughter, and ready for any plan on which she might decide, in order to meet the crisis which she saw was at hand.

The Captain, who, as long as he had a notion that he was wronged, was eager to face and demolish both Pen and his uncle, perhaps shrank from the idea of meeting the former, and asked "what the juice they were to say to the lad if he remained steady to his engagement, and they broke from theirs?" "What? don't you know how to throw a man over?" said Bows; "ask a woman to tell you?" and Miss Fotheringay showed how this feat was to be done simply enough— nothing was more easy. "Papa writes to Arthur to know what settlements he proposes to make in event of a marriage; and asks what his means are. Arthur writes back and says what he's got, and you'll find it's as the Major says, I'll go bail. Then papa writes, and says it's not enough, and the match had best be at an end."

"And, of course, you enclose a parting line, in which you say you will always regard him as a brother"; said Mr. Bows, eyeing her in his scornful way.

"Of course, and so I shall", answered Miss Fotheringay. "He's a most worthy young man, I'm sure. I'll thank ye hand me the salt. Them filberts is beautiful."

"And there will be no noses pulled, Cos, my boy? I'm sorry you're balked", said Mr. Bows.

"'Dad, I suppose not", said Cos, rubbing his own.— "What'll ye do about them letters, and verses, and pomes, Milly, darling?—Ye must send 'em back."

"Wigsby would give a hundred pound for 'em", Bows said, with a sneer.

"'Deed, then, he would", said Captain Costigan, who was easily led.

"Papa!" said Miss Milly.—"Ye wouldn't be for not sending the poor boy his letters back? Them letters and pomes is mine. They were very long, and full of all sorts of nonsense, and Latin, and things I couldn't understand the half of; indeed I've not read 'em all; but we'll send 'em back to him when the proper time comes." And going to a drawer, Miss Fotheringay took out from it a number of the County Chronicle and Chatteris Champion, in which Pen had written a copy of flaming verses celebrating her appearance in the character of Imogen, and putting by the leaf upon which the poem appeared, (for, like ladies of her profession, she kept the favourable printed notices of her performances), she wrapped up Pen's letters, poems, passions, and fancies, and tied them with a piece of string neatly, as she would a parcel of sugar.

Nor was she in the least moved while performing this act. What hours the boy had passed over those papers! What love and longing: what generous faith and manly devotion —what watchful nights and lonely fevers might they tell of! She tied them up like so much grocery, and sate down and made tea afterwards with a perfectly placid and contented heart: while Pen was yearning after her ten miles off: and hugging her image to his soul.[1]

6

And so to Beatrix. We see her first as a child. Her beauty ripens till it dazzles. No novelist, no poet, has produced a fuller effect of it: 'Beatrix is perhaps the finest picture of splendid, lustrous, physical beauty ever given to the world.'[2] That was Roscoe a hundred years ago, and there has been nothing written since, not even by Henry James, to render it out of date. But the 'belle' is completed by the woman, by the addition of character which, while it authenticates her beauty by making it that of a personage felt to be actual, puts us

[1] Ch. xii.   [2] Roscoe, ii, 306.

on tenterhooks because of its coexistence with a will to torture finely. Her power that way is partly thrust upon her by the chance that it is the gentle, self-effacing Esmond who dotes on her—she has no like power, we gather, over the husband she takes later on. Esmond is a 'romantic' person, utterly in love. Generalizing, he thinks men are more 'romantic' than they often know: he well sees that Beatrix would make 'a bad wife...for any man under the degree of a prince', yet would give anything to possess her, as another man would give everything for a certain diamond, or a blue riband, or (if he is a Dutch merchant) a tulip, or the admiration of the town, or in order to write an epic.[1]

It is one of the glories of the book that the author, who was out to draw Queen Anne as she was, could not do the same by the Jacobites without drawing them as 'romantic', Esmond himself in particular. What is rejected as 'romance' had to be retained as realism, the romantic being truthfully part of life, or at least of some lives. A romantic in politics, Esmond is a romantic also in love. The object of his passion is Beatrix for whom it is again a case of

> If to her share some Female Errors fall,
> Look on her Face, and you'll forget 'em all.[2]

Esmond looks on that face all the time. But we cannot. We share with the novelist a more usual, a more just, a more complete estimate of her character. And there is something else we share with him. For, as with the Fotheringay, there is another melancholy stroke of completeness which Esmond during the critical period is spared. Before we begin his memoirs we read their preface, supposedly written by his daughter, in which

[1] Bk III, ch. II.   [2] *The Rape of the Lock*, II, 17f.

occurs this report—a report of what, for the memoirist as he lived his life, still lay in the future:

I did not see the lady, who chose to remain *at her palace* all the time we were in London; but after visiting her, my poor mamma said she had lost all her good looks, and warned me not to set too much store by any such gifts which nature had bestowed upon me. She grew exceedingly stout; and I remember my brother's wife, Lady Castlewood, saying— "No wonder she became a favourite, for the king likes them old and ugly, as his father did before him." On which papa said—"All women were alike; that there was never one so beautiful as that one; and that we could forgive her everything but her beauty." And hereupon my mamma looked vexed, and my Lord Castlewood began to laugh; and I, of course, being a young creature, could not understand what was the subject of their conversation.

Stoutness and fadedness, however, are not the whole picture. In *The Virginians* the character of Beatrix, now the mature Madame de Bernstein, has achieved the constructed richness of a Chinese temple. The passage of time has now created room for this further stage, replacing beauty outlived with a sturdy brilliance, the old spirit domineering now by virtue of money. Even so we have not finished with her. She lives long enough to write of Henry Esmond in these words:

I loved and admired [him] more than any man I think ever I knew in this world: he was greater than almost all, though he made no noyse in it. I have seen very many who have, and, believe me, have found but few with such good heads and good harts as Mr. Esmond.[1]

And to feel for a human being as she feels for the young Harry Warrington (she has burned the compromising letter Harry had sent to Lady Maria, but he refuses to

---

[1] Ch. XLI.

take advantage of the destruction of the material evidence):

"I—I have no more to say. Will you be pleased to ring that bell? I—I wish you a good morning, Mr. Warrington," and, dropping a very stately curtsey, the old lady rose on her tortoiseshell stick, and turned towards the door. But, as she made her first step, she put her hand to her heart, sank on the sofa again, and shed the first tears that had dropped for long years from Beatrix Esmond's eyes.

Harry was greatly moved, too. He knelt down by her. He seized her cold hand, and kissed it. He told her, in his artless way, how very keenly he had felt her love for him, and how, with all his heart, he returned it. "Ah, aunt!" said he, "you don't know what a villain I feel myself. When you told me, just now, how that paper was burned—O! I was ashamed to think how glad I was." He bowed his comely head over her hand. She felt hot drops from his eyes raining on it. She had loved this boy. For half a century past—never, perhaps, in the course of her whole worldly life—had she felt a sensation so tender and so pure. The hard heart was wounded now, softened, overcome. She put her two hands on his shoulders, and lightly kissed his forehead.

"You will not tell her what I have done, child?" she said.

He declared never! never! And demure Mrs. Brett, entering at her mistress's summons, found the nephew and aunt in this sentimental attitude.[1]

And to feel also like this:

As for the Baroness de Bernstein, when that lady took the pains of making a grand toilette, she appeared as an object, handsome still, and magnificent, but melancholy, and even somewhat terrifying to behold. You read the past in some old faces, while some others lapse into mere meekness and content. The fires go quite out of some eyes, as the crow's feet pucker round them; they flash no longer with scorn, or

---

[1] Ch. xxxix.

10-2

with anger, or love; they gaze, and no one is melted by their sapphire glances; they look, and no one is dazzled. My fair young reader, if you are not so perfect a beauty as the peerless Lindamira, Queen of the Ball; if, at the end of it, as you retire to bed, you meekly own that you have had but two or three partners, whilst Lindamira has had a crowd round her all night—console yourself with thinking that, at fifty, you will look as kind and pleasant as you appear now [at] eighteen. You will not have to lay down your coach and six of beauty and see another step into it, and walk yourself through the rest of life. You will have to forego no long-accustomed homage; you will not witness and own the depreciation of your smiles. You will not see fashion forsake your quarter; and remain all dust gloom cobwebs within your once splendid saloons, and placards in your sad windows, gaunt, lonely, and to let! You may not have known any grandeur, but you won't feel any desertion. You will not have enjoyed millions, but you will have escaped bankruptcy. "Our hostess", said my Lord Chesterfield to his friend in a confidential whisper, of which the utterer did not in the least know the loudness, "puts me in mind of Covent Garden in my youth. Then it was the court end of the town, and inhabited by the highest fashion. Now, a nobleman's house is a gaming-house, or you may go in with a friend and call for a bottle."[1]

7

That the characters of men and women are strangely various within themselves is one of the truths that strongly fascinated Thackeray as a novelist. It is the view of human nature the person writing would like to think the fairest. His personages—those hundreds among the thousands whom he has opportunity to approach closely enough—all have their surprises for the reader who concludes too soon that one of them is in this or that category of the moralist. Small kindnesses

[1] Ch. xxvii.

sprout through the case of selfishness. They cost the doers little; if they did, they would remain undone. But they do cost something, and still they are done. Sir Brian Newcome at one tick of the clock 'wish[es] to make the conversation more interesting to the newly-arrived Colonel'.[1] The great often do not know the faces of some of their servants: 'If they were ill, you would not visit them'; but on the other hand,

you would send them an apothecary and of course order that they lacked for nothing. You are not unkind, you are not worse than your neighbours.[2]

"Colonel Newcome's affection for his old nurse does him the greatest honour," said the Baronet, who really meant what he said.[3]

Thackeray's wish to see as much as possible of the truth about his personages is well shown in a paragraph from *Philip*. Its attitude to moral status is, as often in his novels, complicated. He is writing ironically, in part. Philip is 'good', and is wrongly reported in New York; the Twysdens are 'bad'; so are Tregarvan and Ringwood. But that is not the end of the matter. It is on balance that they are one or other:

People there are in our history who do not seem to me to have kindly hearts at all; and yet, perhaps, if a biography could be written from their point of view, some other novelist might show how Philip and *his* biographer were a pair of selfish worldlings unworthy of credit: how uncle and aunt Twysden were most exemplary people, and so forth. Have I not told you how many people at New York shook their heads when Philip's name was mentioned, and intimated a strong opinion that he used his father very ill? When he fell wounded and bleeding, patron Tregarvan dropped him off his horse, and cousin Ringwood did not look behind to see how he fared. But these, again, may have

---

[1] Ch. vi.   [2] Ch. xiv.   [3] Ch. vi.

had their opinion regarding our friend, who may have been misrepresented to them——I protest as I look back at the nineteen past portions of this history, I begin to have qualms, and ask myself whether the folks of whom we have been prattling have had justice done to them; whether Agnes Twysden is not a suffering martyr justly offended by Philip's turbulent behaviour, and whether Philip deserves any particular attention or kindness at all. He is not transcendently clever; he is not gloriously beautiful. He is not about to illuminate the darkness in which the peoples grovel, with the flashing emanations of his truth. He sometimes owes money, which he cannot pay. He slips, stumbles, blunders, brags. Ah! he sins and repents—pray heaven—of faults, of vanities, of pride, of a thousand shortcomings! This I say—*Ego*—as my friend's biographer. Perhaps I do not understand the other characters round about him so well, and have overlooked a number of their merits, and caricatured and exaggerated their little defects.[1]

Personages consistent yet at odds within themselves, an absence of paragons and blackest villains—if the modern reader expects this of a novel, Thackeray is among the novelists he has to thank for it. 'A Novel without a Hero' is the actual sub-title of *Vanity Fair*, and the implied sub-title of the rest. He can have had small respect for Richardson's conception of a Sir Charles Grandison.[2] Rather he is of the school of Fielding, who drew Tom Jones, and who gave Sophia Weston rather too big a chin for perfect beauty of face. 'I hope', he confides on one occasion,

I hope we shall have nobody in this story without his little faults and peculiarities.[3]

[1] Ch. XLI.
[2] "I wish the new novel [*Esmond*] wasn't so grand and melancholy—the hero is as stately as Sir Charles Grandison..." (*Letters*, II, 815).
[3] *Philip*, ch. VI. Cf. *Philip*, ch. XXI: 'In a quarrel, [Philip] would sometimes lose his temper, and speak out his mind; or sometimes, and then he was most dangerous, he would be especially calm and Grandisonian.'

On others he could as well have hoped for little pleasant-nesses, for we are in Chaucer's world where the bright eyes of the monk are at least some compensation for his shortcomings in piety and temperance.

The deliberate provision of heroes who are no heroes carried with it for Thackeray an obvious limitation. If we look to novels to extend the range of our knowledge of men, Thackeray's for the most part will disappoint us. Dickens, Emily Brontë, George Eliot, and others adventure into strange human nature further than he—Thackeray aims rather at confirming our reading of our fellows, and showing us how delicate and vivid it is for one with finer eyes than ourselves. Barry Lyndon was the only major personage who tempted him from his usual haunts. In one or two other instances, personages ought to have been more unusual than Thackeray could manage to make them. One of these is Dr Firmin, who, as far as description goes, is a learned man, but who turns out in practice, measured against a Dr Casaubon, to be a mere schoolboy. Dr Firmin's incomplete-ness as a scholar is Thackeray's own—he freely expressed his want of enthusiasm for the Greek classics and 'an ignorance which is of the most undeniable sort'.[1] The field from which he drew his personages is as vast, or as narrow, as that of most of us, and likewise has a fence round it.

8

I have called the process by which Thackeray gives us the whole of a personage its 'completion'. The term suggests that, although a personage in a novel exists through time, and often through a considerable stretch of time, the whole boxful of him was available from the start, and that as we learn more we are merely having

[1] *From Cornhill to Cairo*, ch. v.

more of him taken out of the box. Thackeray, however, shows himself aware of the notion, then fairly new, that the inner man is a growing organism. When, in the passages of commentary, he considers character, he makes occasional use of the new word 'development'. According to the theory suggested in that word we are born with our characters folded up not as a handker-chief but as a plant inside the restive seed, character growing as by a biological process. I do not think that Thackeray found this new idea engaging—as in so many other matters he remained an eighteenth-century intelligence. The fullest discussion he gives to the puzzle of character in time comes in *Pendennis*, and it shows him clinging to the old concept. During his half-hearted flirtation with Blanche Amory, Pendennis suddenly sees himself against an earlier self:

"And I", thought Pendennis, "am the fellow who eight years ago had a grand passion, and last year was raging in a fever about Briseis!"

Yes, it was the same Pendennis, and time had brought to him, as to the rest of us, its ordinary consequences, consola-tions, developments. We alter very little. When we talk of this man or that woman being no longer the same person whom we remember in youth, and remark (of course to deplore) changes in our friends, we don't, perhaps, calculate that circumstance only brings out the latent defect or quality, and does not create it. The selfish languor and indifference of to-day's possession is the consequence of the selfish ardour of yesterday's pursuit: the scorn and weariness which cries *vanitas vanitatum* is but the lassitude of the sick appetite palled with pleasure: the insolence of the successful *parvenu* is only the necessary continuance of the career of the needy struggler: our mental changes are like our grey hairs or our wrinkles—but the fulfilment of the plan of mortal growth and decay: that which is snow-white now was glossy black once; that which is sluggish obesity to-day was boisterous rosy health a few years back; that calm weariness, benevolent, resigned, and disappointed, was ambition, fierce and violent, but a few years since, and has only settled into submissive repose after many a battle and defeat. Lucky he who can bear his failure so generously, and give up his broken sword to Fate the Conqueror with a manly and humble heart! Are you not awe-stricken, you, friendly reader, who, taking the page up for a moment's light reading, lay it down, perchance, for a graver reflection, —to think how you, who have consummated your success or your disaster, may be holding marked station, or a hopeless and nameless place, in the crowds who have passed through how many struggles of defeat, success, crime, remorse, to yourself only known!—who may have loved and grown cold, wept and laughed again, how often!—to think how you are the same, *You*, whom in childhood you remember, before the voyage of life began? It has been prosperous, and you are riding into port, the people huzzaing and the guns saluting,—and the lucky captain bows from the ship's side, and there is a care under the star on his breast which nobody knows of: or you are wrecked, and lashed, hopeless, to a solitary spar out at sea:—the sinking man and the successful one are thinking each about home, very likely, and remembering the time when they were children; alone on the hopeless spar, drowning out of sight; alone in the midst of the crowd applauding you.[1]

Thackeray does not face the new idea, though he uses some of its terminology. He sees his personages as things made so once for all. If the long life of Beatrix shows her character in several phases, they are rather phases of the moon than of the growth of a tree. When Colonel Newcome turned against Ethel, Thackeray told a friend that 'it was in him to do it. He must',[2] by which he meant that his original nature did not need

[1] Ch. LIX.
[2] *The Works of ... Thackeray with Biographical Introductions by his Daughter, Anne Ritchie,* 13 vols., 1898–9, VIII, xxxvii.

any developing to prompt the surprising act; the first things we see in the Colonel are knightliness, generosity, simplicity, patience, control, but there are others that are disclosed later when, on his second return from India, he begins to manage the life of his son, marrying him to the wrong woman after blazing out in anger against the Ethel he had once valued so justly. 'Time was', writes Thackeray,

when the Colonel himself would have viewed his kinsman more charitably, but fate and circumstance had angered that originally friendly and gentle disposition; hate and suspicion had mastered him, and if it cannot be said that his new life had changed him, at least it had brought out faults for which there had hitherto been no occasion, and qualities latent before.[1]

How shall we interpret the characters of Esmond and Rachel on this score? Esmond's marriage with the mother of the girl who will not have him has always engaged warm discussion. I have mentioned the outrage it was felt to have committed on the taste of the age. But one at least of Thackeray's contemporaries felt himself equal to demonstrating its psychological truth:

the record of Colonel Esmond's life is throughout a record of his attachment to one woman, towards whom his childish gratitude for protection grows with his growth into a complex feeling, in which filial affection and an unconscious passion are curiously blended. So unconscious, indeed, is the passion, that, though the reader has no difficulty in interpreting it, Esmond himself is for years the avowed and persevering though hopeless lover of this very lady's daughter.[2]

[1] Ch. LXIV.
[2] *Essays by the late George Brimley*, ed. W. G. Clarke, 1858, p. 264. To those who were jarred by Esmond's marriage Hannay gave this counsel: 'it would be well worth their while to study, phase by phase, the admirable delicacy with which [his] attachment to Rachel is made to grow, and the exquisite art by which the final result is hinted at, and the spectator gradually reconciled to it in the course of the narrative' (*Studies on Thackeray* [1869], p. 26).

And the critic proceeds to analyse the character of Rachel, so as to show the rightness, from her side also, of the step. His analysis does not need to resort to the concept of development. For Thackeray the marriage was according to the characters each possessed from the start: 'They married themselves',[1] and it was late in the day because the opportunity took a long time to arrive.

9

Seeing his characters as static, Thackeray subscribes to the Popean doctrine of the 'ruling passion'. The danger of this doctrine for any writer wishing to represent human life with the Thackerayan truthfulness is that it encourages him to take men and turn them into 'humours' of the narrowest sort. One way out of the difficulty is to give the personages competing passions even though the 'ruler' repeatedly comes off champion. Another way is to make the ruling passion too subtle to be named—to look at Pope's second 'Moral Essay', that on the characters of women, is to see how un-categorizable in some instances the mastering force can be.

That the ruling passion has rivals is often explicitly argued by Thackeray, as here:

[Major Pendennis] was sincerely vexed at hearing of Arthur's calamity. He would have gone to him, but what good could it do Arthur that he the Major should catch a fever? His own ailments rendered it absolutely impossible that he should attend to anybody but himself....When [Dr.] Goodenough came to see him according to his promise the next day, the Doctor had to listen for a quarter of an hour to an account of the Major's own maladies, before the latter had leisure to hear about Arthur...[and so he] made

[1] *Letters*, III, 47 n.

his appearance in his usual trim order and curly wig, at the dinner-table of the Marquis of Steyne. But we must do the Major the justice to say, that he was very unhappy and gloomy in demeanour. Wagg and Wenham rallied him about his low spirits; asked whether he was crossed in love? and otherwise diverted themselves at his expense. He lost his money at whist after dinner, and actually trumped his partner's highest spade. And the thoughts of the suffering boy, of whom he was proud, and whom he loved after his manner, kept the old fellow awake half through the night, and made him feverish and uneasy.[1]

There is a nicety in the judgment of Mr Bows when he lays his finger on the ruling passion of Captain Costigan: 'The General likes his whiskey-bottle more than anything in life.'[2] As for that same small personage, Mr Bows, he is his essential faithful self on all occasions, but there is enough of sardonic selfishness in him to give his kindness—pathetic in being that of an ageing cripple —a frequent rub. We see the effort it costs his ruling passion to maintain its rule. Here he is, after counselling Fanny, partly for his own ends, not to see Pen again, and Fanny outraged at the counsel:

" . . . you know that if you said a word against him, I would never speak a word to you again—never!" cried Miss Fanny; and clenched her little hand, and paced up and down the room. Bows noted, watched, and followed the ardent little creature with admiration and gloomy sympathy.[3]

The ruling passion of Helen Pendennis rules her other passions only as wild beasts are ruled. Her saintliness is almost as strong as her jealous motherhood, though at one crisis, which I quote below,[4] it is scattered like suffocating feathers. Usually these two main

[1] Ch. LI.   [2] Ch. LV.
[3] Ch. LI.   [4] At p. 169.

passions in Helen are yoked amicably together; usually she is a type of 'sainted', jealous motherhood. On most occasions, here and elsewhere in the novels, the ruling passion rules with the quietest of despotisms. Thackeray is adept at showing the minuteness of the evidence denoting the existence of the regent.

It is already clear that Thackeray gives his personages a ruling passion difficult or impossible to name with exactness. The passions are often subtle, deeply fetched, obscure. To return to *Pendennis*, we could name Helen's ruling passion without much fuss: it is jealous motherhood, that is, passionate motherhood in which the inevitable element of jealousy is strong. But to name Pen's, which as the novel runs its course we are strongly conscious of, would be much more difficult. The title-page describes him as 'his greatest enemy', which goes a certain way toward fixing its complexity.

10

I have said that Thackeray's personages surprise us because, giving us them whole, he lets us see their mingled 'good' and 'bad'. Knowing actual people, we ought not to be surprised by inconsistency of this constitutional kind. But we are, and partly because Thackeray's initial grip on his personages leads us to expect of them that unmixedness we expect of the allegorist. He springs another sort of surprise, however, which the personages of any story-teller, whether novelist or allegorist, would be the better for. Acting out of the firmness of their nature, his personages surprise us by the felicity and inventiveness with which their actions illustrate their natures. I am not yet thinking of the major actions that turn the great wheels of the plot, but of actions that do little more than flash or play a

light into the heart of a character. We are surprised at
Becky's spasm of admiration for the despised Rawdon
as he stands over the unconscious Lord Steyne—
surprised not because it was unforeseeable but because
it was unforeseen by us. The surprise is of the happy sort
that sharpens our sense of her, which we felt to be well
pointed already. Another surprise of this sort comes in
the midst of *The Newcomes*. From the earlier novel we
know that she has made a new life for herself after the
death of Jos, but now we are suddenly shown to what
particular pitch of respectability and distinction: at this
later date she is 'her who wrote the Hymns, you know,
and goes to Mr. Honeyman's chapel'.[1] Another small
instance. It is half-way through *The Virginians*—half-
way, that is, through the second novel containing
Beatrix and her powerful speeches—that we learn that
she was 'slow with her pen, and disliked using it'.[2]
A smaller straw than writing hymns, but a straw in as
strong a wind. And here is a cluster of small surprises
from the same novel. The family of Lord Castlewood
have now learned the news that Harry is no longer heir
to the Virginian estates, which makes a great difference
to their regard for him, but one which they hide behind
the most dazzling of masks:

Only my Lady Castlewood and her daughter Lady
Fanny were in the room into which our young gentlemen
were ushered. Will had no particular fancy to face Harry,
my lord was not dressed, Maria had her reasons for being
away, at least till her eyes were dried. . . .

As the young gentlemen are announced, Lady Castlewood
advances towards them with perfect ease and good humour.
"We have heard, Harry", she says, looking at the latter with
a special friendliness, "of this most extraordinary circum-

[1] Ch. xiii.   [2] Ch. xlii.

stance. My Lord Castlewood said at breakfast that he should wait on you this very day, Mr. Warrington, and Cousin Harry, we intend not to love you any the less because you are poor."

"We shall be able to show now that it is not for your acres that we like you, Harry!" says Lady Fanny, following her mamma's lead.

"And I to whom the acres have fallen?" says Mr. George, with a smile and a bow.

"O, cousin, we shall like you for being like Harry!" replies the arch Lady Fanny.

Ah! who that has seen the world, has not admired that astonishing ease with which fine ladies drop you and pick you up again? Both the ladies now addressed themselves almost exclusively to the younger brother. They were quite civil to Mr. George: but with Mr. Harry they were fond, they were softly familiar, they were gently kind, they were affectionately reproachful. Why had Harry not been for days and days to see them?

"Better to have had a dish of tea and a game at picquet with them than with some other folks", says Lady Castlewood. "If *we* had won enough to buy a paper of pins from you we should have been content; but young gentlemen don't know what is for their own good", says mamma.

"Now you have no more money to play with, you can come and play with us, cousin!" cries fond Lady Fanny, lifting up a finger, "and so your misfortune will be good fortune to us."

George was puzzled. This welcome of his brother was very different from that to which he had looked. All these compliments and attentions paid to the younger brother, though he was without a guinea! Perhaps the people were not so bad as they were painted? The Blackest of all Blacks is said not to be of *quite* so dark a complexion as some folks describe him.[1]

As a further instance take the introduction to that brilliant little scene late in *Vanity Fair* in which Amelia,

[1] Ch. LVI.

159

whose fortunes are now improving, is being honoured by callers. The surprises erupt gently from the normal level of the book. They are those of actions performed when the pressure to act importantly is relaxed to its normal feebleness. This is the first step in the scene:

> The female Bullock, aunt of Georgy [Amelia's son], although despoiled by that little monster of one-half of the sum which she expected from her father, nevertheless showed her charitableness of spirit by being reconciled to the mother and the boy. Roehampton is not far from Richmond, and one day the chariot, with the golden bullocks emblazoned on the panels, and the flaccid children within,[1] drove to Amelia's house at Richmond; and the Bullock family made an irruption into the garden. . . .

I pause here in mid-sentence to point the moment—the Bullocks and ourselves are about to descend on certain well-known people unawares; what shall we find them doing?

> . . . into the garden, where Amelia was reading a book, Jos was in an arbour placidly dipping strawberries into wine, and the Major in one of his Indian jackets was giving a back to Georgy, who chose to jump over him. He went over his head, and bounded into the little advance of Bullocks, with immense black bows in their hats, and huge black sashes, accompanying their mourning mamma.[2]

One small surprise of character I find disappointing —that of Harry Warrington's conscious happiness (in the midst of his misery) at having done a deed of great charity—he had relieved the poor family to which the Reverend Mr Sampson was indebted while his own debts were threatening his imprisonment. This is the

---

[1] Note the complicated irony turned on a feeble family by its name and device: bullocks, though powerful beasts, are not bulls.
[2] Ch. LXI.

short chain of incidents of which I am particularizing one:

"That need not happen", says Mr. Warrington. "Here are eighty guineas, Sampson. As far as they go, God help you! 'Tis all I have to give you. I wish to my heart I could give more as I promised; but you did not come at the right time, and I am a poor devil now until I get my remittances from Virginia."

The Chaplain gave a wild look of surprise, and turned quite white. He flung himself down on his knees and seized Harry's hand.

"Great Powers, sir!" says he, "are you a guardian angel that Heaven hath sent me? You quarrelled with my tears this morning, Mr. Warrington. I can't help them now. They burst, sir, from a grateful heart. A rock of stone would pour them forth, sir, before such goodness as yours! May Heaven eternally bless you, and give you prosperity! May my unworthy prayers be heard in your behalf, my friend, my best benefactor! May ———"

"Nay, nay! get up, friend—get up, Sampson!" says Harry, whom the Chaplain's adulation and fine phrases rather annoyed. "I am glad to have been able to do you a service—sincerely glad. There—there! Don't be on your knees to me!"

"To Heaven who sent you to me, sir!" cries the Chaplain. "Mrs. Weston! Mrs. Weston!"

"What is it, sir?" says the landlady, instantly, who, indeed, had been at the door the whole time. "We are saved, Mrs. Weston! We are saved!" cries the Chaplain. "Kneel, kneel, woman, and thank our benefactor! Raise your innocent voices, children, and bless him!" A universal whimper arose round Harry, which the Chaplain led off, whilst the young Virginian stood, simpering and well-pleased, in the midst of this congregation. They *would* worship, do what he might. One of the children, not understanding the kneeling order, and standing up, the mother fetched her a slap on the ear, crying, "Drat it, Jane, kneel down, and bless the gentleman, I tell 'ee!" ... We leave them performing this sweet benedictory service. Mr. Harry walks off from Long Acre, forgetting almost the griefs of the former four or five days, and tingling with the consciousness of having done a good action.[1]

If I do not care for Harry's tingling it is because at this point I know Harry better than Thackeray did. He is quite capable of the mighty selflessness of sparing, while sore pressed himself, most of his own resources for another's need, and so—if I judge human nature rightly —incapable of tingling. I have strung out the whole chain of incidents because the other links, being firm and true, are characteristic of the firmness of truth which comes on every page. Indeed when one first reads about Harry's tingling, one almost takes it as irony, as if Thackeray were saying that some people would tingle, but not Harry. Our instinct for taking it so is a general tribute to Thackeray.

His personages, then, are almost invariably engaged in illustrating themselves. Otherwise he would not have found them worth writing about, either at that particular point or in general, for his novels are mainly composed of actions which, measured by the scale which, though most ready to hand, is not the true one, are little, nameless, unremembered. I shall quote later a passage in which, assuring us that he knows a great deal about the industrial aristocracy of a new Northern town, he claims that his knowledge is made up of 'interesting particulars'. For Thackeray particulars had to be interesting, that is, significant of the moral nature. I do not recall his ever speaking of a personage's actions as mechanical. If so, it would be because at a climax the primacy of the moral nature was in abeyance. There are several actions so described in the novels of

[1] *The Virginians*, ch. XLIV.

George Eliot, and after her of course came the deluge. Choosing to have the utmost freedom of entry into the mind, many of our modern novelists have almost ceased to read a mental significance into the body. Often we are given actions that have nothing to them beyond themselves. A personage drives a car, and when it runs into rain sets the windscreen wiper wiping and, during the smoking of a cigarette, flicks off the ash. Of this merely physical realism there is none in Thackeray, and at bottom for the same reason that there is none in *The Pilgrim's Progress*. His novels are full of external detail because they are a huge mosaic of allegorical fragments, however much else they are, and however particular or commonplace the moral significance of some of the fragments. He is the critic, as I have said, of everything he invents, and he invents just so because he is a critic. He does not only see things, he reads them. When old Mrs Gashleigh, the dominating mother-in-law in 'A Little Dinner at the Timmins's', leans against the dresser, she is not merely resting. If she were, Thackeray would ignore her till she was doing something less merely animal. She is defeated.

Some of these surprises surprised their author;

Well [he said] when I wrote the sentence [about Becky's admiration for Rawdon], I slapped my fist on the table, and said, '*that* is a touch of genius!'[1]

So he told a friend—and how like him to say 'touch' instead of 'stroke'. To analyse these surprises I go to Dr Johnson's account of the sublime:

the first effect [of which] is sudden astonishment, and the second rational admiration.[2]

---

[1] James Hannay, *Studies on Thackeray* [1869], p. 12.
[2] *Lives of the Poets*, I, 21.

And for naming what produced the effects I go to Ruskin, who asked how Shakespeare knew that Virgilia would remain silent in the din acclaiming Coriolanus's victorious return from the wars, and called the power of knowing it that of 'the penetrative imagination'.[1]

I I

Surprises of action as they are accumulated and ordered in a plot—Thackeray did not care for them. He declared in *The Newcomes*,

I disdain, for the most part, the tricks and surprises of the novelists' art;[2]

and in *Philip*—a 'modest history', in which 'I do not seek to create even surprises'[3]—he strikes this bargain with the reader:

the story is as authentic as many histories, and the reader need only give such an amount of credence to it as he may judge that its verisimilitude warrants.[4]

I have already referred to the 'pushes' that even a good novelist must give his personages from time to time. Thackeray believed they should be as few and as gentle as possible. His way of withholding the pushing hand was to let events be determined wherever possible by the characters of his personages. The first chapter of *Vanity Fair* can be taken as an example. He convinces us that Becky Sharp is actual by the end of the first few paragraphs. Perhaps a hundred words, so far, have been expended on her, but already she has a name and as suggestive a name as ever novelist hit on, and already we have seen her act—she has thrown back over the garden wall the copy of Johnson's Dictionary, the gift

---

[1] *Works*, IV, 227f. (*Modern Painters*, III, ii, 1, 5): Ruskin himself had the power to ask the vital question: 'How did Shakespeare *know* that Virgilia could not speak?'

[2] Ch. LXX.   [3] Ch. VIII.   [4] Ch. III.

of which has cost the younger Miss Pinkerton so much contriving—and we have already felt it ominous that a personage who could become so real at so small a cost of words, and who could act to such purpose, should not already be accorded more prominence—prominence is felt to be already owing her. Meanwhile it is the soft-named Amelia Sedley, on whom words are showered, who is prominent. Already, then, we are awaiting the progress of the story—its progress, for it has already begun, and the rest of the vast novel stretches out before us, like the rest of our own life. We do not trouble ourselves to foresee the course of this progress. The reader of a novel takes what he is given in the order and at the pace he is given it. When, however, he is persuaded that the story ahead will be worth following, he forms expectations vague but not to be thwarted. Once he has grasped the nature of Becky and Amelia he is 'awaiting developments' in accordance with his well-schooled sense of probability. In essentials, as I have said, it is the way we face the remainder of our own lives, not counting on accidents to transform us, but expecting, given our spheres and characters, to continue to exemplify our selves through a course of acts and experiences which in some sort are expected.

This condition of 'awaiting developments' is not unlike the author's when the author is Thackeray. We know that his prevision of a work never had the completeness of a working drawing. As a novelist he is not unfairly reported in the engaging outburst in *The Newcomes*, an apology for the breaking of a promise made in an earlier number:

Not always doth the writer know whither the divine Muse leadeth him. But of this be sure; she is as inexorable as Truth.[1]

[1] Ch. x.

The complex sense he wished to express here must have taxed his powers, but he triumphs over the knot with the nicety of 'not always', the grimace of 'doth' and 'leadeth', the imputation of divinity to a muse caught *flagrante delicto*, and the taunt that the reader must take what he is given. I have already said that this condition, which did not make for the creation of plots to satisfy an exacting craftsman, helped him strongly to attain to an untrimmed verisimilitude towards the flowingness we are aware of in our own lives.

The safest course for a novelist intent on designing an action that shall strike the reader as likely is to make it resemble life even more closely than life itself does. The chance that counts in actual life, even in ordinary actual life, operates freely. So it seems to men. And the only thing they can do about it, when its operation is violent enough to surprise them, is to revise their view, for the time being at least, of what life is like. The task of whatever philosophy they call in for the purposes of consolation is that of digesting what is unalterably given as fact. For men the chance contriving the fact is mysterious, but in novels not necessarily so. Its origin in the author's convenience may be only too patent. When that obviousness is sensed, our instinct is to reject the chance as too clearly not 'heaven-sent'. The 'fate' of the explanatory letter written by Tess on the eve of her wedding is a famous and extreme instance of a heavy act of chance in novels, and only when the philosophy of the book is prepared to bear the consequences of this degree of chance can the reader accept it: we accept this heavy accident only because Hardy is prepared, even eager, to admit that fate is hideously cruel. The humdrum philosophy of Thackeray is not prepared to bear such consequences. Accordingly, he creeps close to the surest probability, and, therefore, close to the appearance of being true to life, a truth which most of us prefer to smart philosophy. Properly investigated, it was no accident that led to Pen's critical collision with Fanny Bolton in Temple Gardens. Ill at ease with repressed guilty love, he has 'taken a fancy' before returning to his rooms to 'take a little walk' in the Gardens:

After walking for a brief space, and looking at the many peaceful and happy groups round about him, he grew tired of the exercise, and betook himself to one of the summer houses which flank either end of the main walk, and there modestly seated himself. What were his cogitations? The evening was delightfully bright and calm; the sky was cloudless; the chimneys on the opposite bank were not smoking; the wharfs and warehouses looked rosy in the sunshine, and as clear as if they, too, had washed for the holiday. The steamers rushed rapidly up and down the stream, laden with holiday passengers. The bells of the multitudinous city churches were ringing to evening prayers,—such peaceful Sabbath evenings as this Pen may have remembered in his early days, as he paced, with his arm round his mother's waist, on the terrace before the lawn at home. The sun was lighting up the little Brawl, too, as well as the broad Thames, and sinking downwards majestically behind the Clavering elms, and the tower of the familiar village church. Was it thoughts of these, or the sunset merely, that caused the blush in the young man's face? He beat time on the bench, to the chorus of the bells without; flicked the dust off his shining boots with his pocket-handkerchief, and starting up, stamped with his foot and said, "No, by Jove, I'll go home." And with this resolution, which indicated that some struggle as to the propriety of remaining where he was, or of quitting the garden, had been going on in his mind, he stepped out of the summer-house.

He nearly knocked down two little children, who did not indeed reach much higher than his knee, and were trotting along the gravel-walk, with their long blue shadows slanting towards the east.

One cried out "Oh!" the other began to laugh; and with a knowing little infantine chuckle, said, "Missa Pen-dennis!" And Arthur, looking down, saw his two little friends of the day before, Mesdemoiselles Ameliar-Ann and Betsy-Jane. He blushed more than ever at seeing them, and seizing the one whom he had nearly upset, jumped her up into the air, and kissed her: at which sudden assault Ameliar-Ann began to cry in great alarm.

This cry brought up instantly two ladies in clean collars and new ribbons, and grand shawls, namely: Mrs. Bolton in a rich scarlet Caledonian Cashmere, and a black silk dress, and Miss F. Bolton with a yellow scarf and a sweet sprigged muslin, and a parasol—quite the lady. Fanny did not say one single word: though her eyes flashed a welcome, and shone as bright—as bright as the most blazing windows in Paper Buildings. But Mrs. Bolton, after admonishing Betsy-Jane, said, "Lor, sir—how *very* odd that we should meet *you* year? I ope you ave your ealth well, sir.—Ain't it odd, Fanny, that we should meet Mr. Pendennis?" What do you mean by sniggering, Mesdames? When young Croesus has been staying at a country-house, have you never, by any singular coincidence, been walking with your Fanny in the shrubberies? Have you and your Fanny never happened to be listening to the band of the Heavies at Brighton, when young De Boots and Captain Padmore came clinking down the Pier? Have you and your darling Frances never chanced to be visiting old widow Wheezy at the cottage on the common, when the young curate has stepped in with a tract adapted to the rheumatism? Do you suppose that, if singular coincidences occur at the Hall, they don't also happen at the Lodge?

It *was* a coincidence, no doubt: that was all. In the course of the conversation on the day previous, Mr. Pendennis had merely said, in the simplest way imaginable, and in reply to a question of Miss Bolton, that although some of the courts were gloomy, parts of the Temple were very cheerful and agreeable, especially the chambers looking on the river and around the gardens, and that the gardens were a very pleasant walk on Sunday evenings and frequented by a great number of people—and here, by the merest chance, all our acquaintances met together, just like so many people in genteel life. What could be more artless, good-natured, or natural?[1]

The coincidence of meeting, then, was no more a coincidence than that other that Thackeray plants but does not draw attention to, the 'coincidence' of the Boltons' being dressed in their best and of Pen's being so dressed also. Thackeray's use of 'fate' and character as contrivers of incident is worth a study in itself. A primary document would be the paragraph two chapters ahead: the rumour of Pen's misconduct has at last reached Fairoaks and has occasioned the outburst of the saintly Helen against poor Laura:

"It *is* true, and you've done it, Laura", cried out Helen fiercely. "Why did you refuse him when he asked you? Why did you break my heart and refuse him? It is you who led him into crime. It is you who flung him into the arms of this—this woman.—Don't speak to me.—Don't answer me. I will never forgive you, never. Martha, bring me my bonnet and shawl. I'll go out. I won't have you come with me. Go away. Leave me, cruel girl; why have you brought this shame on me?" And bidding her daughter and her servants keep away from her, she ran down the road to Clavering.[2]

In the end, of course, the counsels of the vicar prevail and Pen is sent a letter 'earnestly praying that he would break off and repent of a connection so fatal to his best interests and his soul's welfare'. And so in the next chapter comes this:

Unluckily for himself and all parties, Pen never read that homily which Doctor Portman addressed to him, until many

[1] Ch. XLIX.   [2] Ch. L.

weeks after the epistle had been composed; and day after day the widow waited for her son's reply to the charges against him; her own illness increasing with every day's delay....

Those kind readers who have watched Mr. Arthur's career hitherto, and have made, as they naturally would do, observations upon the moral character and peculiarities of their acquaintance, have probably discovered by this time what was the prevailing fault in Mr. Pen's disposition, and who was that greatest enemy, artfully indicated in the title-page, with whom he had to contend. Not a few of us, my beloved public, have the very same rascal to contend with: a scoundrel who takes every opportunity of bringing us into mischief, of plunging us into quarrels, of leading us into idleness and unprofitable company, and what not. In a word, Pen's greatest enemy was himself: and as he had been pampering, and coaxing, and indulging that individual all his life, the rogue grew insolent, as all spoiled servants will be; and at the slightest attempt to coerce him, or make him do that which was unpleasant to him, became frantically rude and unruly. A person who is used to making sacrifices —Laura, for instance, who had got such a habit of giving up her own pleasure for others—can do the business quite easily; but Pen, unaccustomed as he was to any sort of self-denial, suffered woundily when called on to pay his share, and savagely grumbled at being obliged to forego anything he liked.

He had resolved in his mighty mind then that he would not see Fanny; and he wouldn't. He tried to drive the thoughts of that fascinating little person out of his head, by constant occupation, by exercise, by dissipation and society. He worked then too much; he walked and rode too much; he ate, drank, and smoked too much: nor could all the cigars and the punch of which he partook drive little Fanny's image out of his inflamed brain, and at the end of a week of this discipline and self-denial our young gentle-man was in bed with a fever. Let the reader who has never had a fever in chambers pity the wretch who is bound to undergo that calamity.

The reason why Harry Warrington does not receive his brother's letter is not a mechanical disposition of door and carpet, as in *Tess*, but debts, an arrest, a seizure of goods, the newly-arrived letter among them.[1] As for Pen, he does not receive the letter because he is ill, and though he ascribes his illness to 'luck',[2] that is only his way of speaking. The reason for Pen's 'accidental' omission to read springs from incidents moved by his acts, moved in turn by his own psyche and character. Later on, Pen draws a moral from his affair with Miss Fotheringay, the moral that it is 'luckier to fail before marriage than after',[3] but again the word 'luck' is inscribed on only one side of the medal: we have already appreciated the statesmanship of his friends that saved him. If occasionally the author uses the word 'luck'[4] himself, he does so because he speaks as 'a man of the world'.[5] As a constructor of tales he does not believe in it.

If a trick of art comes at the very end of a novel there are aesthetic reasons why we do not always resent it—otherwise, Shakespeare would not have dared to huddle his marital endings in the comedies; or, to take the most minute instance, Browning would not have dared to place his most outrageous rhyme in the final couplet of 'The Pied Piper'. An acceptable ending-trick is played in *Philip*. The long and troubled course of the love of Philip and Charlotte proceeds according to probability till the very end, when Philip achieves money by the sudden discovery of a will. This accident, however, is merely the gilding of an edifice already in place. Another surprise out of the hat comes at the end of

---

[1] *The Virginians*, ch. XLIX.
[2] Ch. LIV.   [3] Ch. LXIV.
[4] E.g., ch. LXIII.   [5] Ch. V.

Lovel the Widower: the charming and wealthy Lovel proposes marriage to Elizabeth, who has been the contention of three, if not four, of the other men in the story, and of course proposes with success. Thackeray first gave the matter of this novel the form of a play, and the surprise it springs would not be objectionable at all on the stage: we should accept it in good humour as a *coup de théâtre*. In a novel it might be very objectionable, in a novel so serious—for all the laughs—as this, since unlike the marriage of Rachel and Esmond it is not prepared for. As in *Philip*, there is excuse. At the very end of novels we do not greatly care, when the act of ending is itself a pleasure, however mixed, by what means things are settled, provided the settlement does not offend our general sense of what is fitting. Or, to put it another way, so long as we feel the author to be laughing as well as ourselves.

12

Though Thackeray's verisimilitude ruled out formal plots, it did not rule out fragments of them. When Brimley remarked that he gives us 'not much more plot than [comes] in one of Defoe's novels', he added:

neither is there, generally speaking, a plot in a man's life, though there may be and often is in sections of it.[1]

An instance of this would be the last lap of the quarrel between the Bayneses and MacWhirters in *Philip*, which is as tightly designed as the quarrel of the lovers in *Midsummer Night's Dream*. And Thackeray will also here and there provide related points of irony. For instance, these three points in *The Virginians*. Madame de Bernstein, who is about seventy years old, stabs the hopes of

[1] *Essays by the late George Brimley*, ed. W. G. Clark, 1858, p. 260.

Lady Maria, who at the age of forty is making young
Harry stand by his proposal of marriage, by dropping
as if casually such a phrase as '[we] two old women'.[1]
In her turn Lady Maria, who knows that Mrs Lambert
has some daughters of Harry's age, inquires how he
went on under their roof, and refers to the daughters,
as if casually, as 'the children'.[2] Mrs Lambert, in a
letter to Harry's mother describes Lady Maria's 'tenderness and concern' for Harry when the road accident
makes him shelter with the Lamberts, as 'maternal'.[3]
Or there are those terminal points of irony of *The Newcomes*, Thomas Newcome starting his promising career,
and ending it penniless, under the roofs of the Grey
Friars. The irony of the balancing fortunes of Amelia
and Becky are formal enough if we look at them away
from the novel. In place they seem no more formal than
life itself warrants.

The bufferless endings of the novels had more meaning
than Saintsbury quite saw. Explaining the way *Pendennis* ends, he says:

Nor is the close in any way objectionable, though closes in
novels, as in life, are rarely quite satisfactory unless they are
tragic. In fact, it is *not* a close, and does not pretend to
be, as, indeed, it need not in this chronicle sort of work.
The author simply cuts you off your most bountiful pennyworth, and keeps the rest for the next time—which next
time in this case was happily no longer in coming than the
beginning of *The Newcomes*.[4]

The endings of *Pendennis* and the rest are not, however,
the lazy gestures of a merchant doling out pennyworths.
Thackeray designed them to be loose so that they represented life more truthfully. It was on that score that he

[1] Ch. xxv.   [2] Ch. xxvii.
[3] Ch. xxi.   [4] Pp. 181 f.

173

justified the ending of *Vanity Fair*. Writing to Robert Bell, who had reviewed the book in *Fraser's*, he declared

I want to leave everybody dissatisfied and unhappy at the end of the story—we ought all to be with our own and all other stories.[1]

In other words, Thackeray stands with our later novelists. Mr Edwin Muir has said that at the end of some of the best novels of the twentieth century

we feel that there is something of the greatest importance to say, and that the ending is really a sort of beginning...we live by an unfinished conception of life, exist in a circle which is never closed.[2]

Unlike Browning, Thackeray may not have judged that any piece of life was arc-like enough to imply a circle. The lives of his personages proceed like wavy lines. At the end of a novel these lines are not knotted into bows. And so as to remind us of the persisting freedom of blood and will he gives us at a later point of time, as time is now being measured in another story, a further glimpse of an old life still pushing independently ahead.

[1] *Letters*, II, 423.
[2] *Essays on Literature and Society*, 1949, p. 147.

CHAPTER VII

The Author's Philosophy

So far it has been in its effects that I have shown the truth that Thackeray admired—in its effects in personage and action. There is more to say of its effects in his personages, and in the furniture of his novels, generally, but it will be said while I attempt to show the nature of the truth that produced these effects.

So amply is this truth present explicitly as a system that Thackeray has not escaped the kind of criticism suitable for a professional philosopher. It was as such, for instance, that a part of Roscoe's criticism dealt with him. I propose to consider that criticism, out of date as some of it is, because it prompts consideration of certain things of permanent importance for Thackeray, and because a part of Roscoe's charge has recently been renewed by Dr Leavis, who has spoken of Thackeray's lack of 'essential substance of interest'.[1]

Roscoe noted that Thackeray's method as a philosopher was never the strict one of the logician:

Thackeray never reasons, he never gains one step by deduction.[2]

But why, we ask, should he? Roscoe has again forgotten that Thackeray is a novelist: on an early occasion he mistook him for an historian. The conditions proper to a logician are as little proper to a novelist as the methods of an historian, even when the novelist pretends to be an historian, or is handling material which the philosopher handles as a logician. Roscoe mistook the category into which his object fell; not, I may say, without

---

[1] See Appendix II, p. 288 below.   [2] II, 276.

invitation from Thackeray. If a novelist gives us history and logic, that is over and above what we expect of him. And of the two, logic is the more unlikely. We do not expect a novelist to care for it. Not much of a logician himself, Thackeray shows us very few specimens of logicians in his writings. The logic of these few fares badly. In *Denis Duval* that of the two disputants is mere straw beside the amorous passion stirring in the mind of the contestant on the Catholic side, M. de la Motte:

It has been said that Monsieur de Saverne loved the sound of his own croaking voice, and to hold forth to his home congregation. Night after night he and his friend M. de la Motte would have religious disputes together, in which the Huguenot gentleman flattered himself that he constantly had the better of the ex-pupil of the seminary. I was not present naturally, not setting my foot on French ground until five-and-twenty years after, but I can fancy Madame the Countess sitting at her tambour frame, and the old duenna ladies at their cards, and the combat of the churches going on between these two champions in the little old saloon of the Hôtel de Saverne. "As I hope for pardon," M. de la Motte said to me at a supreme moment of his life, "and to meet those whom on earth I loved and made unhappy, no wrong passed between Clarisse and me, save that wrong which consisted in disguising from her husband the regard we had for one another. Once, twice, thrice, I went away from their house, but that unhappy Saverne would bring me back, and I was only too glad to return. I would let him talk for hours—I own it—so that I might be near Clarisse. I had to answer from time to time, and rubbed up my old seminary learning to reply to his sermons. I must often have spoken at random, for my thoughts were far away from the poor man's *radotages*, and he could no more change my convictions than he could change the colour of my skin. Hours and hours thus passed away. They would have been intolerably tedious to others: they were not so to me. I preferred that gloomy little château to the finest place in Europe. To see Clarisse, was all I asked. Denis! There is a power irresistible impelling all of us. From the moment I first set eyes on her, I knew she was my fate. I shot an English grenadier at Hastenbeck, who would have bayoneted poor Saverne but for me. As I lifted him up from the ground, I thought, 'I shall have to repent of ever having seen that man.' I felt the same thing, Duval, when I saw you." And as the unhappy gentleman spoke, I remembered how I for my part felt a singular and unpleasant sensation as of terror and approaching evil when first I looked at that handsome, ill-omened face.[1]

More laughable is the fate of the logic of the Rev. Charles Honeyman:

James had not improved in health during Clive's ten months absence. He had never been able to walk well, or take his accustomed exercise, after his fall. He was no more used to riding than the late Mr. Gibbon, whose person James's somewhat resembled, and of whose philosophy our Scottish friend was an admiring scholar. The Colonel gone, James would have arguments with Mr. Honeyman over their claret, bring down the famous XVth and XVIth chapters of the Decline and Fall upon him, and quite get the better of the clergyman. James, like many other sceptics, was very obstinate, and for his part believed that almost all parsons had as much belief as the Roman augurs in their ceremonies. Certainly, poor Honeyman, in their controversies, gave up one article after another, flying from James's assault; but the battle over, Charles Honeyman would pick up these accoutrements which he had flung away in his retreat, wipe them dry, and put them on again.[2]

Even as we laugh at Honeyman, we acknowledge that most men resemble him. In the common view the truth arrived at merely by means of argument has a low status, the truth we live by having been achieved or found by processes more mysterious if more immediate.

---

[1] Ch. II.   [2] *The Newcomes*, ch. XL.

Even great logicians value their skill only for limited purposes. Dr Johnson found it useful for expressing the truth he had already found, and also as a means of discrediting an opponent in post-prandial argument. And Newman, whose logic was used so sensitively as to seem personal, saw that when a practical decision had to be made, what 'moves' is 'the whole man', in whom the logician, if he exists at all, exists merely as a verbal executant. A big decision of this sort was taken by the Countess de Saverne, after the controversies between her husband and lover: she transferred her allegiance to the Church of the latter. But not because of any logical skill on the part of M. de la Motte. Her decision was that of a human being, and it is human beings that make the study of novelists. Pen, an author himself, knows how to rate the logic of his wife:

...there is the fond woman's firm belief that the day will bring its daily bread for those who work for it and ask for it in the proper quarter; against which reasoning many a man knows it is in vain to argue. As to my own little objections and doubts [about Philip's wooing of Charlotte], my wife met them by reference to Philip's former love-affair with his cousin, Miss Twysden. "You had no objection in that case, sir," this logician would say. "You would have had him take a creature without a heart. *You* would cheerfully have seen him made miserable for life, because you thought there was money enough and a genteel connection. Money indeed! Very happy Mrs. Woolcomb is with her money. Very creditably to all sides has *that* marriage turned out!" I need scarcely remind my readers of the unfortunate result of that marriage.[1]

And further:

...this monstrous logician insisted that poverty, sickness, dreadful doubt and terror, hunger and want almost, were

[1] *Philip*, ch. xxx.

all equally intended for Philip's advantage, and would work for good in the end.[1]

Pen sees the logic merely as a means of expressing a truth already mastered, merely as an executant bent on making the truth ungainsayable at that juncture. And even the logic of women has a way of breaking down— as Thackeray noted in *The Virginians*:

The book of female logic is blotted all over with tears, and Justice in their courts is for ever in a passion.[2]

Thackeray roundly admitted his deficiency in this craft of the intellect. In a passage I have already quoted from the preface to *Pendennis* he called himself 'no... thinker', and drew the proper distinction between thinker and novelist:

If truth is not always pleasant; at any rate truth is best, from whatever chair—from those whence graver writers or thinkers argue, as from that at which the story-teller sits as he concludes his labour, and bids his kind reader farewell.

On another occasion he admitted something to the same effect in disclaiming the possession of 'any head above the eyes'.[3]

2

The method that Thackeray did apply to the material of his philosophy was a method, as Roscoe saw, that

appeals to the witness within us; he makes his statement, and leaves it to find its own way to the conviction of his readers.[4]

That Thackeray does no more than this is appropriate for a novelist dealing with the matter of philosophy.

| [1] *Philip*, ch. XL. | [2] Ch. IV. |
| [3] Ray, p. 96. | [4] II, 276. |

But Roscoe has charges to bring against him which touch a novelist of Thackeray's kind more pointedly. He considers him either to lack thoughts or to have thoughts that are feeble:

It is curious how independent he is of thought; how he manages to exist so entirely on the surface of things. Perhaps he is the better observer of manners because he never cares to penetrate below them. He never refers to a principle, or elucidates a rule of action. There is a total absence in his books of what we usually call ideas.[1]

And after the passage I have already quoted about Thackeray's method of making a statement and leaving it for the reader to do anything or nothing with, we get this in conclusion:

The highest moral truths have been thus enunciated, perhaps can only be thus enunciated; but Mr. Thackeray does not enunciate great truths.... He is not absolutely destitute of some of those distilled results of a wide knowledge of men which properly come under the head of wisdom; but they are very disproportioned to the extent and penetration of his perception. He occupies a good deal of space in half-meditative, half-emotional harangues on the phenomena of life. Where these do not immediately deal with the affections, they owe their novelty and value to their form alone....[2]

There is a great difference between having no power to think in the sense of 'think to a conclusion' and having no thoughts. The charge here brought against a novelist who, like Thackeray, mixes musing with his narrative is a serious one, and it can be denied—as it must be roundly denied—both by meeting it on its main ground and by pointing to the exceptions which Roscoe allows but whose status he misjudges.

[1] II, 274.   [2] II, 276.

Roscoe speaks of 'the total absence [from the novels] of what we usually call ideas'. This absence, we cannot but reply, exists only in Roscoe's fancy. What disappointed him, I think, was the lack in Thackeray's novels of ideas about matters much under discussion at the time.[1] In the mid nineteenth century new fields of thought were discovered, in which ideas offered themselves thickly as blackberries. Favourite fields for cogitation—I enumerate them without attention to precedence—were religion, society, anthropology, politics, the sciences, psychology, morality. In most of these fields—I shall speak of the exceptions later—Thackeray had either little to say, or little to say of much contemporary interest. He kept silent for the most part on religion,[2] politics and science. On the latter, for instance, the most we get are a few remarks like this:

Look, gentlemen! Does a week pass without the announcement of the discovery of a new comet in the sky, a new star

[1] Outside the novels, in the articles and travel books there are plenty of ideas of contemporary interest, and much of the description is organized around them. They are usually of the brilliant 'undergraduate' sort: for instance, this delightful passage in *From Cornhill to Cairo*:

> The paddle-wheel is the great conqueror. Wherever the captain cries, "Stop her", Civilization stops, and lands in the ship's boat, and makes a permanent acquaintance with the savages on shore. Whole hosts of crusaders have passed and died, and butchered here in vain. But to manufacture European iron into pikes and helmets was a waste of metal: in the shape of piston-rods and furnace-pokers it is irresistible; and I think an allegory might be made showing how much stronger commerce is than chivalry, and finishing with a grand image of Mahomet's crescent being extinguished in Fulton's boiler. (Ch. vi.)

(Robert Fulton, the American pioneer in steam navigation, failed in 1803 to launch a steamship on the Seine; but succeeded later on the East Hudson River: see H. H. P. Powles, *Steam Boilers*, 1905, p. 57.) In the same work (ch. v) Thackeray organizes his account of Athens around the idea that Athens cannot mean very much to you if, like Michael Angelo Titmarsh, you did not get much out of the Greek you hated at school; and the account of Smyrna (ch. vi) around the idea that the first brief dip into a new country is more rewarding than a prolonged stay, or a second dip.

[2] His views on the religious excitements of the time may be gathered from the quotation from *The Paris Sketch Book* (1840) made below at pp. 228 f.

in the heaven, twinkling dimly out of a yet farther distance, and only now becoming visible to human ken though existent for ever and ever?[1]

A contribution he made to *Punch* is headed: 'Science at Cambridge', and consists of two applications for chairs; but one is for that in the 'trew English Scients of Boxint', and the other, ill-informed if more literate, for that in 'Culinary Science'. The interest of the comet of 1858 for the person writing was its coincidence as if magical with a bumper grape harvest.[2] In *From Cornhill to Cairo* he breaks into the dulcet exclamation:

How delightful is that notion of the pleasant Eastern people about knowledge, where the height of science is made to consist in the answering of riddles! and all the mathematicians and magicians bring their great beards to bear on a conundrum![3]

On the other hand it is worth noting that under his editorship *The Cornhill* found fair space for articles on science. Like all novelists before him, Thackeray at bottom believed that there was nothing new under the sun—which shows how justly he saw his province as a story-teller, but also how little alive he was to the intellectual interests of most of his equals.

3

About society, of course, he has much to say. It is indeed his broadest theme:

The social human heart, man in relation to his kind— that is his subject. His actors are distinct and individual,— truthfully, vigorously, felicitously drawn; master-pieces in their way; but the personal character of each is not the supreme object of interest with the author. It is only a

---

[1] *The Newcomes*, ch. LXV.
[2] See *Lovel the Widower*, ch. IV, and *Philip*, ch. XL.   [3] Ch. VI.

contribution to a larger and more abstract subject of contemplation. Man is his study; but man the social animal,
man considered with reference to the experiences, the aims,
the affections, that find their field in his intercourse with his
fellow-men: never man the individual soul.[1]

Some of his social commentary is direct, more is implicit
in the picture he draws.

He accepts the social structure as it stands, even
though there is much in it that pains him. His position
seems to be that of Pen in his notable debate with
Warrington. On coming into his property, Pen is
obliged by his friend to take stock of the philosophy by
which his life is being conducted. Politics are broached
first, and then the structure of society:

" ...I see men who begin with ideas of universal reform,
and who, before their beards are grown, propound their
loud plans for the regeneration of mankind, give up their
schemes after a few years of bootless talking and vain-
glorious attempts to lead their fellows; and after they have
found that men will no longer hear them, as indeed they
never were in the least worthy to be heard, sink quietly into
the rank and file,—acknowledging their aims impracticable,
or thankful that they were never put into practice. The
fiercest reformers grow calm, and are fain to put up with
things as they are: the loudest Radical orators become dumb,
quiescent placemen: the most fervent Liberals, when out of
power, become humdrum Conservatives, or downright
tyrants or despots in office. Look at Thiers, look at Guizot,
in opposition and in place! Look at the Whigs appealing to
the country, and the Whigs in power! Would you say that
the conduct of these men is an act of treason, as the Radicals
bawl,—who would give way in their turn, were their turn
ever to come? No, only that they submit to circumstances
which are stronger than they,—march as the world marches
towards reform, but at the world's pace, (and the move-

[1] Roscoe, ii, 266.

ments of the vast body of mankind must needs be slow,)—
forego this scheme as impracticable, on account of opposition,—that as immature, because against the sense of the
majority,—are forced to calculate drawbacks and difficulties,
as well as to think of reforms and advances,—and compelled
finally to submit, and to wait, and to compromise."

"The Right Honourable Arthur Pendennis could not
speak better, or be more satisfied with himself, if he was
First Lord of the Treasury and Chancellor of the Exchequer",
Warrington said.

"Self-satisfied? Why self-satisfied?" continued Pen. "It
seems to me that my scepticism is more respectful and more
modest than the revolutionary ardour of other folks. Many
a patriot of eighteen, many a Spouting-Club orator, would
turn the Bishops out of the House of Lords to-morrow, and
throw the Lords out after the Bishops, and throw the throne
into the Thames after the Peers and the Bench. Is that man
more modest than I, who take these institutions as I find
them, and wait for time and truth to develope, or fortify, or
(if you like) destroy them? A college tutor, or a nobleman's
toady, who appears one fine day as my right reverend lord,
in a silk apron and a shovel-hat, and assumes benedictory
airs over me, is still the same man we remember at Oxbridge,
when he was truckling to the tufts, and bullying the poor
under-graduates in the lecture-room. An hereditary legislator, who passes his time with jockeys and black-legs and
ballet-girls, and who is called to rule over me and his other
betters because his grandfather made a lucky speculation in
the funds, or found a coal or tin-mine on his property, or
because his stupid ancestor happened to be in command of
ten thousand men as brave as himself, who overcame twelve
thousand Frenchmen, or fifty thousand Indians—such a
man, I say, inspires me with no more respect than the
bitterest democrat can feel towards him. But, such as he is,
he is a part of the old society to which we belong: and
I submit to his lordship with acquiescence; and he takes his
place above the best of us at all dinner parties, and there
bides his time. I don't want to chop his head off with a

guillotine, or to fling mud at him in the streets. When they call such a man a disgrace to his order; and such another, who is good and gentle, refined and generous, who employs his great means in promoting every kindness and charity, and art and grace of life, in the kindest and most gracious manner, an ornament to his rank—the question as to the use and propriety of the order is not in the least affected one way or other. There it is, extant among us, a part of our habits, the creed of many of us, the growth of centuries, the symbol of a most complicated tradition—there stand my lord the bishop and my lord the hereditary legislator—what the French call *transactions*[1] both of them,—representing in their present shape mail-clad barons and double-sworded chiefs, (from whom their lordships the hereditaries, for the most part, *don't* descend,) and priests, professing to hold an absolute truth and a divinely inherited power, the which truth absolute our ancestors burned at the stake, and denied there; the which divine transmissible power still exists in print—to be believed, or not, pretty much at choice; and of these, I say, I acquiesce that they exist, and no more. If you say that these schemes, devised before printing was known, or steam was born; when thought was an infant, scared and whipped; and truth under its guardians was gagged, and swathed, and blindfolded, and not allowed to lift its voice, or to look out or to walk under the sun; before men were permitted to meet, or to trade, or to speak with each other— if any one says (as some faithful souls do) that these schemes are for ever, and having been changed and modified con- stantly are to be subject to no farther development or decay, I laugh, and let the man speak. But I would have toleration for these, as I would ask it for my own opinions; and if they are to die, I would rather they had a decent and natural than an abrupt and violent death."[2]

Like Pen, Thackeray accepts things as they are and as, left to themselves, they are becoming.

His main concern in the long novels is with the higher

[1] Perhaps in the sense of 'compromises'.
[2] *Pendennis*, ch. LXI.

grades of society. There are several reasons for this choice. One of them is that riches and the social glories that go with them are things of interest to the ordinary man. If a single principle is at work in the social scene it seems to him to be snobbishness, by which he means social climbing. To his sense of the widespread operation of snobbishness there is *The Book of Snobs* as ready witness, a series of some fifty papers on snobs royal, aristocratic, clerical, professional, mercantile, provincial, not to mention 'dinner-giving', Irish and club snobs— the whole representing an effort of sustained criticism as remarkable as the poetical effort that gave the book brilliance and life. It is towards the glory of rank, as he sees it, that society as a whole aspires. In choosing to write much of that glory he knows he will interest readers, who enjoy the sight of the life that most would take the chance of living if they could. On the other hand, he writes much about the poor, especially in his minor writings, because he enjoys their ways with something of a Dickensian relish; and sometimes even out of bravado—the very point of *Catherine* is that she is a rogue who does not exchange drabness for splendour, and her end is so crudely bloody that when the novel was reprinted in the collected edition of 1875 much of it was suppressed. In *Our Street*, which Thackeray may have planned as a companion piece for Miss Mitford's *Our Village*, all the inhabitants are given due attention, even the cheerful 'spawn of the alleys about Our Street'.[1] And there is the squalid household of Dennis Haggarty, and the squalid testimony of James Yellowplush. Then again, Thackeray is the author of a poem of the kind we associate with Ebenezer Elliott, called, as if it were a picture, 'Daddy, I'm Hungry. A Scene

[1] Ch. v, 'What sometimes happens in Our Street'.

in an Irish Coachworker's Family, Designed by Lord Lowther, July 1843', which has verses like the following:

> He turns from their prattle as angry as may be,
>> 'O, daddy, I'm hungry', says each little brat;
> And yonder sits mammy, and nurses the baby,
>> Thinking how long there'll be dinner for that.[1]

Though Thackeray cannot forget his own social position, as Mrs Gaskell and George Eliot could, his examination of members of the lower orders, both in the earlier and later writings, is often thorough. And often tender—in a late piece, a 'Roundabout' paper, 'Autour de mon Chapeau', we hear that

The milkman becomes a study to him; the baker a being he curiously and tenderly examines.

A good instance of tenderness from the earlier writings occurs in *A Shabby Genteel Story* where one of the personages is a servant girl beautifully drawn.

In the later novels there is more of the lower orders than is sometimes credited to Thackeray. They are particularly evident in *Pendennis*, the hero of which has 'sympathy with all conditions of men'.[2]

Having much about the rich and also about the poor, he has much about them as master and servant,

---

[1] This poem is written in the style of those of the 'Hedge Schoolmaster', published in the Dublin *Nation* as part of the campaign for repealing the legislative union between Great Britain and Ireland (see Charles Gavan Duffy's *Young Ireland*, 1880–3, I, 164 and 243, which reproduces Thackeray's verses and his drawing as originally published in the *Nation* of 13 May 1843—the date in the title of the poem shows the poem to be prophetic). Lord Lowther, then Postmaster-General, had angered the Irish nationalists by accepting the tender of a Scottish coachbuilder for the Dublin mail-coaches, a stroke of economy which would have thrown Irish coachmakers out of work. Thackeray's poem may have been written more for the sake of friendship than of politics—the owner of the Dublin coachbuilding firm was the 'Mr P[urcell]' of *The Irish Sketch Book*, ch. II, by whom Thackeray had been entertained. In that same book Thackeray had shown some contempt for the nationalists. Duffy points out that in the end he came to respect their leaders, if not the principles they advanced.   [2] Ch. XLVI.

especially in the big novels, where the picture is on all scales from grand to shabby. The relationship fascinated him, and one of the Roundabout papers, 'On a Chalk-mark on the Door', analyses its moral and human basis with a searchingness fresh and fearless as Johnson's. The standpoint adopted is somewhere in what Roscoe described as his favourite territory, 'the debateable land between the aristocracy and the middle classes'.[1] Taking that standpoint, he cannot but look down at the servants. The perspective is arranged in the first chapter of *Esmond*, which advances a theory of the proper way to write history. Speaking for Thackeray— witness statements in his prose of thinking[2]—Esmond suggests that we widen the range of histories to take in Louis XIV's barber as well as Louis XIV. Hogarth and Fielding, he judges, 'will give our children a much better idea of the manners of the present age in England, than the *Court Gazette* and the newspapers which we get thence'—the instancing of the newspapers as well as the *Court Gazette* shows how wide a meaning Thackeray is here giving to manners. Sometimes the rank of his personages is that of Louis XIV, but his favourite ground, especially in the long novels, is the debatable one discriminated by Roscoe. On this ground the rich and the shabby genteel spring up in their hundreds, complete with domestics, spongers and blackmailers. The poor come into the novels, therefore, mainly as they barber their patrons, and if Thackeray 'knows the secrets of a thousand footmen',[3] the secrets are mainly about their masters. In *Vanity Fair* a chapter is headed 'How to live well on nothing a-year': we note the word

[1] II, 274.
[2] E.g. 'Caricatures and Lithography in Paris' and 'Meditations at Versailles' in *The Paris Sketch Book*.
[3] I have failed to trace the source of this quotation.

'well', and know that it means 'very well'. The downward range of the long novels is not unfairly suggested by the principle advanced in the commentary of *Pendennis*, that there is no

more effectual plan...to get a knowledge of London society, than to begin at the foundation—that is, at the kitchen-floor.[1]

This principle determines the structure of *Lovel the Widower*, in which 'the parlour and kitchen...are on the same level'.[2] That is not so in any of the other later works, unless it be *Denis Duval*, but in the middle sections of *Pendennis* and in the relevant sections of *Vanity Fair* the reader is given a sense of London society complete. In any of these novels we come on remarks such as

A pauper child in London at seven years old knows how to go to market, to fetch the beer, to pawn father's coat, to choose the largest fried fish or the nicest ham-bone, to nurse Mary Jane of three...[3]

Thackeray is not so much at home when he invites us to visit the new industrial northerly town of Newcome. The visit, we are told in advance, will be brief, and we are to see little of the chief interest of the place:

My design does not include a description of that great and flourishing town of Newcome, and of the manufactures which caused its prosperity; but only admits of the introduction of those Newcomites who are concerned in the affairs of the family which has given its respectable name to these volumes.

Thus in previous pages we have said nothing about the Mayor and Corporation of Newcome, the magnificent bankers and manufacturers who had their places of business

[1] Ch. xxxvi.   [2] Ch. i.   [3] *The Newcomes*, ch. liii.

in the town, and their splendid villas outside its smoky precincts; people who would give their thousand guineas for a picture or a statue, and write you off a cheque for ten times the amount any day; people who if there was talk of a statue to the Queen or the Duke, would come down to the Town All and subscribe their one, two, three undred apiece (especially if in the neighbouring city of SLOWCOME they were putting up a statue to the Duke or the Queen)—not of such men have I spoken, the magnates of the place; but of the humble Sarah Mason in Jubilee Row—of the Reverend Dr. Bulders the Vicar, Mr. Vidler the apothecary, Mr. Puff the baker—of Tom Potts the jolly reporter of the "Newcome Independent", and — Batters, Esq., the proprietor of that journal—persons with whom our friends have had already, or will be found presently to have, some connection. And it is from these that we shall arrive at some particulars regarding the Newcome family, which will show us that they have a skeleton or two in *their* closets, as well as their neighbours.

When later he says:

I could go on giving you interesting particulars of a hundred members of the Newcome aristocracy....[1]

we have little doubt that he could, though it is by the thousand that he gives us interesting particulars of the London aristocracy. We suspect, however, that he might be hard put to it to give us a hundred about its plebs—rather, of course, because they are northern than that they are plebs: as Hannay observed,

He was...too honest to draw fancy pictures of classes with whom he had never lived.[2]

In the period of writing his great novels, and on several occasions earlier, he bears some resemblance to his own

---

[1] Ch. LV.   [2] *Studies on Thackeray* [1869], p. 6.

Captain Fitz-Boodle, whose papers he invented in 1842, and who is still on his legs in 1860:

Captain Fitzb—dle, who belongs to a dozen clubs, and knows something of every man in London;[1]

—by 'man' he means 'gentleman'—or his own Tom Eaves, the gossip who

knew all the great folk in London, and the stories and mysteries of each family;[2]

—by 'each family' he means 'each great family'. Thackeray's commentary cannot be considered of topical importance for his times. By and large it shows him to be still virtually living in the eighteenth century. We have only to remember that *Culture and Anarchy* was published six years after his death to see the old-fashionedness of his social sense, and the feebleness of his concern with the changes that mattered most. A lack of up-to-date interest in such things appeared a grave deficiency in the mid-nineteenth century, even in a novelist, seeming graver still after the advent of George Eliot, in whose novels, as Brownell noted, there was the very 'taste of science', and the taste of most other intellectual interests as well. The strength of Thackeray's mind lay in other quarters, as Fitzjames Stephen well noted. His instance was the character of Warrington:

Warrington is represented as being a man of great originality —full of powerful thought, scholarship, and knowledge of various kinds; but we have none of the powerful thought, or scholarship, or knowledge, produced in the book; still less are any incidents introduced to give scope to them.

[1] *Lovel the Widower*, ch. IV.
[2] *Vanity Fair*, ch. XLVII; cf. *Philip*, ch. XL.

And so to the positive side:

We certainly get the impression that Warrington was a man of vigorous understanding; but we get it from learning that he behaved in the commonest affairs of life as such a man might be supposed to behave, not from any description of the remarkable things which he did.[1]

The inferences drawn by Thackeray's imagination were often sound, for all their slender basis in the sort of knowledge that the intellect can give an account of. In making the commentary of the novels, as distinct from the personages, there was more opening for thinking than Thackeray could always take advantage of. George Eliot, who learnt from him how to place commentary in the novel, had more penetrating political comments to place. When it came to politics the political animal was for Thackeray little more than another name for the moral animal.[2]

The moral interests of his novels are brilliantly served by that part of society given most attention in them. Thackeray would not have allowed himself to specialise on a part, even to the extent he did, if it had imperilled any universality on the plane that mattered to him first and foremost—the plane of human nature and morals. Like Wordsworth and Pope, he believed that we have all of us one human heart, but he did not effectively share Wordsworth's further belief that the heart shows

[1] 'The Relation of Novels to Life', included in *Cambridge Essays, contributed by Members of the University. 1855*, p. 161.
[2] For a summary of Thackeray's interests in politics see John W. Dodds, *Thackeray: A Critical Portrait*, 1941, pp. 211 ff., who concludes: 'To say...that Thackeray was not interested in the political currents of his time is to do an injustice to his active and inquiring mind. It would be foolhardy, however, to declare that his political opinions were always pertinent or ever really profound. In politics he was always more or less the big, beaming, enthusiastic outsider, with liberal instincts and a judgment guided by a warm and sympathetic heart rather than by a clear political head. The best that Thackeray had to say to his generation cut across political lines and went much deeper than party affiliations.'

itself best when there is least artificiality. Rather he shared the belief of Pope that it is the contrast between the heart and civilization that best reveals the cardiac condition:

> Bare the mean Heart that lurks beneath a Star[1]

and how much more is the meanness apparent. To have the Pretender is to make this contrast—whether or not out of invented matter does not concern me:

> The heir of one of the greatest names, of the greatest kingdoms, and of the greatest misfortunes in Europe, was often content to lay the dignity of his birth and grief at the wooden shoes of a French chambermaid, and to repent afterwards (for he was very devout) in ashes taken from the dustpan;

and to draw this generalization:

> 'Tis for mortals such as these that nations suffer, that parties struggle, that warriors fight and bleed. A year afterwards gallant heads were falling...whilst the heedless ingrate, for whom they risked and lost all, was tippling with his seraglio of mistresses in his *petite maison* of Chaillot.[2]

To have the vicious Lord Steyne is to have the opportunity of belittling him with his titles:

> ...the Most Honourable George Gustavus, Marquis of Steyne, Earl of Gaunt and of Gaunt Castle, in the Peerage of Ireland, Viscount Hellborough, Baron Pitchley and Grillsby, a Knight of the Most Noble Order of the Garter, of the Golden Fleece of Spain, of the Russian Order of Saint Nicholas of the First Class, of the Turkish Order of the Crescent, First Lord of the Powder Closet and Groom of the Back Stairs, Colonel of the Gaunt or Regent's Own Regiment of Militia, a Trustee of the British Museum, an Elder Brother of the Trinity House, a Governor of the White Friars, and D.C.L.[3]

---

[1] *Imitations of Horace*, Sat. II, i, 108.
[2] Bk III, ch. IX.   [3] *Vanity Fair*, ch. LXIV.

To have Colonel Newcome is to have that interesting thing, a contrast of manners because of the return from long absence abroad. To have the Sedleys is to have people who are high enough to come down in the world. To have the Reverend Charles Honeyman is to be able to write:

I fancy Saint Peter of Alcantara, and contrast him with such a personage as the Incumbent of Lady Whittlesea's chapel, May Fair.

His hermitage is situated in Walpole Street let us say, on the second floor of a quiet mansion, let out to hermits by a nobleman's butler, whose wife takes care of the lodgings. His cells consist of a refectory, a dormitory, and an adjacent oratory where he keeps his shower-bath and boots—the pretty boots trimly stretched on boot-trees and blacked to a nicety (not varnished) by the boy who waits on him. The barefooted business may suit superstitious ages and gentlemen of Alcantara, but does not become May Fair and the nineteenth century. If St. Pedro walked the earth now with his eyes to the ground he would know fashionable divines by the way in which they were shod. Charles Honeyman's is a sweet foot. I have no doubt as delicate and plump and rosy as the white hand with its two rings, which he passes in impassioned moments through his slender flaxen hair.

...By his bedside are slippers lined with blue silk and worked of an ecclesiastical pattern, by some of the faithful who sit at his feet....Purses are sent to him—pen-wipers—a portfolio with the Honeyman arms—yea, braces have been known to reach him by the post (in his days of popularity), and flowers, and grapes, and jelly when he was ill, and throat comforters, and lozenges for his dear bronchitis. In one of his drawers is the rich silk cassock presented to him by his congregation at Leatherhead (when the young curate quitted that parish for London duty), and on his breakfast-table the silver tea-pot, once filled with sovereigns and presented by the same devotees. The devoteapot he has, but the sovereigns, where are they?

What a different life this is from our honest friend of Alcantara, who eats once in three days![1]

Again, how little there would have been to seize on had Mrs Newcome—Sophia Alethea Newcome—been denied a palette of expensive colours:

When his father married, Mr. [later Colonel] Thomas Newcome, jun., and Sarah his nurse were transported from the cottage where they had lived in great comfort to the palace hard by, surrounded by lawns and gardens, pineries, graperies, aviaries, luxuries of all kinds. This paradise, five miles from the standard at Cornhill, was separated from the outer world by a thick hedge of tall trees, and an ivy-covered porter's-gate, through which they who travelled to London on the top of the Clapham coach could only get a glimpse of the bliss within. It was a serious paradise. As you entered at the gate, gravity fell on you; and decorum wrapped you in a garment of starch. The butcher-boy who galloped his horse and cart madly about the adjoining lanes and common, whistled wild melodies (caught up in abominable play-house galleries), and joked with a hundred cook-maids, on passing that lodge fell into an undertaker's pace, and delivered his joints and sweet-breads silently at the servants' entrance. The rooks in the elms cawed sermons at morning and evening; the peacocks walked demurely on the terraces; the guinea-fowls looked more quaker-like than those savoury birds usually do. The lodge-keeper was serious, and a clerk at a neighbouring chapel. The pastors who entered at that gate, and greeted his comely wife and children, fed the little lambkins with tracts. The head-gardener was a Scotch Calvinist, after the strictest order, only occupying himself with the melons and pines provisionally, and until the end of the world, which event he could prove by infallible calculations, was to come off in two or three years at farthest. Wherefore he asked should the butler brew strong ale to be drunken three years hence; or the housekeeper (a follower of Joanna Southcote), make

[1] *The Newcomes*, ch. XI.

provisions of fine linen and lay up stores of jams? On a Sunday (which good old Saxon word was scarcely known at the Hermitage), the household marched away in separate couples or groups to at least half a dozen of religious edifices, each to sit under his or her favourite minister, the only man who went to Church being Thomas Newcome, accompanied by Tommy his little son, and Sarah his nurse, who was I believe also his aunt, or at least his mother's first cousin. Tommy was taught hymns very soon after he could speak, appropriate to his tender age, pointing out to him the inevitable fate of wicked children, and giving him the earliest possible warning and description of the punishment of little sinners. He repeated these poems to his step-mother after dinner, before a great, shining mahogany table, covered with grapes, pine-apples, plum-cake, port-wine, and Madeira, and surrounded by stout men in black, with baggy white neckcloths, who took the little man between their knees, and questioned him as to his right understanding of the place whither naughty boys were bound. They patted his head with their fat hands if he said well, or rebuked him if he was bold as he often was.[1]

And so on. If Thackeray had limited himself to 'the short and simple annals of the poor' he might not have seen less humanity but he would have foregone the spectacle of men who have access to materials adequate for the thorough display of their natures.

4

Thackeray has something to say about the conditions of writers in his day. It is true that, as Fitzjames Stephen noted, 'nothing turns upon [the] law or [the] literature'[2] of the personages in *Pendennis* described as literary barristers, any more than upon the medical business of Philip's father. But on the other hand we are told much

[1] *The Newcomes*, ch. II.
[2] *Cambridge Essays, contributed by Members of the University. 1855*, p. 161.

about Clive's attempts at painting and John James Ridley's career as a painter—he ended as an Academician—and a great deal about the struggles of Pen and Warrington to make writing a profession. The account of Warrington's literary career, for instance, throws up the following paragraph of thinking:

"I am a prose labourer," Warrington said; "you, my boy, are a poet in a small way, and so, I suppose, consider you are authorised to be flighty. What is it you want? Do you want a body of capitalists that shall be forced to purchase the works of all authors, who may present themselves, manuscript in hand? Everybody who writes his epic, every driveller who can or can't spell, and produces his novel or his tragedy,—are they all to come and find a bag of sovereigns in exchange for their worthless reams of paper? Who is to settle what is good or bad, saleable or otherwise? Will you give the buyer leave, in fine, to purchase or not? Why, sir, when Johnson sate behind the screen at Saint John's Gate, and took his dinner apart, because he was too shabby and poor to join the literary bigwigs who were regaling themselves round Mr. Cave's best table-cloth, the tradesman was doing him no wrong. You couldn't force the publisher to recognise the man of genius in the young man who presented himself before him, ragged, gaunt, and hungry. Rags are not a proof of genius; whereas capital is absolute, as times go, and is perforce the bargain-master. It has a right to deal with the literary inventor as with any other;—if I produce a novelty in the book trade, I must do the best I can with it; but I can no more force Mr. Murray to purchase my book of travels or sermons, than I can compel Mr. Tattersall to give me a hundred guineas for my horse. I may have my own ideas of the value of my Pegasus, and think him the most wonderful of animals; but the dealer has a right to his opinion, too, and may want a lady's horse, or a cob for a heavy timid rider, or a sound hack for the road, and my beast won't suit him."[1]

[1] *Pendennis*, ch. XXXII.

5

Thackeray's deficiencies as a thinker on matters dear to the thinkers of his time do not trouble the reader of to-day. And even in his own age of intellectual stress, there must have been many readers who were no more troubled than we are, and who therefore better repre-sented the 'common' reader than Roscoe. At best, we may say in general, a good commentary on matters of intellectual interest made by a good novelist will be an additional reason why certain readers take pleasure in his fictions. Other readers, well able to appreciate the fine points of a story, may be put off by the intellectual content. If so, they have a better right to complain of the superfluity than the Roscoes of the deficiency—a novel on principle being first and foremost a story, what-ever its proportion of inner and outer event. Excellent as are her views on matter still of great interest to us, George Eliot—and that is her best achievement—is read mainly for her story. As I have suggested, Thackeray had partly himself to blame for Roscoe's complaint. He did throw a web of commentary over his story, and so raised the hopes of Roscoe and his like, which, had he been a George Eliot, he would have satisfied.

Roscoe, however, allows exceptions to his generaliza-tions. He allows some 'novelty' to Thackeray's thoughts when 'the affections' are in question, and he is aware also of the 'form' of Thackeray's commentary. But he allows these exceptions without seeing their full force.

The term 'affections' he employs, I think, in its widest sense, still current at that time, which pertained to the full range of feelings—anger, fear, pity, love, and so on—and not merely to the pleasanter ones of love, fondness, kind feelings. The affections in this wide sense are things a novelist is very much concerned with. He need not provide any explicit thought about them. His first job, which he is free to make his last, is to show them in personage and action. If he provides thoughts, that is over and above the necessity, and, other things being equal, we are lucky in getting more than we bargained for, the luck shining increasingly as the value of the thoughts rises. Thackeray does give us this advantage. Here is a bundle of instances of his thoughts, including some about matters other than the affections. In some of them the thought is expressed aphoristically, in others it is conveyed in narrative and description.

The ladies—Heaven bless them!—are, as a general rule, coquettes from babyhood upwards. Little shes of three years old play little airs and graces upon small heroes of five; simpering misses of nine make attacks upon young gentlemen of twelve; and at sixteen, a well-grown girl, under encouraging circumstances,—say, she is pretty, in a family of ugly elder sisters, or an only child and heiress, or an humble wench at a country inn, like our fair Catherine—is at the very pink and prime of her coquetry: they will jilt you at that age with an ease and arch infantine simplicity that never can be surpassed in maturer years.[1]

that perspicuity and ingenuity and enterprise which only belongs to a certain passion.[2]

it was curious how emotion seemed to olden him.[3]

watching the pair with that anxiety with which brooding women watch over their sons' affections—and in acknowledging which, I have no doubt there is a sexual jealousy on the mother's part, and a secret pang.[4]

There are stories to a man's disadvantage that the women who are fondest of him are always the most eager to believe. Isn't a man's wife often the first to be jealous of him?[5]

[1] *Catherine*, ch. I. [2] *Pendennis*, ch. XL.
[3] Ibid. ch. LII. [4] Ibid. ch. XXIV.
[5] Ibid. ch. LIII.

The satire of people who have little natural humour is seldom good sport for bystanders. I think dull men's *facetiae* are mostly cruel.[1]

A woman who scarcely ever does any wrong, and rules and governs her own house and family, as my ——, as the wife of the reader's humble servant most notoriously does, often becomes—must it be said?—too certain of her own virtue, and is too sure of the correctness of her own opinion. We virtuous people give advice a good deal, and set a considerable value upon that advice. We meet a certain man who has fallen among thieves, let us say. We succour him readily enough. We take him kindly to the inn, and pay his score there: but we say to the landlord, "You must give this poor man his bed; his medicine at such a time, and his broth at such another. But, mind you, he must have that physic, and no other; that broth when we order it. *We* take his case in hand, you understand. Don't listen to him or anybody else. We know all about everything. Good-by. Take care of him. Mind the medicine and the broth!" and Mr. Benefactor or Lady Bountiful goes away, perfectly self-satisfied.[2]

The father and son loved each other so, that each was afraid of the other. A war between two such men is dreadful....

"My boy's heart is gone from me," thinks poor Thomas Newcome; "our family is insulted, our enterprises ruined, by that traitor, and my son is not even angry! he does not care for the success of our plans—for the honour of our name even; I make him a position of which any young man in England might be proud, and Clive scarcely deigns to accept it."

"My wife appeals to my father," thinks poor Clive; "it is from him she asks counsel, and not from me. Be it about the ribbon in her cap, or any other transaction in our lives, she takes her colour from his opinion, and goes to him for advice, and I have to wait till it is given, and conform myself to it. If I differ from the dear old father, I wound him; if I yield up my opinion, as I do always, it is with a bad

---

[1] *The Virginians*, ch. xiii.   [2] *Philip*, ch. xxxix.

grace, and I wound him still. With the best intentions in the world, what a slave's life it is that he has made for me!"[1]

So the Lady of Honour and the Prime Minister hated Giglio because they had done him a wrong.[2]

She would accept benefits, you see, but then she insulted her benefactors, and so squared accounts.[3]

She didn't wish to marry him, but she wished to keep him. She wished to give him nothing, but that he should give her all. It is a bargain not unfrequently levied in love.[4]

He tried by indulgence to the grandson to make up for harshness to the [dead] elder George.[5]

There is scarce any parent, however friendly or tender with his children, but must feel sometimes that they have thoughts which are not his or hers; and wishes and secrets quite beyond the parental control.[6]

And then there is the happy class about whom there seems no doubt at all: the spotless and white-robed ones, to whom virtue is easy...who are children, and good; young men, and good; husbands and fathers, and yet good.[7]

Scandal almost always does master people; especially good and innocent people.[8]

Emmy was not very happy after her heroic sacrifice. She was very *distraite*, nervous, silent, and ill to please. The family had never known her so peevish. She grew pale and ill.[9]

I don't know that it is always at the best jokes that children laugh:—children and wise men too.[10]

You read the past in some old faces, while some others lapse into mere meekness and content.[11]

[1] *The Newcomes*, ch. LXVI. [2] *Rose and the Ring*, ch. VI.
[3] *Lovel the Widower*, ch. IV. [4] *Vanity Fair*, ch. LXVI.
[5] Ibid. ch. LVI. [6] *The Newcomes*, ch. XXI.
[7] *Philip*, ch. V. [8] *The Virginians*, ch. XXVIII.
[9] *Vanity Fair*, ch. LXVII. [10] *Philip*, ch. XV.
[11] *The Virginians*, ch. XXVII.

...Do you suppose Skinflint is tortured with remorse at the idea of the distress which called to him in vain, and of the hunger which he sent empty away? Not he. He is indignant with Prodigal for being a fool: he is not ashamed of himself for being a curmudgeon. What? a young man with such opportunities throw them away? A fortune spent amongst gamblers and spendthrifts? Horrible, horrible! Take warning, my child, by this unfortunate young man's behaviour, and see the consequences of extravagance. According to the great and always Established Church of the Pharisees, here is an admirable opportunity for a moral discourse, and an assertion of virtue.[1]

What matters if you are considered obtrusive, provided that you obtrude?[2]

...though Philip fancied he hid his anxieties from his wife, be sure she loved him too much to be deceived by one of the clumsiest hypocrites in the world. Only, being a much cleverer hypocrite than her husband, she pretended to be deceived, and acted her part so well that poor Philip was mortified with her gaiety, and chose to fancy his wife was indifferent to their misfortunes.[3]

This is to begin to compile a commonplace book from the novels. The truth expressed in its items is old truth. How could it be otherwise, being truth and being about mankind? Hoariness in these things does not necessarily imply staleness. Some of the old truth in Thackeray will strike even some of ourselves as novel. But whether it is novel or not scarcely matters for a story-teller. A story-teller given to commenting can be happy for ever, and keep his readers happy, among such primary moral commonplaces, which his personages and their actions show working on another plane—such truths, in a word, as find their place in the old epics, and which, as Johnson said, story-tellers have continued to arrange

[1] *The Virginians*, ch. L.   [2] *The Newcomes*, ch. VIII.
[3] *Philip*, ch. XXXIX.

and re-arrange ever since Homer. 'What stories are new?' asked Thackeray in his turn, and gave the old answer:

All types of all characters march through all fables: tremblers and boasters; victims and bullies; dupes and knaves; long-eared Neddies, giving themselves leonine airs; Tartuffes wearing virtuous clothing; lovers and their trials, their blindness, their folly and constancy. With the very first page of the human story do not love and lies too begin? So the tales were told ages before Æsop: and asses under lion's manes roared in Hebrew; and sly foxes flattered in Etruscan; and wolves in sheep's clothing gnashed their teeth in Sanscrit, no doubt. The sun shines to-day as he did when he first began shining; and the birds in the tree over-head, while I am writing, sing very much the same note they have sung ever since there were finches. Nay, since last he besought good-natured friends to listen once a month to his talking, a friend of the writer has seen the New World, and found the (featherless) birds there exceedingly like their brethren of Europe. There may be nothing new under and including the sun; but it looks fresh every morning, and we rise with it to toil, hope, scheme, laugh, struggle, love, suffer, until the night comes and quiet. And then will wake Morrow and the eyes that look on it; and so *da capo*.[1]

When Brownell wrote of Thackeray's being above all a lover of truth, it was, as I have already noted, of such truth first of all, the word 'truth' not being more important than the identity of the subject of his sentence, Thackeray, which limits it to the truth most proper to the interests of a novelist. When Roscoe allowed Thackeray some status as an authority on the affections, he was rating the novelist more highly than he knew. He grudgingly allowed him some worldly wisdom. Thackeray, however, had a whole treasury of it, at

---

[1] *The Newcomes*, ch. I.

latest by the time he had written *The Great Hoggarty Diamond*, in which there is some wobble and uncertain judgment. And for a novelist it is a necessary endowment.

6

Roscoe's second favourable exception was of the 'form' in which Thackeray expressed his philosophy. And again he did not see that the virtue of the exception overpowers its principal.

A novelist deals in old truth which, it is his main business, as I have said, to show in personage and action. When he is the first to bring a piece of it to light, we are duly pleased, being enlightened; when he has expressed old truth in personage and action, all is well. If the old truth he draws on is already known, it is still acceptable provided he expresses it in personage and action that are unexpectedly novel, or expresses it in statements that justify themselves by presenting it with a new felicity. The theory and practice of a writer's duty towards old truth were well understood in Thackeray's favourite century. 'True wit', Pope had said, by which he meant good thought, and so old truth, consists in

> What oft was thought but ne'er so well expressed.

And it was Johnson's belief that the best thought was old thought with something new added—a new angle from which to see it, a new application of it, a new refinement of it, perhaps also a new grace in its expression. That Thackeray grasped this for himself is clear from the remark of his that I have already quoted, and which exemplifies what I am discussing as well as contributes to formulating its sense:

There may be nothing new under and including the sun; but it looks fresh every morning.

It is this fresh look that the purveyor of old truth must express. Thackeray's purveying of it is justified because his expression, what Roscoe called 'its 'form', honoured the novelty old truth wore for him. His wording of an old idea usually has a virtue nearer that of verse than prose. The 'truisms' in the verse of Gray were 'divine' for Tennyson, which divine truisms, he confessed, 'make me weep'.[1] Truisms out of metre may also exercise this power: witness those of Newman, and perhaps those of Sterne. Witness also those of Thackeray. The power is partly due to the quality of the prose: these writers give their aphorisms a subtle rhythm.

Thackeray's aphorisms come mainly in the passages of extended commentary. In these the art of his expression exists at its fullest. I have already tried to justify them as intimately of their context. If we tear them out of it and look at them for the occasion as things of art, they show as masterpieces in the discursive manner, done with a flying pen by the best English writer of the best sort of essay—the grounds for my superlative being of course the *Roundabout Papers*. These passages of commentary are lively indeed. They are a lavishly coiling music, light as on strings, rapid but marked with emphases and pauses. They are a sort of informal psalm or ode made of conversation and amicable harangue. Informal as movements of air, they yet bristle with points of art—they cry out in formal invocation, they apostrophize, they fling out imperatives. And yet for all their passionate gestures, they so express themselves as to seem enveloped in a flowing coolness and quietness.

[1] The Allingham MSS., quoted by Birkbeck Hill, Johnson's *Lives*, III, 445.

7

Thackeray the novelist honoured this kind of truth throughout his career. In a letter to Mark Lemon, which I am soon to quote at large, he speaks of 'the solemn prayer to Almighty God that...we may never forget truth'—words all the more forceful in a context concerned with things in the novels that he saw as changing.

Those aspiring words could stand as motto for his work early, middle and late. In *The Luck of Barry Lyndon*, the first version of the novel we know as *The Memoirs of Barry Lyndon, Esq.*, the idea takes another form:

If this [picture of the triumphs of the wicked] be true of the world, those persons who find their pleasure or get their livelihood by describing its manners and the people who live in it are bound surely to represent to the best of their power life as it really appears to them to be; not to foist off upon the public figures pretending to be delineations of human nature,—gay and agreeable cut-throats, otto-of-rose murderers, amiable hackney-coachmen, Prince Rodolphs[1] and the like, being representatives of beings that never have or could have existed. At least, if not bounden to copy nature, they are justified in trying.[2]

Later, in the Preface to *Pendennis*, we revert to brevity: 'If there is not [truth], there is nothing'. And among other metamorphoses this from *Vanity Fair*:

the moralist...is bound to speak the truth as far as [he] knows it...and a deal of disagreeable matter must come out in the course of such an undertaking.[3]

[1] An incredible personage in Eugène Suc's *Mystères de Paris*, which Thackeray had reviewed in 'Thieves' Literature of France' published in *The Foreign Quarterly Review*, July 1843.
[2] Op. cit., from the final paragraph.   [3] Ch. VIII.

These last words echo the oath of the law-courts, an oath which also includes the words 'the whole truth'. Items of truth do not always add up to something we agree to be 'the whole truth'. It is often said of Thackeray that he selected certain bits of truth and failed to give us truth in the round. He himself gave some encouragement to this view, as in his remark to Dr John Brown:

[I was] created with a sense of the ugly, of the odd, of the meanly false, the desperately wicked.[1]

[1] *Horae Subsecivae*, Third Series, ed. 1882, p. 180. Thackeray's self-sketch was intended, I think, to carry a literary allusion, and if so the tongue may not have been wholly absent from the cheek. During the 1830's Hans Andersen had begun to be known in England as a writer of stories. Thackeray, as we should have expected, 'was wild about him' (*Letters*, II, 263; letter of 2 Jan. 1847). Among the stories already translated was 'The Snow-Queen', the first chapter of which contains the following:

Once upon a time there was a wicked sprite, indeed he was the most mischievous of all sprites. One day he was in a very good humour, for he had made a mirror with the power of causing all that was good and beautiful when it was reflected therein to look poor and mean; but that which was good for nothing and looked ugly was shown magnified and increased in ugliness. In this mirror the most beautiful landscapes looked like boiled spinach [how Thackeray must have enjoyed this image!], and the best persons were turned into frights, or appeared to stand on their heads; their faces were so distorted that they were not to be recognised; and if any one had a mole, you might be sure that it would be magnified and spread over both nose and mouth. "That's glorious fun!" said the Sprite. If a good thought passed through a man's mind, then a grin was seen in the mirror, and the Sprite laughed heartily at his clever discovery. All the little sprites who went to his school—for he kept a sprite-school—told each other that a miracle had happened; and that now only, as they thought, it would be possible to see how the world really looked. They ran about with the mirror; and at last there was not a land or a person who was not represented distorted in the mirror. So then they thought they would fly up to the sky, and have a joke there. The higher they flew with the mirror, the more terribly it grinned: they could hardly hold it fast. Higher and higher still they flew, nearer and nearer to the stars, when suddenly the mirror shook so terribly with grinning, that it flew out of their hands and fell to the earth, where it was dashed into a hundred million and more pieces. And now it worked much more evil than before; for some of these pieces were hardly so large as a grain of sand, and they flew about in the wide world, and when they got into people's eyes, there they stayed; and then people saw every thing perverted, or only had an eye for that which was evil. This happened because the very

It is only *Vanity Fair* that need hold us up at this juncture—*Catherine* and *Barry Lyndon* remove themselves from the discussion by being studies of persons who are exceptional, and the long novels other than *Vanity Fair* range vividly over enough of the beautiful, noble and generous for their 'imitation' of life to be seen as satisfyingly whole even by the grossest eyesight. It takes a keener glance, admittedly, to see that *Vanity Fair* wears this larger look of truth. That it was partly intended, like the earlier work, to take a special line is evinced by all three forms of its title—the title of the manuscript of the opening chapters *Pen and Pencil Sketches of English Society*, the title of the edition in parts *Vanity Fair: Pen and Pencil Sketches of English Society*, and the title of the first edition in book form, which was final, *Vanity Fair: A Novel without a Hero*. In defence of its ending, however, Thackeray claimed an application wider than to Mayfair:

I want to leave everybody dissatisfied and unhappy at the end of the story—we ought all to be with our own and all other stories.[1]

---

smallest bit had the same power which the whole mirror had possessed. Some persons even got a splinter in their heart, and then it made one shudder, for their heart became like a lump of ice. Some of the broken pieces were so large that they were used for window-panes, through which one could not see one's friends. Other pieces were put in spectacles; and that was a sad affair when people put on their glasses to see well and rightly. The wicked Sprite laughed till he almost choked, for all this tickled his fancy....

(*The Shoes of Fortune, and other tales*, trans. by Charles Bower, 1847, pp. 63 ff.). Thackeray seems to allude to this story again in the letter justifying the 'dissatisfying' ending of *Vanity Fair*: he speaks of 'that may-be cracked and warped looking glass in which I am always looking' (*Letters*, II, 423 f.; letter of 3 Sept. 1848). If the letters and travel writings are to be taken as affording the soundest evidence, Thackeray's eye was 'healthy'; he enjoyed looking at whatever offered ugly or beautiful, which was according to the principles advanced at the close of *The Luck of Barry Lyndon*: that the novelist should describe 'not only what is beautiful, but what is ill-favoured too, faithfully, so that each may appear as like as possible to nature. It is as right to look at a beauty as at a hunchback; and, if to look, to describe too: nor can the most prodigious genius improve upon the original.'

[1] *Letters*, II, 423.

Among knaves, good people—people in whom goodness preponderates—usually appear as fools. *Vanity Fair* has its foolish good—Dobbin, Amelia and several small personages—and enough of them to suggest that more complete truthfulness towards the whole picture of truth which, because it is a novel deliberately 'unpleasant', it does not undertake to show squarely.

8

Thackeray, then, gives us truth constantly, if not always with the same degree of fulness, exhibiting it always in personages, action and commentary.

Exception has been taken to the last of these categories: showing truth in personage and action, he has not always been credited with placing a constant value on the act of commenting on it, and taking it as the text for sermons; nor has he always been seen as referring it to a constant scale of values.

My own views on all this I can perhaps make clear by discussing those of Mr Ray, set out in his interesting lecture to the Royal Society of Literature a few years ago, '*Vanity Fair*: One Version of the Novelist's Responsibilities'. It may be that on a matter of this extent and complexity, various views are possible, especially at this stage of our ignorance. As Thackeray's writings come to be studied more closely, views will be tested and will shed their crudeness, coming to rest on a subtler justice which, lacking a sufficiency of worthy criticism, we cannot yet discern. Here then are my views, which, despite the footprints of Mr Ray and others, are those of a timid pioneer.

To begin where Mr Ray begins. If we were looking for an explanation why Thackeray, hitherto without wide fame, acquired it during the publication of

Vanity Fair, is there any doubt where we should find it? The welcome that Lady Eastlake gave that novel in an anonymous review is the welcome Thackeray must have expected:

...much as we were entitled to expect from its author's pen, [*Vanity Fair*] has fairly taken us by surprise. We were perfectly aware that Mr. Thackeray had of old assumed the jester's habit, in order the more unrestrainedly to indulge the privilege of speaking the truth;—we had traced his clever progress through 'Fraser's Magazine' and the ever improving pages of 'Punch'—which wonder of the time has been infinitely obliged to him—but still we were little prepared for the keen observation, the deep wisdom, and the consummate art which he has interwoven in the slight texture and whimsical pattern of Vanity Fair.[1]

And Mr Ray himself has recovered for us this rousing advertisement from *The Athenæum*:

NEW WORK BY MICHAEL ANGELO TITMARSH

This day is published, price 1s. with numerous Illustrations on Steel and Wood, Part VII. of

VANITY FAIR:
PEN AND PENCIL SKETCHES OF ENGLISH SOCIETY.

By W. M. THACKERAY

Author of 'Mrs. Perkins's Ball', &c.

'Everything is simple, natural and unaffected. Common sense sits smiling on the top of every page.'—*Morning Chronicle*.
'If Mr. Thackeray were to die to-morrow, his name would be transmitted down to posterity by his "Vanity Fair." He is the Fielding of the nineteenth century.'—*Sun*.[2]

[1] *Quarterly Review*, LXXXIV, Dec. 1848–Mar. 1849, p. 155.
[2] *Letters*, II, 311f.

This emergence into fame during the publication of *Vanity Fair* needs no more explaining than Dickens's during the publication of *The Pickwick Papers*. Good and better as all the fiction of Thackeray had been hitherto, *Vanity Fair* was great fiction and on a great scale. Mr Ray, however, imputes the fame to its commentary, and this, I think, because he has misjudged as a critic what he has found as a researcher. He has examined what survives of the manuscript of its early chapters and has made this interesting discovery about the history of their composition:

It would appear that Thackeray began his novel early in 1845 and soon completed enough for two monthly parts. These eight chapters he wrote in his slanting hand. When Colburn and two or three other publishers refused "Pen and Pencil Sketches of English Society", as the story was first called, Thackeray laid the manuscript temporarily aside. By March of 1846 Bradbury and Evans had accepted it; but other work intervened, and Thackeray did not return to his novel until the last months of that year. The changes he made at this time are readily identifiable, for they were entered, perhaps at the printer's request, in his more legible upright hand.[1]

These revisions insert passages of moral commentary, and they 'everywhere bear the marks' of what Mr Ray thinks to be Thackeray's 'new view of fiction'. But why impute novelty to this interspersing of moral commentary? Thackeray was born a commentator. Writing— as if he were merely talking—on moral matters came to him as naturally as narration did. In the early work such writing is abundant. I have already said that it would be difficult to imagine any story with more of it than *The Ravenswing*. In *Catherine* there is much, and

[1] Pp. 92f.

even much in 'Dennis Haggarty's Wife'. It would almost seem, then, that what stands in need of explanation is why moral commentary is ever absent from his writings.

The textual history of *Barry Lyndon* may be taken as a test case. Thackeray contributed *The Luck of Barry Lyndon* to *Fraser's*, in 1844, under the pseudonym of Fitz-Boodle. The words 'our family...the Barrys' in the first sentence declare the form of the novel to be that of autobiography. As we read it in any modern reprint except that in the 'Oxford Thackeray', which by means of typographical devices gives us both texts together, we find it almost wholly lacking in commentary. Given to unscrupulous calculation and action, Lyndon finds little time for the moral reflection most of us cannot but practise. At some junctures in the story, however, it is forced on him—I have already quoted an instance of it.[1]

But the novel as it now stands is proof that, when he wished, Thackeray could strip a story fairly clear of commentary. In the earlier form of the work, however, we are given a different picture. There the autobiography is a thing *presented*, and Fitz-Boodle, the alleged presenter, is recognizably Thackerayan. To begin with, like the unpseudonymous author of *Vanity Fair* himself, Fitz-Boodle finds it necessary to dissociate himself from his 'puppet'. To a passage in which Lyndon brazenly confesses to pandering and double-dealing Fitz-Boodle adds a footnote:

In the original MS. the words 'my master' have often been written, but afterwards expunged, by Mr. Barry, and 'my captain' written in their stead. If we have allowed the passage which describes his occupation under Monsieur de

[1] See above, p. 126.

Potzdorff to remain, it is not, we beseech the reader to suppose, because we admire the autobiographer's principles or professions.[1]

And Fitz-Boodle steps in and introduces what was originally Part II of the text of 1844 with a disclaimer on similar lines:

It is, perhaps, as well for the reader that in the following part of his Memoirs, which details the history of Mr. Lyndon's life after his marriage and during the first years of his fashionable life, the autobiographer has not been more explicit. His papers at this period contain a mass of very unedifying and uninteresting documents,—such as tavern-bills of the Star and Garter and the Covent Garden houses of entertainment; paid I O U's, indicating gambling transactions with some of the most fashionable personages of the day; letters in female handwriting, which show that he was anything but constant to the wife whom he had won; drafts of letters to lawyers and money-brokers relative to the raising of money, the insuring of Lady Lyndon's life, and correspondence with upholsterers, decorators, cooks, housekeepers, bailiffs and stewards. Indeed, he appears to have docketed all these testimonials of his extravagance with the most extraordinary punctuality, and kept every possible voucher of his want of principle. What he says of himself in the present section of the Memoirs, "that he was clever at gaining a fortune, but incapable of keeping one", is a statement (not like all the statements he makes) worthy of entire credit; and a professional accountant, were he to go through the voluminous Lyndon papers, might, no doubt, trace every step which the adventurer took in the destruction of the splendid property which he acquired through his lady. But this is a calculation not in the least profitable or necessary here; it is only sufficient to know the process, without entering into the interminable particulars. And the editor of the Memoirs, in placing these few lines of preface before the second part of them, is glad to think that

[1] Ch. VII.

the reader is speedily about to arrive at that period in the history where poetical justice overtakes the daring and selfish hero of the tale. After enumerating the bribes he paid his agents in consequence of their marriage, Mr. Lyndon proceeds as follows to recount the pleasures of their honeymoon:[1]

and so to the account of its miseries, an account I have already quoted.[2]

Nor are such things all. The Lyndon of the earlier version has enough commentary in his own right to give his nature a colour lacking from the revised version. In the earlier he is almost as much a commentator as Esmond is. Esmond's commentary is always in character—he is another Thackeray, though a Thackeray less unbuttoned—but Lyndon's is not always so. When Lyndon's commentary is bright with military imagery, well and good. But not so good when he is allowed to write as in the second half of this passage:

What a change now!—ah, gods, what a royal change! How different is Fanny Edwards! What has happened to her that she has become an angel since yesterday, or what strange enchantment has fallen upon you, that she should seem like one? Shall we go on in this strain, and discourse through this entire chapter upon the nature and peculiarities of love, and its influences upon the youthful bosom? No, no! such things had best be thought about, not spoken of. Let any man who has a mind to do so, fall back in his chair, dropping the book out of his hand—fall back into his chair, and call back the sleeping sweet reminiscences of his early love-days, long before he ever saw Mrs. Jones. She, good woman, has sent down half a dozen times already to say that tea is waiting. Never mind; sit still, Jones, and dream on. Call back again that early, brilliant, immortal first love. What matters what the object of it was?[3]

[1] Ch. xvii.   [2] See above, p. 126.   [3] Ch. i.

214

This is the maturest of Thackerayan commentary; and its date is 1844, three years before *Vanity Fair*.

Why Thackeray expunged most of the authorial commentary from the second edition (that of the *Miscellanies* of 1855–7) I do not know. The likely reason is his coming to feel that despite the appropriate form given to much of Lyndon's disquisition—for Thackeray's style is designed in general to be in character—it was unlikely that Lyndon would think discursively at all, that what was usually a darling virtue of Thackeray's own was in this instance a darling sin. At any rate here was Thackeray in 1856, at a time when he was lacing his new fiction ever more and more generously with commentary, cutting out brilliant specimens of it from an earlier novel.

In most of his other works the principles of art called for no suppression. Among these is *The Pen and Pencil Sketches of English Society*, and it remains a puzzle why Thackeray forgot to avail himself of the congenial opportunities until a first draft of those eight chapters was complete. But the lapse is the less significant in that he returned to the manuscript in order to complete its Thackerayization. According to his view of it, fiction was people and their actions seen always with the moral eye, commented on always with the moral voice. His revision, therefore, does not show him as a Dr Johnson revising the work of a Virginia Woolf, but the same Thackeray now trying to enlarge what he felt not to be yet big enough. In other words, he resembles Pope, who in the last important reconsideration of *The Rape of the Lock*, already once thoroughly revised, added the speech of Clarissa to a poem drenched in moral, in order 'to open [the moral] more clearly'.

9

And the second point, the sermonizing. Mr Ray assumes too readily, I think, that Thackeray in the earlier years saw moralizing as humbug, and so a thing that he had vowed 'morbidly, perhaps, [to] eschew'.[1] The humbug to be eschewed was, early as well as late, the moralizing of hypocrites. His own practice shows moralizing about truth, as truth pertained to novelists, to have been welcome enough so long as the moralist included himself in the charge. I shall have more to say on this later on. Mr Ray draws support for his theory that Thackeray began by disliking moral teaching from the review of Lever's *St Patrick's Eve* that he contributed anonymously to *The Morning Chronicle*. I suspect that it is due to Mr Ray's researches that this interesting piece is now known to be Thackeray's. When we read it at length, however, and not in the excerpt which Mr Ray gives from it, we see Thackeray's position clearly. The review is headed 'Lever's St Patrick's Eve—Comic Politics', and opens as follows:

Since the days of Æsop, comic philosophy has not been cultivated so much as at present. The chief of our pleasant writers—Mr. Jerrold, Mr. Dickens, Mr. Lever—are assiduously following this branch of writing; and the first-named jocular sage [i.e. Æsop], whose apologues adorned our spelling-books in youth, was not more careful to append a wholesome piece of instruction to his fable than our modern teachers now are to give their volumes a moral ballast. To some readers—callous, perhaps, or indifferent to virtue or to sermons—this morality is occasionally too obtrusive. Such sceptics will cry out—We are children no longer; we no longer want to be told that the fable of the dog in the

[1] P. 89.

manger is a satire against greediness and envy; or that the
wolf and lamb are types of Polk[1] gobbling up a meek
Aberdeen, or innocence being devoured by oppression.
These truths have been learned by us already. If we want
instruction, we prefer to take it from fact rather than fiction.
We like to hear sermons from his reverence at church; to
get our notions of trade, crime, politics, and other national
statistics, from the proper papers and figures; but when
suddenly, out of the gilt pages of a pretty picture book, a
comic moralist rushes forward, and takes occasion to tell us
that society is diseased, the laws unjust, the rich ruthless, the
poor martyrs, the world lop-sided, and *vice-versâ*, persons
who wish to lead an easy life are inclined to remonstrate
against this literary ambuscadoe. You may be very right,
the remonstrant would say, and I am sure you are very
hearty and honest, but as these questions you propound
here comprehend the whole scheme of politics and morals,
with a very great deal of religion, I am, I confess, not
prepared at the present moment to enter into them. Without wishing to be uncomplimentary, I have very shrewd
doubts as to your competency to instruct upon all these
points; at all events, I would much rather hear you on your
own ground—amusing by means of amiable fiction, and
instructing by kindly satire, being careful to avoid the discussion of abstract principles, beyond those of the common
ethical science which forms a branch of all poets and
novelists' business—but, above all, eschewing questions of
politics and political economy, as too deep, I will not say for
your comprehension, but for your readers'; and never, from
their nature, properly to be discussed in any, the most
gilded, story-book. Let us remember, too, how loosely some
of our sentimental writers have held to political creeds;—
thus we all know that the great philosopher, Mrs. Trollope,
who, by means of a novel in shilling numbers, determined
to write down the poor-laws, somewhere towards the end
of her story came to a hitch in her argument, and fairly

[1] For the relations of the American President Polk and Aberdeen, the
British Foreign Secretary, see *D.N.B.*, s.v. Gordon, George Hamilton.

broke down with a confession that facts had come to light, subsequent to the commencement of her story, which had greatly altered her opinions regarding the law; and so the law was saved for that time. Thus, too, we know that the famous author of "Coningsby", before he propounded the famous New England philosophy, had preached many other respectable doctrines, viz., the Peel doctrines, the Hume doctrines, &c.: all this Sir Robert Peel himself took the pains to explain to the House of Commons the other night, when the great philosopher alluded to called the right honourable baronet an organised hypocrite.

Lever's novel has been seized by Thackeray as the occasion for

enter[ing] a protest against sentimental politics altogether ...because the practice amongst novelists is prodigiously on the increase, and can tend, as we fancy, to little good. You cannot have a question fairly debated in this way.

The upshot of his argument is that

we had better have some other opinion than that of the novelist to decide upon the dispute between [the landlord and the labourer].

'Has any sentimental writer', Thackeray asks, 'organised any feasible scheme for bettering the poor?' In tales of this kind all that really happens is that 'there somehow arrives a misty reconciliation between the poor and the rich...the characters make their bow, grinning, in a group'. And he proceeds:

This is not the way in which men seriously engaged and interested in the awful question between rich and poor meet and grapple with it. When Cobden thunders against the landlords, he flings figures and facts into their faces, as missiles with which he assails them; he offers, as he believes, a better law than their's as a substitute for that which they uphold. When Sir Robert Peel resists or denies, or takes up the standard which he has planted, and runs away, it is because he has cogent prudential reasons for his conduct of the day. But on one side or the other it is a serious contest which is taking place in the press and Parliament over the " Condition of England question ". The novelist, as it appears to us, ought to be a non-combatant. But if he persists in taking a side, don't let him go into the contest unarmed; let him do something more effectual than call the enemy names. The cause of either party in this great quarrel requires a stronger championship than this, and merits a more earnest warfare.[1]

Thackeray does not think that the claims made by Lever for his moral—he made them in the dedication of the book to his children—can be fairly drawn from the story itself; but that is not really the question that interests him, which is the broader question whether fiction is the place for political morals at all. Whatever the answer to that may be, it is clear that for Thackeray morals drawn from truth, in the sense I am using it here, were another matter: he makes the explicit statement that they 'form...a branch of all poets and novelists' business'. In drawing this distinction he is honouring the human fact that at all times, except the worst, life can be lived without recourse to political thinking, but never without recourse to ethical. It is from no ambush that the novelist speaks of ethics, a novel being a ground where moral walks the highway freely as the personages themselves, accompanying them closely as their shadow.

Thackeray, in this review, makes his imaginary remonstrator prefer sermons from his reverence at church to those from the comic novelists under discussion. For his assumption that the readers of his own books were not unready to take the preaching they contained we

[1] This and the preceding quotations are from *The Morning Chronicle*, 3 April 1845, p. 5.

have much evidence, earlier and later. If they took his commentary, they were almost committed to take his preaching. Conditions were propitious: here was a situation carved out of human nature, a commentator and a reader. Assured of the soundness of the comment, it was an easy step for the commentator to apply the case to that of the reader himself, which he could only too shrewdly guess to be not unlike. But I have already sought to justify the directing of the Thackerayan commentary *at* the reader.[1] That directing was no new thing in *Vanity Fair*.

10

And so to the last matter raised by Mr Ray's article, the view that Thackeray's attitude to truth changed, that he adopted a new tone in speaking of it, that he came to change that something in himself he mixed with it.

In cautioning against any account that sees a sudden change, or a change due to more than the oscillation of ingredients that had existed from the start, I have Thackeray the letter-writer against me as well as Mr Ray. For about the time of *Vanity Fair* Thackeray himself thought he adopted a new tone in speaking of truth.

The moment when he expressed that 'development' pointedly comes in his letter to Mark Lemon of 24 February 1847, from which I have already quoted. We can see from the immediately preceding letters that conditions for making a statement were ripening. Indeed, the batch of letters he wrote at that season are among his most searching.

On 3 February, while making a journey by train, he had written to his friend William Brookfield to explain and ask forgiveness for some indiscretion of speech

[1] See above, pp. 96 f.

which broke out apparently when he was being medically treated with an anaesthetic. The letter deserves quotation in full:

Under the confessional seal in the railway.

My dear old Reverence,

I think from some words you let drop about 30 miles off, about my insanity yesterday, explanation is necessary on my part.

Without the ether I should never have broken out as I did about a certain personage (we are just come to a station) but in the etherial or natural state, my opinion is the same. I think the personage you know what. Her innocence, looks, angelical sweetness and kindness charm and ravish me to the highest degree; and every now and then in contemplating them I burst out into uncouth raptures. They are not the least dangerous—it is a sort of artistical delight (a spiritual sensuality so to speak)—other beautiful objects in Nature so affect me, children, landscapes, harmonies of colour, music, etc. Little Minny[1] and the Person most of all. By my soul I think my love for the one is as pure as my love for the other—and believe I never had a bad thought for either. If I had, could I shake you by the hand, or have for you a sincere and generous regard? My dear old fellow, you and God Almighty may know all my thoughts about your wife;—I'm not ashamed of one of them—since the days of the dear old twopenny tart dinner till now.

The misfortune is in incautious speaking about her. Such a person ought not to be praised in public and in my fits of enthusiasm I cannot refrain. I shall try to correct this, and beg your pardon for it. Indeed I didn't intend that the Joseph the carpenter simile should go to her ears; and write you now under the seal of confession. My breast is so clean that you will have no difficulty I think in giving me absolution.

'Evins! Here is Wimbledon Station. Well, I have opened my bowels to you. Indeed there has not been much secret

[1] His second daughter, then six years old.

before; and I've always admired the generous spirit in which you have witnessed my queer raptures. If I had envy, or what you call passion, or a wicked thought...I should have cut you long ago, and never could have had the rascality to say as I do now that I'm yours sincerely and affectionately,

W. M. T.[1]

On 18 February, Thackeray wrote to his old friend John Allen, and again on 22 February, sending on this later date a still further letter on the same matter to Henry Reeve, in all of which he pleaded for a more up-to-date and well-informed view of the character of Brookfield, to which Allen had been called on to testify by an appointing body, and which he had charged with 'levity & looseness of talk'.[2] In these characteristic letters, Thackeray pleads for a truer judgment, taking practical measures to see it instated. He goes into the matter deeply, and with the subtlety we expect of him, winding up by crediting Brookfield with a certain practical reform:

Now it is not Punch that has perverted Brookfield; but Brookfield has converted Punch! & that's something to have done in these days. Two years ago I used only to make a passive opposition agst the Anti-church and Bishop sneers—last year I made an active one (Jerrold & I had a sort of war & I came off conqueror) and it was through his influence—It's something to stop half a million of people from jeering at the Church every week—No cry is more popular. At this minute we might be turning the Bishop of London into such scorn & ridicule upon perfectly just grounds too, and to the delight of the public. It's William Brookfield who stopped it, & you may tell the Bench so and I wish you would—by his kindness, his tenderness, his honest pious life.[3]

[1] *Letters*, II, 271 f. [2] Op. cit. II, 277.
[3] Op. cit. II, 274 f.

Thackeray concluded by saying that 'this long letter is more about me than about Brookfield'. It was about himself because he felt that his career as a writer was taking a turn. Of this turn he spoke more fully in his letter to Lemon from which I have already quoted. The letter begins by referring to 'That concluding benedictory paragraph' in the articles on snobs (later collected as *The Book of Snobs*), a conclusion which, he hopes, 'wont be construed in any unpleasant way by any other laborer on [*Punch*]'. It reads as follows:

To laugh at such is *Mr. Punch's* business. May he laugh honestly, hit no foul blow, and tell the truth when at his very broadest grin—never forgetting that if Fun is good,[1] Truth is still better, and Love best of all

—an illustration of which scale of values is neatly provided in the letter just quoted; it would have been fun to gird at the Bishop of London; nor would it have flouted truth, the 'grounds' being 'perfectly just';[2]

[1] On the status given to fun in this passage some general remarks of Roscoe provide a brilliant comment: 'Wickedness has its funny side; but it grates on our ears to hear [actual] English ladies talking as they do sometimes of "that charming wicked little Becky". We don't say that a vicious or even a degraded nature is not a fit subject for the artist, —no doubt it is [cf. p. 206 above]; we do not say it is an unfit subject even for comedy; but we do say it ought not to be comically treated... Sin is fire; and Mr. Thackeray makes fireworks of it.' (II, 299f.)

[2] Charles James Blomfield, the Bishop of London at this time, was concerned, unsuccessfully and with much loss of dignity, in trying to draw a line between what could be allowed to Tractarian reformers and what not. That the full annotation of this passage would be of interest is indicated by these items: (1) Thackeray pokes fun at the Bishop in his letter written in Paris on 19 March 1841 to Mrs Proctor:

What shall I tell you? Last night there were at least two hundred thousand persons of both sexes disguised in various costumes, dancing madly from ten until five this morning: as I suppose the Bishop of London was at Drury Lane when he cried out so against the French rabble. Did his Lordship dance with his apron on? It would have been a fine sight and a pretty subject for a picture. Odry says in one of the farces, "I saw a beautiful carp in the market to-day, and when I go next week I am determined to buy it." I was just on the point of covering this paper with a picture of the Bishop dancing, but have put

nevertheless it is better if the laugh is restrained by love. Thackeray then launches out into this statement:

What I mean applies to my own case & that of all of us—who set up as Satirical-Moralists—and having such a vast multitude of readers whom we not only amuse but teach. And indeed, a solemn prayer to God Almighty was in my thoughts that we may never forget truth & Justice and kindness as the great ends of our profession. There's something of the same strain in Vanity Fair. A few years ago I should have sneered at the idea of setting up as a teacher at all, and perhaps at this pompous and pious way of talking about a few papers of jokes in Punch—but I have got to

it off till next week or till the next exhibition, or till the next time that I venture to send you a letter. Indeed I have hardly the impertinence to despatch such nonsense as this.

(*Letters*, II, 12 f.); (2) That the Bishop came near touching Thackeray himself there is evidence in the following letter from Catherine Winkworth to her sister Susanna:

VENTNOR,

Sept. 20, 1849

When Emily was walking with Mrs. White yesterday they met Mr. S. and his sisters—the latter reside in Bonchurch, and the former is very intimate with, or at least a very old friend of the Whites'. But Mr. W. does not give him by any means a good character. He says he is undoubtedly clever, but that he has no real principles at all, except an intense aversion to evangelical clergymen, and that his one object is to obtain preferment and celebrity. "And so sure enough he has got promoted lately by the Bishop of London—not that it's any honour to have been promoted by that old scoundrel." Of course we wanted to know why the Bishop of London was a scoundrel, and Mr. W. said because he was so bigoted and tyrannical. "Not long ago he sent for a friend of mine, a clergyman in London, and asked whether it was true that he had had Douglas Jerrold and one or two more *Punch* writers at his house. My friend said it was; for he's a very sensible man, and would rather associate with clever men than with the old snobs of Archdeacons and so-on—an excellent man he is, too—and the Bishop answered: 'Sir, I don't choose that my clergymen should be clever men themselves, or should associate with clever men, and I beg you to understand that if you continue your acquaintance with such people, you need not look for any preferment at my hands.' So my friend told Lord Lyndhurst of this, and Lord L. got him made an Inspector of Schools." Don't you think this rather an odd style of conversation for a clergyman?

(*Memorials of Two Sisters Susanna and Catherine Winkworth*, ed. Margaret J. Shaen, 1908, pp. 48 f.). I owe to my wife the identification of the London clergyman who became a school inspector with Thackeray's old friend Brookfield.

believe in the business, and in many other things since then. And our profession seems to me to be as serious as the Parson's own.[1]

That February was a month of stock-taking, perhaps as never before, and a month or two later came more of it over the quarrel with Forster—for which I refer interested readers to *Letters*, II, 294–304.

One of the first things to note is that in these letters Thackeray is not being fair to his earlier work—what person is who thinks he has taken a turn for the better? Much tenderness, as I have already remarked, and much love exist in the earlier writings, fiercely as they sometimes blaze. Thackeray is always as much a Maria Edgeworth as he is a satirist. Here is the opinion of Roscoe on some of these writings, though two of his instances come from the middle of Thackeray's career:

Some of Mr. Thackeray's lesser works are pervaded throughout with a genial kindly spirit; such are the *History of Mr. Samuel Titmarsh and the Great Hoggarty Diamond* (which it is pleasant to hear is a favourite with the author), and *The Kickleburys on the Rhine, Dr. Birch's School.* &c. In these, foibles are pleasantly touched with cheerful happy raillery, and a light, gay, yet searching tone of ridicule, and a tender pleasing pathos, pervade the story: "the air nimbly and sweetly recommends itself;" the wit plays freshly and brightly, like the sun glittering through the green leaves on the wood-paths.[2]

Nor is ferocity noticeably absent from *Vanity Fair*: one of the passages which Thackeray added to his manuscript, and which I have already quoted, recommended ridicule as medicine for the 'Faithless, Hopeless, Charityless':

let us have at them, dear friends, with might and main. Some there are, and very successful too, mere quacks and fools: and it was to combat and expose such as those, no doubt, that Laughter was made.[3]

[1] *Letters*, II, 282.   [2] II, 298.   [3] Ch. VIII.

Ferocity is not so effectively absent from *Vanity Fair* as Mr Ray's argument requires. Its first readers did not find it absent. Mr Ray quotes some contemporary comments on the novel, of which several repudiate it with distaste, or worse. Evidently for these readers the force of 'love is best of all' had not made itself felt. More love, perhaps, is shown in the novels that followed, which were drawing nearer to the Indian summer of *The Roundabout Papers*, but there is also much fierceness, much Ruskinian fierceness, in these also. Thackeray, as I see it, is like any of his own personages—a whole thing from the start undergoing little that we can call development, but from time to time receiving a shake-up.

And assuredly that complete man never harboured anything like a 'treasure of meditated hatred'.[1] This Satanic equipment was accorded him by Taine, writing in the year after Thackeray's death, and it is endorsed by Mr Ray in his account of Thackeray up to the writing of *Vanity Fair*.[2] Surely the view of James Hannay is nearer to soundness; he spoke of

his hearty and pleasant satire, always Horatian rather than Juvenalian,—always exciting Mirth rather than Hate.... His satire was never at any time malignant.[3]

Hatred of the meditated sort was outside his scope. Carlyle was right in thinking him 'not a strong man',[4] and no man less than strong can embosom so settled a vice. Hatred in more than short occasional spurts was even unlikely on general grounds—a novelist deeply versed in ordinary human nature is too much aware of

---

[1] 'un trésor de haine méditée' (*Histoire de la Littérature Anglaise*, 1863–4, IV, 73).

[2] P. 89.

[3] James Hannay, *A Brief Memoir of the late Mr Thackeray*...[*Reprinted from the Edinburgh Courant*], 1864, pp. 4, 14.

[4] [Thackeray's] *Letters*, I, cviii.

complexity, and too much fascinated by it, to find anything complete and unrelieved enough to incite hatred. The last word on all this seems that letter of John Blackwood declining for his magazine an article called forth by Thackeray's death:

> I do not feel that it describes Thackeray, and consequently I did not like to put it into the Magazine as our portrait and tribute to his memory. I do not much care for the stories you give. He used to tell such stories in a pitying half-mocking way in which it was impossible to say how much was sincerity and how much sham. But when he dropped that vein, and spoke with real feeling of men and things that he liked, the breadth and force of his character came out, and there was no mistake about his sincerity. None of the numerous sketches I have read give to me any real picture of the man with his fun and mixture of bitterness with warm good feeling. I have stuck in this note. Writing about old "Thack." has set me thinking about him, and all the scenes we have had together. I feel so truly about him that I am frightened to give a wrong impression of him to one who did not know him.[1]

I do not think Thackeray felt hatred as a man, but I am sure he did not feel it as a novelist.

Much is at stake here for Thackeray in general. And this because he would have elected to be judged by the ordinary man, to whom the person writing especially addresses himself. One great merit of the ordinary man is that he will not respect a writer who holds in his heart a treasure of meditated hatred. And to appeal, finally, to grounds the most general of all—no such 'treasure' is owned by any writer we can call great: not even the much misjudged Swift.

[1] Mrs Gerald Porter, *Annals of a Publishing House John Blackwood* [being] *The Third Volume of William Blackwood and his Sons*, 1898, p. 99.

II

I have invoked the ordinary man. The standards he sets cannot but be borne in mind by anyone trying to see Thackeray aright, and I shall go on invoking them till the end of my argument. How far can the 'ordinary man' be grasped as a concept? Johnson's expansion of his term 'the common reader' helps to body him forth a little—he describes him as a man possessing his share of the 'common sense', who is 'uncorrupted with literary prejudices', and who ignores 'all the refinements of subtilty and the dogmatism of learning'.[1] The surest way of finding him is to look within ourselves, cutting away characteristics which are too personal, too national, too much of a class, too religious, too professional. He represents that portion of the mind within us all that likes to see fair play, dislikes speaking ill of the dead, looks forward to the green of spring, and the foods and drinks of 'merry' Christmas, prefers not to spend a night alone in a church, fears when a storm strikes a lake

for boat or vessel where none was,[2]

honours birthdays...and so on for a long time; in short the commonplace in the minds of millions of men who prefer *Twelfth Night* to *All's Well*, *Hamlet* to *Troilus and Cressida*, Goldsmith to Sterne, Wordsworth's poems to Keats's, Chaucer's to Langland's, like *The Vicar of Wakefield* and think Sir Roger de Coverley the best thing in Addison. He is the creature whom Thackeray appeals to explicitly in his essay on the novels of George Sand.[3]

---

[1] *Lives*, III, 441.

[2] From a discarded scrap of *The Prelude* (ed. de Selincourt, 1926, p. 601).

[3] In one of these novels, *Spiridion*, the hero forsakes one creed after another with what Thackeray calls 'a fiery versatility of belief'. Here is some of the criticism Thackeray directs against the novel:

I think that Madame Sand's novel of Spiridion may do a vast deal of good, and bears a good moral with it; though not such an one, perhaps,

It is a testimonial to the greatness of Thackeray's novels that they address themselves squarely to the ordinary man. Look again at those matters I began by discussing. The effect of the means that help towards unifying the novels, the means of dynasty, place, length of historic time, increase the reader's sense—a sense dear to the ordinary man—that the world of the novelist is the world of newspapers rather than of fiction. His effect this way may be distinguished from Trollope's, who used some of the same means. When the repeated names of Thackeray's fictitious personages exist along-side those of persons known to historians, and the repeated names of his fictitious places—Chatteris, Pumpernickel and the rest—alongside those of places known to cartographers, the novels and everything in them are planted in the reader's own world, not in a Barsetshire containing Framley, Allington and Plum-stead Episcopi, with its Mrs Proudie and its Mr Harding, but in the world containing London, with its Holborn, Hampstead and Pentonville, and its Queen Anne,

as our fair philosopher intended. For anything he learned, [the hero] might have remained a Jew from the beginning to the end. Wherefore be in such a hurry to set up new faiths? Wherefore, Madame Sand, try and be so preternaturally wise? Wherefore be so eager to jump out of one religion, for the purpose of jumping into another? See what good this philosophical friskiness has done you, and on what sort of ground you are come at last. You are so wonderfully sagacious, that you flounder in mud at every step; so amazingly clear-sighted, that your eyes cannot see an inch before you, having put out, with that ex-tinguishing genius of yours, every one of the lights that are sufficient for the conduct of common men.... I wish the State would make a law that one individual should not be allowed to preach more than one doctrine in his life; or, at any rate, should be soundly corrected for every change of creed. How many charlatans would have been silenced,—how much conceit would have been kept within bounds,—how many fools, who are dazzled by fine sentences, and made drunk by declamation, would have remained quiet and sober, in that quiet and sober way of faith which their fathers held before them.

('Madame Sand and the New Apocalypse' in *The Paris Sketch Book*).

Dr Johnson, Georges I, II, III and IV. To use the words of Roscoe:

Many novelists have a world of their own which they inhabit. Thackeray thrusts his characters in among the moving every-day world in which we live.[1]

When his novels treat, as they often do, of the past, it is felt more poignantly because it is the past as actual people once knew it. It draws on the reader's experience as directly as a book of history or topography. His older personages look back often, and it is on what was once a solid present, that of memoirs and biographies. Thackeray grounded all his novels in the one world that claimed his interest almost entirely:

> ...the very world, which is the world
> Of all of us,—the place where, in the end,
> We find our happiness, or not at all![2]

Then again, the personages living in this worldly scene fall well within the ordinary human range. If they are given enough chance to prove it, all of them are individuals, some few of them striking individuals; but most of them not more striking than any ordinary human being. Though he paid most attention to rich people, he did not forget that rich and poor have one human heart. From his writings, therefore, emerges a normal psychology, an account of how ordinary men act in response to a run of events like that making up ordinary existence. Rachel, alarmed as her husband's return is upon her because the plague he has bolted from has spoiled her looks; Laura, at one point during Pen's infatuation for the Fotheringay, practising the piano 'for hours' before breakfast; the Fotheringay cleaning her slippers while her beliquored father

---

[1] II, 271.   [2] Wordsworth, *The Prelude*, XI, 142 ff.

threatens a duel with Pen; the 'solemn happiness'[1] of Colonel Newcome almost bemusedly blissful in the domestic company of his daughter-in-law, 'perform[ing] all the courtship part of [his son's] marriage'[2]—all such things in their thousands are felt by the personages experiencing them as they are felt by ordinary people, not by a Pater or a Henry James or a Virginia Woolf, any more than by a Mr Micawber, a Golden Dustman or a Mr Venus.

Thackeray's truthfulness here honours the average human response. There was some wisdom in Saintsbury's odd recommendation that the tyro should approach the novels by way of *The Roundabout Papers*. No one reading those papers can miss the centre of Thackeray's interest. This centre, of course, can be discerned as clearly in the novels, but not on the evidence so infallibly. It was because he prized most highly the sort of experience that cannot but fall generously to the lot of all men that he found something dishonourable in the very idea of fiction. He turned to writing novels, as Fielding did, partly because of a dislike for certain contemporary novels in which life was misrepresented. He wrote novels as any man might, given the literary power. It is said that a good novel could be made out of each of our lives. Essentially that novel exists somewhere in Thackeray's, wherein, as Chesterton said, every man reads his own past.[3] Thackeray is one of those geniuses who do not puzzle the rest of us. There is much in Dickens that we honour while we see that it is foreign to ordinary men: his mind is not often ours. But what we honour in Thackeray is our own mind at a finer pitch, working on our own experience widened and deepened. We could

---

[1] Ch. LXII.   [2] Ch. LXV.
[3] *The Victorian Age in Literature*, 1912, p. 126.

all be Thackerays if we could improve what we have got. In him the novelist stands with the poet as Wordsworth saw him, a man speaking to men because he is a man and because he has the power of speech.

13

There is a further recommendation to the ordinary man in the sort of knowledge Thackeray draws on. He has the gift for keeping the reader assured that his personages occupy houses and rooms which exist. Roscoe's remark I have already quoted that it is only one step from doubting the existence of Becky's finished little house in Curzon Street to accepting the philosophy of Berkeley.[1] Thackeray did not doubt the existence of the houses in his fiction, if only because he took them, as it were literally, from his actual life:

he once pointed out to us [wrote Hannay] the very house in Russell Square where his imaginary Sedleys lived,—a curious proof of the reality his creations had for his mind.[2]

To mention houses and rooms is to be reminded that Thackeray's genius preferred the shelter of a roof and walls. If there is landscape, it is as a house has it, or as two or more of them are linked by it. In this he resembles Fielding, but, unlike him, deliberately abstains from doing something he could have done well: witness the brilliant and also poetical descriptions in his travel books. His power that way was equal to Henry James's—I am content to stake my proof on one scrap of description, that of the aged carp at Potsdam 'with hunches of blue mould on their back'.[3]

If he has little space in his novels for the purely aesthetic, that is because the common man has little

[1] See above, p. 121.   [2] *Studies on Thackeray* [1869], pp. 17f.
[3] *The Roundabout Papers*, 'On some carp at Sans Souci'.

space for it in his life. A beautiful setting claims notice in ordinary life only because the man in it is happy and free enough to notice it; if it makes him happier still, that is because he chooses to let it; it is unlikely that it will be noticed by a man who is unhappy. Ruskin took a long time to learn what Thackeray knew from the start—that a beautiful sunset requires a man of leisure to see it. The act of seeing is, in Thackeray, a prompted act. His descriptions are instances of the principle of the pathetic fallacy. Here is an example of landscape being put in its place:

Before the dinner was served, the guests met on the green of the hotel, and examined that fair landscape, which surely does not lose its charm in our eyes because it is commonly seen before a good dinner. The crested elms, the shining river, the emerald meadows, the painted parterres of flowers around, all wafting an agreeable smell of *friture*, of flowers and flounders exquisitely commingled.[1]

And another from 'Round about the Christmas Tree':

When you read this, will Clown still be going on lolling his tongue out of his mouth, and saying, "How are you to-morrow?" To-morrow, indeed! He must be almost ashamed of himself (if that cheek is still capable of the blush of shame) for asking the absurd question. To-morrow, indeed! To-morrow the diffugient snows will give place to Spring; the snowdrops will lift their heads; Ladyday may be expected, and the pecuniary duties peculiar to that feast; in place of bonbons, trees will have an eruption of light green knobs; the whitebait season will bloom.[2]

Thackeray knows that, when all is said, external nature is the source of man's food. In *The Irish Sketch Book* he has this laugh at the tourists:

Next day, instead of going back to the race-course, a car drove me out to Muckross, where, in Mr. Herbert's beautiful grounds, lies the prettiest little *bijou* of a ruined

---

[1] *Philip*, ch. XL.   [2] *Roundabout Papers*.

abbey ever seen—a little chapel with a little chancel, a little cloister, a little dormitory, and in the midst of the cloister a wonderful huge yew-tree which darkens the whole place. The abbey is famous in book and legend; nor could two young lovers, or artists in search of the picturesque, or picnic parties with the cold chicken and champagne in the distance, find a more charming place to while away a summer's day than in the park of Mr. Herbert. But depend on it, for show-places and the due enjoyment of scenery, that distance of cold chickens and champagne is the most pleasing perspective one can have. I would have sacrificed a mountain or two for the above, and would have pitched Mangerton into the lake for the sake of a friend with whom to enjoy the rest of the landscape.[1]

And he reminds his readers that even poets—let alone mere prose-writers, let alone ordinary people—are not poetical all the time:

A woman melodiously crying "Dublin Bay herrings", passed just as we came up to the door, and as that fish is famous throughout Europe, I seized the earliest opportunity and ordered a broiled one for breakfast. It merits all its reputation: and in this respect I should think the Bay of Dublin is far superior to its rival of Naples—are there any herrings in Naples Bay? Dolphins there may be, and Mount Vesuvius to be sure is bigger than even the Hill of Howth, but a dolphin is better in a sonnet than at a breakfast, and what poet is there that, at certain periods of the day, would hesitate in his choice between the two?[2]

The proportions of his interest in man and in what is beautiful in external nature, and the connections between them, are well represented by this small scene from *The Newcomes*: the family party is assembled to see the colonel off to India:

Charles Honeyman came down and preached one of his very best sermons. Fred Bayham was there, and looked

[1] Ch. XII.   [2] Ch. I.

particularly grand and noble on the pier and the cliff. I am inclined to think [comments 'Pendennis' the supposed narrator] he had had some explanation with [Colonel] Thomas Newcome, which had placed F.B. in a state of at least temporary prosperity. Whom did he not benefit whom he knew, and what eye that saw him did not bless him? F.B. was greatly affected at Charles's sermon, of which our party of course could see the allusions. Tears actually rolled down his brown cheeks; for Fred was a man very easily moved, and as it were a softened sinner. Little Rosey and her mother sobbed audibly, greatly to the surprise of stout old Miss Honeyman, who had no idea of such watery exhibitions, and to the discomfiture of poor Newcome, who was annoyed to have his praises even hinted in that sacred edifice. Good Mr. James Binnie came for once to church; and, however variously their feelings might be exhibited or repressed, I think there was not one of the little circle there assembled who did not bring to the place a humble prayer and a gentle heart. It was the last sabbath-bell our dear friend was to hear for many a day on his native shore. The great sea washed the beach as we came out, blue with the reflection of the skies, and its innumerable waves crested with sunshine. I see the good man and his boy yet clinging to him, as they pace together by the shore.[1]

The sea is a thing to notice just then because water is the medium of the Colonel's sad impending separation from Clive. But it is noticed also because its mingle of surface sparkle and dragging depths is the snatched-up emblem of the lives of the onlookers and so of life itself.

14

Strong among the recommendations which the novels offer the ordinary man is the nature of the authorial person himself. Much of it has been exhibited already in the passages I have quoted. Not attempting to study

[1] Ch. xxvi.

it here in detail I propose to note two matters which go together. They shade off from the more purely intellectual to the more purely moral.

Thackeray contemplates what offers with an openness of mind, an untendentious readiness to see all sides of a thing. Whereas the fanatic or too forceful mind snatches and hastens on, Thackeray rests his gaze, though not relaxing for a moment the gaiety and business of the prolonged experience. I propose to explore first an instance from one of his travel books, his account of the approach to Constantinople.[1] In this account he starts by giving us truth as it is patent fact:

When we rose at sunrise to see the famous entry to Constantinople, we found, in the place of the city and the sun, a bright white fog, which hid both from sight, and which only disappeared as the vessel advanced towards the Golden Horn. There the fog cleared

—to stop in mid-sentence, because the account proceeds with truth as it struck one person, Thackeray—

There the fog cleared off as it were by flakes; and as you see gauze curtains lifted away, one by one, before a great fairy scene at the theatre, this will give idea enough of the fog;

so far so good; though speaking for himself, the truth in question is so commonplace that he feels he can speak for everyone. At this point he becomes aware of truth far from commonplace, and appearing different to different people:

this will give idea enough of the fog; the difficulty is to describe the scene afterwards;

yet he can still plump down his own version with some confidence:

which was in truth the great fairy scene, than which it is impossible to conceive anything more brilliant and magnificent.

[1] *From Cornhill to Cairo*, ch. VII.

And then with less confidence, though with a hope he carries his readers with him:

I can't go to any more romantic place than Drury Lane to draw my similes from—Drury Lane, such as we used to see it in our youth, when, to our sight, the grand last pictures of the melodrama or pantomime were as magnificent as any objects of nature we have seen with maturer eyes. Well, the view of Constantinople is as fine as any of Stanfield's best theatrical pictures, seen at the best period of youth, when fancy had all the bloom on her—when all the heroines who danced before the scene appeared as ravishing beauties, when there shone an unearthly splendour about Baker and Diddear—and the sound of the bugles and fiddles, and the cheerful clang of the cymbals, as the scene unrolled, and the gorgeous procession meandered triumphantly through it—caused a thrill of pleasure, and awakened an innocent fulness of sensual enjoyment that is only given to boys.

Not the truth of Drury Lane as men know it, but as men remember it. And so the further establishment of his version of truth by means of persuasion, and the rejection of different truths as irrelevant:

The above sentence contains the following propositions:—The enjoyments of boyish fancy are the most intense and delicious in the world. Stanfield's panorama used to be the realization of the most intense youthful fancy.[1] I puzzle my brains and find no better likeness for the place. The view of Constantinople resembles the *ne plus ultra* of a Stanfield diorama, with a glorious accompaniment of music, spangled houris, warriors, and winding processions, feasting the eyes and the soul with light, splendour, and harmony. If you were never in this way during your youth ravished at the play-house, of course the whole comparison is useless: and

[1] Clarkson Stanfield, R.A., the friend of Thackeray, Dickens and others, who 'at the request of Macready painted a diorama for the pantomime at Covent Garden in 1837, and refused to accept more than 150 *l*. for it, though offered twice that amount by the great actor'. (*D.N.B.*, s.n. Stanfield.)

you have no idea, from this description, of the effect which Constantinople produces on the mind. But if you were never affected by a theatre, no words can work upon your fancy, and typographical attempts to move it are of no use. For, suppose we combine mosque, minaret, gold, cypress, water, blue, caïques, seventy-four,[1] Galata, Tophana, Ramadan, Backallum, and so forth, together, in ever so many ways, your imagination will never be able to depict a city out of them. Or, suppose I say the Mosque of St. Sophia is four hundred and seventy-three feet in height, measuring from the middle nail of the gilt crescent, surmounting the dome, to the ring in the centre stone; the circle of the dome is one hundred and twenty-three feet in diameter, the windows ninety-seven in number—and all this may be true, for anything I know to the contrary; yet who is to get an idea of St. Sophia from dates, proper names, and calculations with a measuring line? It can't be done by giving the age and measurement of all the buildings along the river, the names of all the boatmen who ply on it. Has your fancy, which pooh-poohs a simile, faith enough to build a city with a foot-rule? Enough said about descriptions and similes...
it is a scene not perhaps sublime, but charming, magnificent, and cheerful beyond any I have ever seen—the most superb combination of city and gardens, domes and shipping, hills and water, with the healthiest breeze blowing over it, and above it the brightest and most cheerful sky.[2]

The omission near the end of the above passage contains this parenthesis:

(though whenever I am uncertain of one I am naturally most anxious to fight for it)

which is a truth flashed from a different quarter again— that of psychological truth. To how many things and

---

[1] A warship carrying seventy-four guns.

[2] This passage may have suggested to Newman the famous two-sided description of Athens in the third volume of his *Historical Sketches*, first as 'Athens, the city of the mind, as radiant, as splendid, as delicate, as young, as ever she had been', and of exquisite charm for the senses, and then as the Athens of a report drawn up by 'the agent of a London company'—'plenty of good marble...fisheries productive', etc.

aspects of things is Thackeray being faithful at one and the same time—to the changing face of the earth, to this man and to that, and to the experience of young and old.

As random instances from the novels take first the ending of *Catherine*. Besides recording the events called for by history and discussing the principles on which rogues should be portrayed in novels, Thackeray parcels out the narrative among various styles—that of the sentimental historical novel, that of theatre advertisements, that of newspapers contemporary with the crime (paragraphs are quoted with a rough accuracy from *The Daily Post* and *The Daily Journal* of 1726), that of the Newgate ordinary.[1] As the second instance there is the courtship of Pen. Thackeray gives us Pen's feelings in all their swooning completeness and truth, but to the accompaniment of the truth about the theatre as a part of the world of business—the company both as men and players, the Fotheringay whom some half-dozen men see differently, even the band that accompanies the performance and that 'blew by kind permission of Colonel Swallowtail'[2]—and of the truth, adult and worldly, supplied by Major Pendennis and his following.

I have said that Thackeray took no worthy interest in the science of his day, but in this fair unhastening comprehensiveness of vision is there not something that earns the term scientific? Carlyle missed strength in Thackeray, moral strength: what was strong in him was the endurance of his sensitiveness to ordinary experience.

[1] The chaplain who prepared the condemned prisoner for death.
[2] Ch. IV.

15

With this intellectual fairmindedness goes his indecisiveness as a moralist. He lacks a burning need to rid himself of vacillation, because matters seem to him, as to the ordinary man, too mixed and obscure. His biographers tell us that he was indecisive as a person. Carlyle thought him 'very uncertain and chaotic in all points except his outer breeding'.[1] Professor Greig felt justified in introducing his 'reconsideration' with a chapter headed 'The Indecisive Thackeray'. One result of this hovering was *The Book of Snobs*, upwards of fifty chapters and a long conclusion, all of which are concerned with verbal picture and allegoric incident, and allow discussion of a wide, impalpable phenomenon—which he repeatedly attempts to define. Another of its results was the ambiguous light that hangs over *Vanity Fair*, and another the strange vacillation in *Esmond* between first and third person. The most extended result is the character of Pendennis, of whom Fitzjames Stephen wrote:

The irresolute, half-ashamed, sceptical hero, conscious of his own weakness, conscious of his own ignorance... governed by tastes and circumstances instead of principles, but clinging, firm to old habits, to traditional lessons of truth and honour...not very bad, nor very good, nor very anything...is one of the saddest, as it is one of the most masterly memorials of the times in which he lived which any writer ever drew for posterity.[2]

But is not Pendennis eternal, and that because he is essentially like the rest of us? 'Pen, if anybody in modern fiction', wrote Saintsbury, 'is *l'homme sensuel moyen*.'[3]

[1] Quoted, *Letters*, I, cviii.
[2] *Cambridge Essays, contributed by Members of the University. 1855*, p. 184.
[3] P. 183.

The most intense indecisiveness comes from Mr Batchelor. Borrowing Thackeray's practised pen, as it were, he begins *Lovel the Widower* with a paragraph pages long of which this is the first half:

Who shall be the hero of this tale? Not I who write it. I am but the Chorus of the Play. I make remarks on the conduct of the characters: I narrate their simple story. There is love and marriage in it: there is grief and disappointment: the scene is in the parlour, and the region beneath the parlour. No: it may be the parlour and kitchen, in this instance, are on the same level. There is no high life, unless, to be sure, you call a baronet's widow a lady in high life; and some ladies may be, while some certainly are not. I don't think there's a villain in the whole performance. There is an abominable selfish old woman, certainly: an old highway robber; an old sponger on other people's kindness; an old haunter of Bath and Cheltenham boarding-houses (about which how can I know anything, never having been in a boarding-house at Bath or Cheltenham in my life?); an old swindler of tradesmen, tyrant of servants, bully of the poor—who, to be sure, might do duty for a villain, but she considers herself as virtuous a woman as ever was born. The heroine is not faultless (ah! that will be a great relief to some folks, for many writers' good women are, you know, so *very* insipid). The principal personage you may very likely think to be no better than a muff. But is many a respectable man of our acquaintance much better? and do muffs know that they are what they are, or, knowing it, are they unhappy? Do girls decline to marry one if he is rich? Do we refuse to dine with one? I listened to one at Church last Sunday, with all the women crying and sobbing; and, oh, dear me! how finely he preached! Don't we give him great credit for wisdom and eloquence in the House of Commons? Don't we give him important commands in the army? Can you, or can you not, point out one who has been made a peer? Doesn't your wife call one in the moment any of the children are ill? Don't we read his dear poems, or even novels? Yes;

perhaps even this one is read and written by—Well! *Quid rides?* Do you mean that I am painting a portrait which hangs before me every morning in the looking-glass when I am shaving? *Après?* Do you suppose that I suppose that I have not infirmities like my neighbours? Am I weak? It is notorious to all my friends there is a certain dish I can't resist; no, not if I have already eaten twice too much at dinner. So, dear sir, or madam, have *you* your weakness— *your* irresistible dish of temptation? (or if you don't know it, your friends do). No, dear friend, the chances are that you and I are not people of the highest intellect, of the largest fortune, of the most ancient family, of the most consummate virtue, of the most faultless beauty in face and figure. We are no heroes nor angels; neither are we fiends from abodes unmentionable, black assassins, treacherous Iagos, familiar with stabbing and poison—murder our amusement, daggers our playthings, arsenic our daily bread, lies our conversation, and forgery our common handwriting. No, we are not monsters of crime, or angels walking the earth— at least I know *one* of us who isn't, as can be shown any day at home if the knife won't cut or the mutton comes up raw. But we are not altogether brutal and unkind, and a few folks like us. Our poetry is not as good as Alfred Tennyson's, but we can turn a couplet for Miss Fanny's album: our jokes are not always first-rate, but Mary and her mother smile very kindly when papa tells his story or makes his pun. We have many weaknesses, but we are not ruffians of crime. No more was my friend Lovel. On the contrary, he was as harmless and kindly a fellow as ever lived when I first knew him. At present, with his changed position, he is, perhaps, rather *fine* (and certainly I am not asked to his *best* dinner-parties as I used to be, where you hardly see a commoner—but stay! I am advancing matters). At the time when this story begins, I say, Lovel had his faults—which of us has not? He had buried his wife, having notoriously been henpecked by her. How many men and brethren are like him! He had a good fortune—I wish I had as much—though I daresay many people are ten times as rich....

Thackeray had some fellow-feeling for Costigan, who was unable to *think* truth, let alone tell it—'fact and fiction reeled together in his muzzy, whiskified brain'.[1]

It was rightly noted by Roscoe that there is no personage of strong conviction in Thackeray's novels.[2] This did not mean, however, that there were no personages with strength of purpose behind their actions. Barry Lyndon is one of the most terrifying instances of such strength—terrifying because he is as credibly a man as Hamlet or Othello, and more credibly so than Iago. Lady Kew and several others are scarcely less terrifying. To make these personages Thackeray acquired strength from somewhere in his nature: we know, however, that *Barry Lyndon* caused him special pains in the writing.[3] Again, is not Thackeray standing by the rest of us? It is only rarely that conviction is strong.

As an inventor of stories he shrinks from employing the utmost rigour possible. He is not sure that the poetic justice which novelists mete out to villains is indeed justice, even were he sure that it is in accordance with probability. Here is the passage in which 'Fitz-Boodle' concludes the autobiography of Barry Lyndon, a passage cancelled in the revised edition:

When [Barry Lyndon] lost his income, his spirits entirely fell. He was removed into the paupers' ward, where he was known to black boots for wealthier prisoners, and where he was detected in stealing a tobacco-box. It was in this plight his staunch old mother found him, and from it she withdrew him; and if, upon being restored to bread-and-cheese, he despised blacking boots and no longer stole snuff-boxes, the reader must not fancy that he was a whit more virtuous than when, under the strong temptation of necessity, he performed those actions unworthy of a man and a gentleman.

---

[1] *Pendennis*, ch. v.   [2] II, 277.
[3] See John W. Dodds, *Thackeray: A Critical Portrait*, 1941, p. 72.

16-2

To break the chain of the quotation—does not this principle dispose of Becky Sharp's brilliant sophism 'I think I could be a good woman if I had five thousand a year',[1] though not of the astute implications that with riches she would have been accounted virtuous? and does not the quotation as it proceeds well account for her many successes?

If the tale of his life have any moral (which I sometimes doubt), it is that honesty is *not* the best policy. That was a pettifogger's maxim, who half admits he would be a rogue if he found his profit in it, and has led astray scores of misguided people both in novels and the world, who forthwith set up the worldly prosperity or adversity of a man as standards by which his worth should be tried. Novelists especially make a most profuse, mean use of this pedlar's measure, and mete out what they call poetical justice.

Justice, forsooth! Does human life exhibit justice after this fashion? Is it the good always who ride in gold coaches, and the wicked who go to the workhouse? Is a humbug never preferred before a capable man? Does the world always reward merit, never worship cant, never raise mediocrity to distinction? never crowd to hear a donkey braying from a pulpit, nor ever buy the tenth edition of a fool's book? Sometimes the contrary occurs, so that fools and wise, bad men and good, are more or less lucky in their turn, and honesty is 'the best policy', or not, as the case may be.

Lacking faith in justice of the sort called poetical, which is the author's earthly anticipation of the Old Testament judgment of God, he shrinks from this possible office of the 'poet'. In 'De Finibus' he tells how he once held his hand, because he saw that a certain chance might be taken even by villains:

In the story of Philip, just come to an end, I have the permission of the author to state that he was going to drown the

[1] *Vanity Fair*, ch. XLI.

two villains of the piece—a certain Doctor F—— and a certain Mr. T. H—— on board the *President*, or some other tragic ship—but you see I relented. I pictured to myself Firmin's ghastly face amid the crowd of shuddering people on that reeling deck in the lonely ocean, and thought, "Thou ghastly lying wretch, thou shalt not be drowned: thou shalt have a fever only; a knowledge of thy danger; and a chance—ever so small a chance—of repentance." I wonder whether he *did* repent when he found himself in the yellow-fever, in Virginia? The probability is, he fancied that his son had injured him very much, and forgave him on his death-bed. Do you imagine there is a great deal of genuine right-down remorse in the world? Don't people rather find excuses which make their minds easy; endeavour to prove to themselves that they have been lamentably belied and misunderstood; and try and forgive the persecutors who *will* present that bill when it is due; and not bear malice against the cruel ruffian who takes them to the police-office for stealing the spoons?

Taking man for his matter, Thackeray sometimes sees that attack is called for; but the sword after a few passes melts in his hand. 'Let us not be too angry...' is how he begins a characteristic sentence in *The Ravenswing*.[1] The novels of Charlotte Brontë prompted him to say that

Novel writers should not be in a passion with their characters as I imagine, but describe them, good or bad, with a like calm.[2]

When he does make attacks he takes full advantage of their being attacks in words. Is it not a law of literature that literature does not take kindly to the expression of anger that is unmixed? To express fierce emotions whether in speech or writing is to find some relief from them, and to express them adequately is to leave room

[1] Ch. I.   [2] *Letters*, III, 67.

245

for a new emotion, which is more noticeable when the expression is in writing—the purer, aesthetic emotion at having adequate expression to look at. For the reader aesthetic emotion is usually paramount, by however narrow a margin. As an instance see the passage I quoted above, in which Thackeray rounds on the novels that occasioned *Catherine*:[1] we laugh at what is exhibited as ridiculous, but we also respond aesthetically to the wit of the exhibition:

The amusing novel of *Ernest Maltravers*...opens with a seduction; but then it is performed by people of the strictest virtue on both sides....

And when Thackeray is on the attack something else complicates the emotions. I have shown how fairminded he is by authorial nature. He sees things too completely to want to attack them complete. Unlike Swift in this, he is more like Pope and Dickens, who cannot but allow the aesthetic good in the moral bad. Thackeray knows that what is sham on the moral may be delightful on other grounds. He sometimes allows the truth that he loves first and foremost to make an addition to falsity rather than to supplant it. The mind has many sides, and Thackeray listens to their separate pleas for attention. Judgment is made, if at all, at the gate, after the tour of the serpent-haunted garden. It is a judgment therefore against which there is no reasonable ground for appeal. Here are two random instances of his fairness all round. When he laughs at the play the Fotheringay is acting in he sees that for all its silliness it has Nature in it:

Those who know the play of the "Stranger", are aware that the remarks made by the various characters are not valuable

[1] Pp. 133 f. above.

in themselves, either for their sound sense, their novelty of observation, or their poetic fancy. In fact, if a man were to say it was a stupid play, he would not be far wrong. Nobody ever talked so. If we meet idiots in life, as will happen, it is a great mercy that they do not use such absurdly fine words. The Stranger's talk is sham, like the book he reads and the hair he wears, and the bank he sits on, and the diamond ring he makes play with—but, in the midst of the balderdash, there runs that reality of love, children, and forgiveness of wrong, which will be listened to wherever it is preached, and sets all the world sympathising.[1]

And here for instance is the grotesque and the false with beauty mixed in it, and an honest account of the much mixed feelings of Esmond when confronted with it:

Here in her ladyship's saloon, the young man saw again some of those pictures which had been at Castlewood, and which she had removed thence on the death of her lord, Harry's father. Specially, and in the place of honour, was Sir Peter Lely's picture of the Honourable Mistress Isabella Esmond as Diana, in yellow satin, with a bow in her hand and a crescent in her forehead; and dogs frisking about her. 'Twas painted about the time when royal Endymions were said to find favour with this virgin huntress; and, as goddesses have youth perpetual, this one believed to the day of her death that she never grew older: and always persisted in supposing the picture was still like her.

After he had been shown to her room by the groom of the chamber, who filled many offices besides in her ladyship's modest household; and after a proper interval, his elderly goddess Diana vouchsafed to appear to the young man. A blackamoor in a Turkish habit, with red boots and a silver collar, on which the viscountess's arms were engraven, preceded her and bore her cushion; then came her gentle-woman; a little pack of spaniels barking and frisking about preceded the austere huntress—then, behold, the viscountess herself "dropping odours". Esmond recollected from his

[1] *Pendennis*, ch. IV.

childhood that rich aroma of musk which his mother-in-law (for she may be called so) exhaled. As the sky grows redder and redder towards sunset, so, in the decline of her years, the cheeks of my lady dowager blushed more deeply. Her face was illuminated with vermilion, which appeared the brighter from the white paint employed to set it off. She wore the ringlets which had been in fashion in King Charles's time; whereas the ladies of King William's had head-dresses like the towers of Cybele. Her eyes gleamed out from the midst of this queer structure of paints, dyes, and pomatums. Such was my lady viscountess, Mr. Esmond's father's widow.

He made her such a profound bow as her dignity and relationship merited: and advanced with the greatest gravity, and once more kissed that hand, upon the trembling knuckles of which glittered a score of rings—remembering old times when that trembling hand made him tremble. "Marchioness", says he, bowing, and on one knee, "is it only the hand I may have the honour of saluting?" For, accompanying that inward laughter, which the sight of such an astonishing old figure might well produce in the young man, there was goodwill too, and the kindness of consanguinity. She had been his father's wife, and was his grandfather's daughter. She had suffered him in old days, and was kind to him now after her fashion. And now that bar-sinister was removed from Esmond's thought, and that secret opprobrium no longer cast upon his mind, he was pleased to feel family ties and own them—perhaps secretly vain of the sacrifice he had made, and to think that he, Esmond, was really the chief of his house, and only prevented by his own magnanimity from advancing his claim.[1]

16

With this indecisiveness, this passiveness that the common man respects as wise, goes the author's low estimate of his own moral worth. He knows the

[1] Bk II, ch. III.

characters of his personages so thoroughly because that is how he knows his own. On whatever level he shows himself there is little he finds to commend. I have already shown that in effect he applied to himself that line which Pope applied to others:

Sleepless [himself] to give his readers sleep.[1]

In *The Ravenswing* comes this description of the career of Sir George Thrum, with the thought it prompts:

He was the author of several operas...and, of course, of songs which had considerable success in their day, but are forgotten now, and are as much faded and out of fashion as those old carpets which we have described in the professor's house, and which were, doubtless, very brilliant once. But such is the fate of carpets, of flowers, of music, of men, and of the most admirable novels—even this story will not be alive for many centuries. Well, well, why struggle against Fate?[2]

The arch-analyst of snobbery admits that there is a touch of it in himself:

You must not judge hastily or vulgarly of Snobs: to do so shows that you are yourself a Snob. I myself have been taken for one.[3]

Later we get:

When a man goes into a great set company of dinner-giving and dinner-receiving Snobs, if he has a philosophic turn of mind, he will consider what a huge humbug the whole affair is...the philosopher included.[4]

If prelates have darling sins, what about ourselves?

I confess, that when those Right Reverend Prelates come up to the gates of Paradise with their probates of wills in their

---

[1] *Dunciad*, I, 94. [2] Ch. VII.
[3] *The Book of Snobs*, Prefatory Remarks.
[4] *The Book of Snobs*, ch. xx.

249

hands, I think that their chance is.... But the gates of
Paradise is a far way to follow their Lordships; so let us trip
down again, lest awkward questions be asked there about
our own favourite vices too.[1]

For summary of his constant attitude we might take
this from *The Newcomes*:

I am not here to scourge sinners; I am true to my party.[2]

Rousseau began his *Confessions* by calling around him
the innumerable swarm of his fellows and daring them,
after they had read his account, to tell God that they
are better men than he. Baudelaire, confessing much in
his turn, called on his reader to own to the same sins:

Hypocrite lecteur,—mon semblable,—mon frère![3]

Both seek to excuse themselves by reference to their
brother. Thackeray excuses his brother by reference to
himself. There cannot have been many satirists who
included themselves in the object of their satire both at
its mildest and fiercest. The possessor of that humility
does not earn the label sentimentalist, the mark of the
sentimentalist being a half-conscious rosy ignorance of
the whole truth.

This humility helped, no doubt, to prompt his method
of writing fiction as if he were an historian. Being a
novelist and so having access to omniscience, he could
have entered the hearts of his personages at will. To
have a power so godlike, however, even over puppets,
he did not think seemly. He shrank from entering the
hearts of his 'saints'. The author of *Pendennis* shrinks
from knowing how Helen Pendennis and Laura conduct
their prayers. And it is the same with his blackguards.
When Barnes repents, the question cannot but be

---

[1] Ibid. ch. XI.   [2] Ch. XXVIII.
[3] The last line of 'Au Lecteur', before *Spleen et Idéal*.

raised whether his repentance is sincere or altogether so. Thackeray will not even try to decide:

There is some hypocrisy, of which one does not like even to entertain the thought.[1]

For the same reason at bottom he will not pry closely even into Becky's doings. When he does look into a heart it is sometimes because he knows he will see there this same becoming delicacy. For instance:

And presently Dobbin had the opportunity which his heart coveted, and he got sight of Amelia's face once more. But what a face it was! So white, so wild and despair-stricken, that the remembrance of it haunted him afterwards like a crime.... Our gentle-hearted Captain felt a guilty shock as he looked at her. "Good God", thought he, "and is it grief like this I dared to pry into?"[2]

And here is both the author and his creature towards the close of *Philip*:

It had wounded her pure heart to be obliged to think that her father could be other than generous, and just, and good. That he should humble himself before her, smote her with the keenest pang of tender commiseration. I do not care to pursue this last scene. Let us close the door as the children kneel by the sufferer's bedside, and to the old man's petition for forgiveness, and to the young girl's sobbing vows of love and fondness, say a reverent Amen.[3]

(In *Philip*, as in *The Newcomes*, we are reminded of the late plays of Shakespeare: older people do wrong, and find peace in blessing the younger.)

17

Knowing so much about himself he was much aware of the weakness of ordinary men.

In a striking paragraph of her anonymous review of *Vanity Fair*—a review from which I have already quoted

---

[1] *The Newcomes*, ch. LXIX.   [2] *Vanity Fair*, ch. XXX.   [3] Ch. XXIX.

—Lady Eastlake pleaded with the author on a score he could not but respect:

We almost long for a little exaggeration and improbability to relieve us of that sense of dead truthfulness which weighs down our hearts, not for the Amelias and Georges of the story, but for poor kindred human nature. In one light this truthfulness is even an objection. With few exceptions the personages are too like our every-day selves and neighbours to draw any distinct moral from. We cannot see our way clearly. Palliations of the bad and disappointments in the good are perpetually obstructing our judgment, by bringing what should decide it too close to that common standard of experience in which our only rule of opinion is charity. For it is only in fictitious characters which are highly coloured for one definite object, or in notorious personages viewed from a distance, that the course of the true moral can be seen to run straight—once bring the individual with his life and circumstances closely before you, and it is lost to the mental eye in the thousand pleas and witnesses, unseen and unheard before, which rise up to overshadow it. And what are all these personages in Vanity Fair but feigned names for our own beloved friends and acquaintances, seen under such a puzzling cross-light of good in evil, and evil in good, of sins and sinnings against, of little to be praised virtues, and much to be excused vices, that we cannot presume to moralise upon them—not even judge them,—content to exclaim sorrowfully with the old prophet, "Alas! my brother!" Every actor on the crowded stage of Vanity Fair represents some type of that perverse mixture of humanity in which there is ever something not wholly to approve of or to condemn. There is the desperate devotion of a fond heart to a false object, which we cannot respect; there is the vain, weak man, half good and half bad, who is more despicable in our eyes than the decided villain. There are the irretrievably wretched education, and the unquenchably manly instincts, both contending in the confirmed *roué*, which melt us to the tenderest pity. There is the selfishness and self-will which the possessor of great wealth and fawning relations can hardly avoid. There is the vanity and fear of the world which assist mysteriously with pious principles in keeping a man respectable; there are combinations of this kind of every imaginable human form and colour, redeemed but feebly by the steady excellence of an inward man, and the genuine heart of a vulgar woman, till we feel inclined to tax Mr. Thackeray with an underestimate of our nature, forgetting that Madame de Staël is right after all, and that without a little conventional rouge no human complexion can stand the stage-lights of fiction.[1]

How well this reader has taken the whole point of the book. And how powerful the plea for a retreat from the whole of truth. The same plea rose indirectly from a complaint made by Roscoe against the method Thackeray sometimes chose for presenting his 'cynicism':

...both [the characters of Beatrix and Rachel] are masterpieces of poetical insight; the latter blemished, however, here and there with the author's unconquerable hankering to lay his finger on a blot. He must search it out, and give it at least its due blackness. He will not leave you to gather that it must be there,—he parades it to the day, and presses it to your reluctant eyes. It comes partly from the truthfulness of his nature, which cannot bear that a weakness should be concealed, and partly probably from a mistaken apprehension of the truth that the artist must be true to nature....When in a character, especially a woman's, he comes upon a defect, he does not allow it to speak itself, or show itself naturally, and sink with its own proper significance into the reader's mind. He rushes in as author, seizes on it, and holds it up with sadness or triumph: "See", he says, "this is what you find in the best women." Thus he gives it an undue importance and vividness, and troubles and distorts the true impression of the whole character.[2]

[1] *The Quarterly Review*, LXXXIV, Dec. 1848–March 1849, 155f.
[2] II, 306f.

Was not Roscoe pleading, though he did not know it, for a part only of Thackeray's truth? In offering to supply blemishes for himself, was he not self-deceived? would they ever have been supplied by one whose 'eyes' were 'reluctant'? Thackeray's truth was too much for Roscoe in another direction also: taking his stand on the conception of a 'gentleman', he scented a 'vulgarity in the tone of [Thackeray's] work'.[1] This unpleasantness he found it hard to locate, but adduced one instance:

In the first volume of the *Newcomes* we are told how Warrington and Pendennis gave a little entertainment at the Temple, including among their guests little Rosey and her mother. It is a very pleasant charming picture, and the narrator speaks of the 'merry songs and kind faces', the 'happy old dingy chambers illuminated by youthful sunshine.' What unhappy prompting, then, makes him drop this blot on his description: 'I may say, without false modesty, that our little entertainment was most successful. The champagne was iced to a nicety. The ladies did not perceive *that our laundress, Mrs. Flanagan, was intoxicated very early in the afternoon.*' And before the end of the description we are not spared another allusion to 'Mrs. Flanagan in a state of excitement'. It is vulgar, surely, to mar the pure and pleasant impression of the scene with this image of the drunken laundress not only introduced, but insisted on.[2]

Roscoe's 'surely' suggests a doubt in his mind. Surely, we rejoin, if this is vulgar, it is because to the man interested in truthfulness life itself must include vulgarity as inevitably as it includes nobility.

In offering to supply blemishes for himself Roscoe was giving another proof that the novels were for him so truthful as to qualify for documents in a court of law: he spoke as a man rather than as a novel reader. In a

[1] II, 281. [2] Ibid.

novel we can only take what we are given by the novelist. If Thackeray told him—'with glee', as he reckoned—that blemishes exist, might not that be because he observed the unwillingness in readers like Roscoe to know the truth as well and truly as he himself knew it? Thackeray put his finger on the trouble when replying to a common complaint about *Vanity Fair*:

I am quite aware of the dismal roguery w[hich] goes all through the Vanity Fair story—and God forbid that the world should be like it altogether: though I fear it is more like it than we like to own.[1]

It is there, and so we must own it, but we do not like to. In his essay on *The Newcomes* the young Edward Burne-Jones threw the blame on to the complaining reader, convicting him out of his own Sunday-morning mouth:

how comes this inconsistency of ours, that we reject our own testimony against ourselves in the mouth of a brother; that we do perseveringly seek to turn into a charge of spleen and sneering against a writer his faithful picturing of an evil we cannot deny, and a life of broken promises we are ever confessing[?][2]

18

Moving towards a summary, I begin by reproducing more of the eloquence of Pen in his big debate with Warrington. I have already quoted much of the social and political part; here is the more general:

"If I doubt whether I am better than my neighbour," Arthur continued,—"if I concede that I am no better,— I also doubt whether he is better than I...."...

---

[1] *Letters*, ii, 354.
[2] 'Essay on the Newcomes' ['this masterpiece of all novel writing']. *The Oxford and Cambridge Magazine*, i, Jan. 1856, p. 50.

"You would have sacrificed to Jove", Warrington said, "had you lived in the time of the Christian persecutions."

"Perhaps I would", said Pen, with some sadness. "Perhaps I am a coward,—perhaps my faith is unsteady; but this is my own reserve. What I argue here is that I will not persecute. Make a faith or a dogma absolute, and persecution becomes a logical consequence; and Dominic burns a Jew, or Calvin an Arian, or Nero a Christian, or Elizabeth or Mary a Papist or Protestant; or their father both or either, according to his humour; and acting without any pangs of remorse,—but, on the contrary, with strict notions of duty fulfilled. Make dogma absolute, and to inflict or to suffer death becomes easy and necessary; and Mahomet's soldiers shouting 'Paradise! Paradise!' and dying on the Christian spears, are not more or less praiseworthy than the same men slaughtering a townfull of Jews, or cutting off the heads of all prisoners who would not acknowledge that there was but one prophet of God."

"A little while since, young one," Warrington said, who had been listening to his friend's confessions neither without sympathy nor scorn, for his mood led him to indulge in both, "you asked me why I remained out of the strife of the world, and looked on at the great labour of my neighbour without taking any part in the struggle? Why, what a mere dilettante you own yourself to be, in this confession of general scepticism, and what a listless spectator yourself! You are six-and-twenty years old, and as *blasé* as a rake of sixty. You neither hope much, nor care much, nor believe much. You doubt about other men as much as about yourself. Were it made of such *pococuranti* as you, the world would be intolerable; and I had rather live in a wilderness of monkeys, and listen to their chatter, than in a company of men who denied everything."

"Were the world composed of Saint Bernards or Saint Dominics, it would be equally odious," said Pen, "and at the end of a few scores of years would cease to exist altogether. Would you have every man with his head shaved, and every woman in a cloister,—carrying out to the full the ascetic principle? Would you have conventicle hymns twanging from every lane in every city in the world? Would you have all the birds of the forest sing one note and fly with one feather? You call me a sceptic because I acknowledge what *is*; and in acknowledging that, be it linnet or lark, a priest or parson, be it, I mean, any single one of the infinite varieties of the creatures of God (whose very name I would be understood to pronounce with reverence, and never to approach but with distant awe), I say that the study and acknowledgment of that variety amongst men especially increases our respect and wonder for the Creator, Commander, and Ordainer of all these minds, so different and yet so united,— meeting in a common adoration, and offering up each according to his degree and means of approaching the Divine centre, his acknowledgment of praise and worship, each singing (to recur to the bird simile) his natural song."

"And so, Arthur, the hymn of a saint, or the ode of a poet, or the chant of a Newgate thief, are all pretty much the same in your philosophy," said George.

"Even that sneer could be answered were it to the point," Pendennis replied; "but it is not; and it could be replied to you, that even to the wretched outcry of the thief on the tree, the wisest and the best of all teachers we know of, the untiring Comforter and Consoler, promised a pitiful hearing and a certain hope. Hymns of saints! Odes of poets! who are we to measure the chances and opportunities, the means of doing, or even judging, right and wrong, awarded to men; and to establish the rule for meting out their punishments and rewards? We are as insolent and unthinking in judging of men's morals as of their intellects. We admire this man as being a great philosopher, and set down the other as a dullard, not knowing either, or the amount of truth in either, or being certain of the truth any where. We sing Te Deum for this hero who has won a battle, and De Profundis for that other one who has broken out of prison, and has been caught afterwards by the policeman. Our measure of rewards and punishments is most partial and incomplete, absurdly inadequate, utterly worldly, and we wish to continue it into the next world. Into that next and awful world we strive to pursue men, and send after them our impotent party verdicts of condemnation or acquittal. We set up our paltry little rods to measure Heaven immeasurable, as if, in comparison to that, Newton's mind or Pascal's or Shakespeare's was any loftier than mine; as if the ray which travels from the sun would reach me sooner than the man who blacks my boots. Measured by that altitude, the tallest and the smallest among us are so alike diminutive and pitifully base, that I say we should take no count of the calculation, and it is a meanness to reckon the difference."

"Your figure fails there, Arthur", said the other, better pleased; "if even by common arithmetic we can multiply as we can reduce almost infinitely, the Great Reckoner must take count of all; and the small is not small, or the great great, to his infinity."

"I don't call those calculations in question", Arthur said; "I only say that yours are incomplete and premature; false in consequence, and, by every operation, multiplying into wider error. I do not condemn the man who murdered Socrates and damned Galileo. I say that they damned Galileo and murdered Socrates."

"And yet but a moment since you admitted the propriety of acquiescence in the present, and, I suppose, all other tyrannies?"

"No: but that if an opponent menaces me, of whom and without cost of blood and violence I can get rid, I would rather wait him out, and starve him out, than fight him out. Fabius fought Hannibal sceptically. Who was his Roman coadjutor, whom we read of in Plutarch when we were boys, who scoffed at the other's procrastination and doubted his courage, and engaged the enemy and was beaten for his pains?"

On that schoolboy question the debate pauses for a moment while the person writing appends this comment:

In these speculations and confessions of Arthur, the reader may perhaps see allusions to questions which, no doubt, have occupied and discomposed himself, and which he has answered by very different solutions to those come to by our friend. We are not pledging ourselves for the correctness of his opinions, which readers will please to consider are delivered dramatically, the writer being no more answerable for them, than for the sentiments uttered by any other character of the story: our endeavour is merely to follow out, in its progress, the development of the mind of a worldly and selfish, but not ungenerous or unkind or truth-avoiding man. And it will be seen that the lamentable stage to which his logic at present has brought him, is one of general scepticism and sneering acquiescence in the world as it is; or if you like so to call it, a belief qualified with scorn in all things extant. The tastes and habits of such a man prevent him from being a boisterous demagogue, and his love of truth and dislike of cant keep him from advancing crude propositions, such as many loud reformers are constantly ready with; much more of uttering downright falsehoods in arguing questions or abusing opponents, which he would die or starve rather than use. It was not in our friend's nature to be able to utter certain lies; nor was he strong enough to protest against others, except with a polite sneer; his maxim being, that he owed obedience to all Acts of Parliament, as long as they were not repealed.

And to what does this easy and sceptical life lead a man? Friend Arthur was a Sadducee, and the Baptist might be in the Wilderness shouting to the poor, who were listening with all their might and faith to the preacher's awful accents and denunciations of wrath or woe or salvation; and our friend the Sadducee would turn his sleek mule with a shrug and a smile from the crowd, and go home to the shade of his terrace, and muse over preacher and audience, and turn to his roll of Plato, or his pleasant Greek song-book babbling of honey and Hybla, and nymphs and fountains and love. To what, we say, does this scepticism lead? It leads a man to a shameful loneliness and selfishness, so to speak—the more shameful, because it is so good-humoured and conscienceless and serene. Conscience! What is conscience?

17-2

Why accept remorse? What is public or private faith? Mythuses alike enveloped in enormous tradition. If seeing and acknowledging the lies of the world, Arthur, as see them you can with only too fatal a clearness, you submit to them without any protest farther than a laugh; if, plunged yourself in easy sensuality, you allow the whole wretched world to pass groaning by you unmoved: if the fight for the truth is taking place, and all men of honour are on the ground armed on the one side or the other, and you alone are to lie on your balcony and smoke your pipe out of the noise and the danger, you had better have died, or never have been at all, than such a sensual coward.

Whereupon the debate moves to this conclusion:

"The truth, friend!" Arthur said, imperturbably; "where is the truth? Show it me. That is the question between us. I see it on both sides. I see it in the Conservative side of the House, and amongst the Radicals, and even on the ministerial benches. I see it in this man who worships by Act of Parliament, and is rewarded with a silk apron and five thousand a-year; in that man, who, driven fatally by the remorseless logic of his creed, gives up everything, friends, fame, dearest ties, closest vanities, the respect of an army of churchmen, the recognised position of a leader, and passes over, truth-impelled, to the enemy, in whose ranks he will serve henceforth as a nameless private soldier:— I see the truth in that man, as I do in his brother, whose logic drives him to quite a different conclusion, and who, after having passed a life in vain endeavours to reconcile an irreconcileable book, flings it at last down in despair, and declares, with tearful eyes, and hands up to Heaven, his revolt and recantation. If the truth is with all these, why should I take side with any one of them? Some are called upon to preach: let them preach. Of these preachers there are somewhat too many, methinks, who fancy they have the gift. But we cannot all be parsons in church, that is clear. Some must sit silent and listen, or go to sleep mayhap. Have we not all our duties? The head charity-boy blows the bellows; the master canes the other boys in the organ-loft; the clerk sings out Amen from the desk; and the beadle with the staff opens the door for his Reverence, who rustles in silk up to the cushion. I won't cane the boys, nay, or say Amen always, or act as the church's champion or warrior, in the shape of the beadle with the staff; but I will take off my hat in the place, and say my prayers there too, and shake hands with the clergyman as he steps on the grass outside. Don't I know that his being there is a compromise, and that he stands before me an Act of Parliament? That the church he occupies was built for other worship? That the Methodist chapel is next door; and that Bunyan the tinker is bawling out the tidings of damnation on the common hard by? Yes, I am a Sadducee; and I take things as I find them, and the world, and the Acts of Parliament of the world, as they are; and as I intend to take a wife, if I find one—not to be madly in love and prostrate at her feet like a fool—not to worship her as an angel, or to expect to find her as such—but to be good-natured to her, and courteous, expecting good-nature and pleasant society from her in turn. And so, George, if ever you hear of my marrying, depend on it, it won't be a romantic attachment on my side: and if you hear of any good place under Government, I have no particular scruples that I know of, which would prevent me from accepting your offer."

"O Pen, you scoundrel! I know what you mean", here Warrington broke out. "This is the meaning of your scepticism, of your quietism, of your atheism, my poor fellow. You're going to sell yourself, and Heaven help you! You are going to make a bargain which will degrade you and make you miserable for life, and there's no use talking of it. If you are once bent on it, the devil won't prevent you."

"On the contrary, he's on my side, isn't he, George?" said Pen with a laugh. "What good cigars these are! Come down and have a little dinner at the Club; the *chef*'s in town, and he'll cook a good one for me. No, you won't? Don't be sulky, old boy, I'm going down to—to the country to-morrow."

261

Surely this is a conclusion in which nothing is concluded except that action, blind or more clear-sighted, is inevitable—Pen is preparing to marry Blanche Amory, not the girl he needs most. Who is to say for certain where the author himself stands in it all? Perhaps, like Warrington, he is 'neither without sympathy nor scorn, for his mood led him to indulge in both'. As near as matters his position is that of Mr Irwine, the rector, in *Adam Bede*, for whom even so good a thinker as George Eliot cannot conceal her approval:

He...had no very lofty aims, no theological enthusiasm: if I were closely questioned, I should be obliged to confess that he felt no serious alarms about the souls of his parishioners, and would have thought it a mere loss of time to talk in a doctrinal and awakening manner to old 'Feyther Taft', or even to Chad Cranage the blacksmith. If he had been in the habit of speaking theoretically, he would perhaps have said that the only healthy form religion could take in such minds was that of certain dim but strong emotions, suffusing themselves as a hallowing influence over the family affections and neighbourly duties. He thought the custom of baptism more important than its doctrine, and that the religious benefits the peasant drew from the church where his fathers worshipped and the sacred piece of turf where they lay buried, were but slightly dependent on a clear understanding of the Liturgy or the sermon. Clearly the Rector was not what is called in these days [George Eliot is writing *c.* 1850, and the action of the story takes place *c.* 1800] an 'earnest' man: he was fonder of church history than of divinity, and had much more insight into men's characters than interest in their opinions....[1]

Writing his stories, Thackeray has the Irwines in mind, even the Tafts and Cranages. He knows that the readers of novels are ordinary men who prefer old truth to smart philosophy and the earnest driving of views.

[1] Bk I, ch. v.

And where the old truth available is self-contradictory —it is a truism that proverbs often exist in contradictory pairs—he has some respect for the honesty that admits to bafflement or which can keep contradictory principles suspended in the mind. Much of our daily life the mind spends in sitting, in coiling about, in wriggling, hovering and dithering, rather than in marching or darting ahead.

The philosophy in Thackeray's novels was not such as to satisfy Roscoe. He discussed it at some length, and found it false: Thackeray, he says,

never cultivated [light literature, which we accept merely as entertainment] in spirit, though he may for a time have availed himself of its ordinary forms [Roscoe is thinking of the work Thackeray did as a journalist and writer of sketches]. His genius is too large, too penetrating, too grave to move in this sphere. He professes to paint human life; and he who does so, and who does not base his conception on that religious substructure which alone makes it other than shreds of flying dreams, is an incomplete artist and a false moralist. And Mr. Thackeray cannot be sheltered behind the assertion that a fitting reverence precludes the intermingling of religious ideas with light literature,—first, because what we ask for does not demand a constant presence of the religious element on the surface, or indeed that it should appear there at all,—only that the spirit of the work and the picture of life should recognise it as at the foundation, or even only not utterly lose sight of it as a fundamental element in the conception of this world; and secondly, because he does not scruple (and fitly, we think) reverently to introduce the topic of religion, and to picture a humble spirit looking upwards for consolation and support;—because, while he includes the *sentiment*, he excludes the *realities* of religion, and has no place for those aspirations of the higher life, only to form the field for which was this world he deals with created.[1]

[1] II, 292f.

The case against Thackeray as a philosopher un-
acceptable to religious people could not be better
stated. It only remains to say that the ordinary man
could not honestly make the criticism that Roscoe
makes. Nor could he assent to the belief that Thackeray
missed 'the true scope of life' and 'those higher connections from which alone it acquires a purpose': or again
that he 'reduce[s] it to a medley fit only to move the
laughter of fools and the tears and scorn of the wise'.[1]
The ordinary man is satisfied with much less from life than
Roscoe looked for. 'Is it so small a thing', he would ask,

> Is it so small a thing
> To have enjoy'd the sun,
> To have liv'd light in the spring,
> To have lov'd, to have thought, to have done;
> To have advanc'd true friends...?[2]

The ordinary man is satisfied during much of his
course with the lot that falls to his senses and with the
commonplace affections during all of it. To demand more
of life before you accept it as worth having is in itself
a sort of blasphemy, the addition being so often not
forthcoming. In any event religious people can still read
Thackeray because he gives as complete a picture of

---

[1] II, 291.

[2] The question is that of Empedocles, in the great ode he speaks
towards the end of the first act of Arnold's *Empedocles on Etna*, when he
tries to form a just estimate of the destiny of man. A poet more nearly
of our own time has justified that destiny on even narrower grounds.
In his poem 'After' Mr Ralph Hodgson imagines the soul of man being
asked after the death of the body how it went with him 'on my peopled
star', and giving the answer:

> "Oh well enough...
> It went for me where mortals are!
> I saw blue flowers and the merlin's flight
> And the rime on the wintry tree,
> Blue doves I saw and summer light
> On the wings of the cinnamon bee."

Or there is the evidence of Hardy's poem 'Afterwards'. Roscoe had
forgotten the sound testimony of Lamb in his essay 'New Year's Eve'.

the world of men as any man has ever given, and because by example as well as precept he can positively teach the humility that people who are truly religious do not wish to fail to practise. Certainly the religious person alluded to in those speculations of Pendennis did not find him negligible. When Thackeray died at Christmas 1863, Newman mourned him in a letter to a friend, Thackeray's old friend Mary Holmes:

I...write...to express the piercing sorrow that I feel in Thackeray's death.

You know I never saw him, but you have interested me in him, and one saw in his books the workings of his mind—and he has died with such awful suddenness.

A new work of his had been advertised, and I had looked forward with pleasure to reading it; and now the drama of his life is closed, and he himself is the greatest instance of the text of which he was so full, *Vanitas vanitatum, omnia vanitas.* I wonder whether he has known his own decay, for a decay I think there has been. I thought his last novel betrayed lassitude and exhaustion of mind, and he has lain by apparently for a year. His last (fugitive) pieces in the 'Cornhill' have been almost sermons. One should be very glad to know that he had presentiments of what was to come.

What a world this is! how wretched they are who take it for their portion! Poor Thackeray! it seems but the other day since we [i.e. his correspondent and himself] became Catholics; now all his renown has been since that—he has made his name, has been made much of, has been fêted, and has gone out, all since 1846 or 1847.[1]

Thackeray, now that his death has brought a piercing sorrow, is 'poor Thackeray!'; nevertheless Newman was looking forward with pleasure to reading *Denis Duval.*

Thackeray is a wise practical moralist because he does not expect too much. Which is the better psychologist,

[1] *Letters and Correspondence of John Henry Newman,* ed. Anne Mozley, 1891, II, 478f.

Roscoe or he? Roscoe blamed him for pointing to the meanness and selfishness of all men instead of 'raising men out of the atmosphere of them'.[1] Thackeray, like Newman, had said that we cannot be too suspicious of ourselves. It is the old quarrel between those who would raise us and those who would humble us.

19

If we wish to summarize the essentials of Thackeray's philosophy, they do not make much of a show. Life is a mixed affair of which the tone deepens with the years. Mankind is made up of men who are what Pope said they were:

> Virtuous and vicious every man must be.

You being a man and this being so, try to be as kindly as you can and as little of a humbug. Revere the affections of the family, which are sacred,[2] and enjoy the comforts of friends without asking too much of those friends. Avail yourself in a practical way of all the pleasures of company and creature comforts—food and drink are sometimes good for cheering you up, even when you are downcast as a result of your own folly; the simple pleasures of play, pantomime, Punch and Judy are sovereign for a time against the spleen; whistling keeps up the courage, and wit freshens like paint. And so on for a few more steps, ending perhaps with 'vanity of vanities, all is vanity', though even here remembering that there is much to be said for vanity before it begins to look vain. Out of his mouth, fleshed like our own, flows the brook of talk, touching all the terrors, but accepting them without knowing very well what else to do about them.

[1] II, 294.　　[2] See below, pp. 282, 294.

20

'Nature', the core of what is human, addresses itself to man, to man in his prime. Thackeray addressed the Nature that he provided so much of to men rather past their prime. Life being brief, we cannot postpone the reading of the great literature of the world until we are ripe for all aspects of its greatness, but Thackeray's great novels are, more than most writings, the better for keeping. So much of his tone is scarcely discernible by the young. On one occasion he noted that 'the greater number of story readers are young',[1] and armed, it seems, with this assurance, Saintsbury conducted an experiment:

A company of young men and maidens to whom [*Esmond*] was not long ago submitted pronounced it (with one or two exceptions) inferior as a work of humour. The hitting of little Harry in the eye with a potato was, they admitted, humorous, but hardly anything else.[2]

The reason for the failure of this experiment is suggested by the remainder of the sentence I have just quoted from Thackeray:

and those who are ever so old remember that their own young days occurred but a very, very short while ago.

Thackeray usually wrote for readers who are old or 'ever so old'. 'Thackeray is everybody's past', said Chesterton, from which it follows that he wrote for readers with a past to remember. When Chesterton added '—is everybody's youth', he ought to have added further that the youth we get from Thackeray is often youth remembered. Like Major Pendennis Thackeray

---

[1] *Philip*, ch. xviii.
[2] Pp. 192f.

was a 'veteran moralist'.[1] A characteristic sentence of
his is this from *Esmond*:

Her words as she spoke struck the chords of all his memory,
and the whole of his boyhood and youth passed within
him....[2]

The experiment that Saintsbury conducted was
doomed from the start. No young person, however
intelligent and mature, can truly appreciate *Esmond* or
any of Thackeray's great novels, all of which, as I began
by saying, were written in Thackeray's older age which,
counted by years, came on him early. It is not merely
a question of any individual reader's power of imagination. The imagination of a few young readers might
possibly imagine the emotions of an 'oldster'—to use
Thackeray's term. But the ripe tone of the novels speaks
to more than the imagination of older readers: it speaks
to a possessed fact within them, as close as hands and
feet. Literature does not readily allow the psychical
distance strung out between the page and the reader to
be reduced beyond a certain point, unless the page concerned deliberately sets out to arouse the reader's
practical sense. When older readers read the work of the
older Thackeray, I do not say that that distance is reduced to nothing. The emotions aroused remain literary,
but it makes a difference that we have felt them ourselves on our own behalf and not merely on behalf of
the personages, that the emotions aroused by the
imaginary fact are accompanied by similar emotions
aroused by actual fact. The young have merely the first
green shoots of memory to look at or ignore. If they
know sadness, it is expressed for them in the poems of
Keats or the music of Chopin. Missing the sad bloom

---

[1] *Pendennis*, ch. XXXVII.   [2] Bk II, ch. I.

on words that seem as dry as Addison's, the young cannot but find Thackeray's most characteristic philosophy distasteful, even foreign. His writings ought to be denied them, as wines should, and the latest music of Mozart and Beethoven.

We do not need to wish for Thackeray's direct comment on the well-intentioned experiment of Saintsbury. It is writ large by implication in the novels, and largest of all in *The Roundabout Papers*, one of which bears the title, Ciceronian with a new difference, 'De Juventute'. When he found a boy reading a novel, he hailed him as 'sensible' only because it was a thriller. The schoolboys playing in the distant prospect were kept by Gray, on second thoughts, from knowing that they were men; Schumann described his *Kinderscenen*, which have at most an autumnal gaiety, as for men of his own age; and Thackeray gave this injunction to his daughters: 'So please to be young and to be merry as long as you can'.[1] The 'locus classicus' of all this is surely the climax of that little scene towards the close of 'Round about the Christmas Tree', one of *The Roundabout Papers*:

One more Christmas sight we had, of course; and that sight I think I like as well as Bob himself at Christmas, and at all seasons. We went to a certain garden of delight, where, whatever your cares are, I think you can manage to forget some of them, and muse, and be not unhappy; to a garden beginning with a Z, which is as lively as Noah's ark; where the fox has brought his brush, and the cock has brought his comb, and the elephant has brought his trunk, and the kangaroo has brought his bag, and the condor his old white wig and black satin hood. On this day it was so cold that the white bears winked their pink eyes, as they plapped up and down by their pool, and seemed to say, "Aha, this weather reminds us of dear home!" "Cold!

[1] *Letters*, III, 56.

bah! I have got such a warm coat", says brother Bruin, "I don't mind"; and he laughs on his pole, and clucks down a bun. The squealing hyænas gnashed their teeth and laughed at us quite refreshingly at their window; and, cold as it was, Tiger, Tiger, burning bright, glared at us red-hot through his bars, and snorted blasts of hell. The woolly camel leered at us quite kindly as he paced round his ring on his silent pads. We went to our favourite places. Our dear wombat came up, and had himself scratched very affably. Our fellow-creatures in the monkey-room held out their little black hands, and piteously asked us for Christmas alms. Those darling alligators on their rock winked at us in the most friendly way. The solemn eagles sate alone, and scowled at us from their peaks; whilst little Tom Ratel[1] tumbled over head and heels for us in his usual diverting manner. If I have cares in my mind, I come to the Zoo, and fancy they don't pass the gate. I recognize my friends, my enemies, in countless cages. I entertained the eagle, the vulture, the old billy-goat, and the black-pated, crimson-necked, blear-eyed, baggy, hook-beaked, old marabou stork yesterday at dinner; and when Bob's aunt came to tea in the evening, and asked him what he had seen, he stepped up to her gravely, and said—

> "First I saw the white bear, then I saw the black,
> Then I saw the camel with a hump upon his back.
> *Chorus of* Then I saw the camel with a HUMP upon his back!
> *Children*
>
> Then I saw the gray wolf, with mutton in his maw;
> Then I saw the wombat waddle in the straw;
> Then I saw the elephant with his waving trunk,
> Then I saw the monkeys—mercy, how unpleasantly
> they smelt!"

There. No one can beat that piece of wit, can he, Bob? And so it is all over; but we had a jolly time, whilst you were with us, hadn't we? Present my respects to the doctor; and I hope, my boy, we may spend another merry Christmas next year.

[1] This honey-badger was a Zoo favourite: see J. G. Wood, *The Illustrated Natural History*, 1861, I, 373.

This one sentence—'No one can beat that piece of wit, can he, Bob?'—may be given to a reader of Thackeray as the test of ripeness. Boys disqualify themselves by giving an answer, whether negative or affirmative does not matter, and youths by thinking it a joke on Bob. Only their elders can sense the wan halo round the jest— a jest indulgent not ironical, impossibly envious not detached, and which into the bargain sadly accepted what could not be altered. Those words are Thackeray's version, light and economical, of the *danza tedesca* in that late quartet of Beethoven, and of the quiet words towards the close of the latest play of Shakespeare:

> *Miranda*: O wonder!
> How many goodly creatures are there here!
> How beauteous mankind is! O brave new world
> That has such people in't.
> *Prospero*: 'Tis new to thee.

Young people may remember the thrown potato in *Esmond*—I have quite forgotten it myself: and then more potatoes are thrown in Dickens, and more still in the films of Laurel and Hardy. But where else do you get Thackeray's tone of sadness, earthly yet tender as if otherworldly? It is sunnier than Newman's, and lighter than Tennyson's. Perhaps it is nearest to certain phases of Hamlet's. Thackeray shares with him his vivid indecisiveness, his rapidity and lightness of mind, his liking to hear his own voice. When Hamlet speaks prose, it is violent and swift as Thackeray's, and the tone of 'Alas, poor Yorick...' is nearer Thackeray's than Sterne's.

And so the 'cynic' and 'sentimentalist' commends himself to the rest of us by his honesty and humility: we cease to be angered, disgusted, sickened, in being sobered. But any views advanced by Thackeray the novelist are, as I have said, not of first importance; what matters is that the novels should show us human life as truthfully as possible. We may occupy ourselves trying to enlarge the truth by thinking, but a novel exists, as poetry does, to show us pictures. These, when the novelist and poet are good, are beyond the explanation of intellect, as life is, to which they hold up the mirror. But what is beyond the intellect is not necessarily beyond the man: he has his emotions and imagination to help him.

Thackeray's Personages
and His Friends

In my preface I said that critics had neglected Thackeray. That will do as a generalization, though it applies more completely to the non-academic critics than to the academic. An essay on *Vanity Fair* in Mr V. S. Pritchett's *In my Good Books* (1942) is all that I remember from the non-academic, whereas from university teachers we have had Mr John W. Dodds's *Thackeray: a Critical Portrait* (1941), Professor J. Y. T. Greig's *Thackeray: a Reconsideration* (1950), Mr Lambert Ennis's *Thackeray: the Sentimental Cynic* (1950)—which I have not read—and now Mr Gordon N. Ray's *The Buried Life: a Study of the Relation between Thackeray's Fiction and his Personal History* (1952). Of these books the three I have read concern themselves, much or wholly, with what the first of them called 'criticism with some biographical infiltration'.[1] They have all something to commend them: Mr Dodds is sound and well-balanced, Professor Greig is lively, Mr Ray cares for the art of the novel in general and has come to know more than anybody else about the people Thackeray knew well in actual life.

Mr Dodds's book was published in 1941 and its date may —as I see things—have proved its salvation. The soundness I admire in it may be due to the non-existence of Mr Ray's noble edition of the *Letters and Private Papers* of Thackeray, which followed in 1945–6. Those four volumes showed, more perfectly and fully than ever before, the extraordinarily subtle mind of Thackeray the letter-writer and diarist, matched with a pen nimble to catch the shimmer of the moment, a mind, moreover, of a novelist whose emotions were deeply engaged in several quarters. Dazzled by these volumes, as I see it, students have yielded to the temptation of explaining the faults nowadays commonly, and

[1] P. vii.

I think indolently, ascribed to Thackeray the novelist by referring them to Thackeray the man. The combination of criticism of the life with criticism of the novels appeals to us moderns very much. We are all psychologists these days, and it is not difficult, having hit on the faults of any writer, to account for them to our own satisfaction by reference to his life. The snag is surely obvious. Biographical truth, let alone psychological truth that is adequately whole, is hard to arrive at, especially for the dead, who survive only in records. But even if it were easy, there is nothing in the necessity of things to make it of primary use to the literary critic. Literature is the work of one man who designs it for others, indeed for strangers. Being planned to be shown widely, it is made mainly out of what he can readily share with the swarm of his fellows. Even the few writers who are free with their intimate thoughts edit those thoughts, consciously or unconsciously, in wording them for others. Even letters are works of art. Newman thought them to contain 'the true life of a man';[1] it may be so, but only after the serious reservations prompted by these words of Johnson:

It has been so long said as to be commonly believed that the true characters of men may be found in their letters, and that he who writes to his friend lays his heart open before him. But the truth is that such were simple friendships of the *Golden Age*, and are now the friendships only of children. Very few can boast of hearts which they dare lay open to themselves, and of which, by whatever accident exposed, they do not shun a distinct and continued view; and certainly what we hide from ourselves we do not shew to our friends.[2]

It is even true that conscious but unspoken thoughts are things edited. When spoken, they are coloured still further. And that this is no modern discovery there is useful confirmation in Matthew Arnold:

> Below the surface-stream, shallow and light,
> Of what we *say* we feel—below the stream,
> As light, of what we *think* we feel—there flows
> With noiseless current strong, obscure and deep,
> The central stream of what we feel indeed.[3]

[1] *Letters...of John Henry Newman*, ed. Anne Mozley, 1891, I, I.
[2] *Lives of the Poets*, III, 206f.
[3] *Poetical Works*, ed. C. B. Tinker and H. F. Lowry, 1950, p. 483.

When the person is a 'literary' man, editing is pursued cunningly as in a photographer's 'studio'. Thackeray himself said, apropos of a letter Newman contributed to a controversy—a letter which, he conceded, 'read[s] very honest'—that

It is very difficult for literary men to keep their honesty. We are actors more or less all of us[. W]e get to be public personages *malgré nous*. I stick at an invitation to dinner sometimes, knowing that the lady will keep it as an autograph.[1]

Which leads us to Mr Eliot's remark, all the more weighty coming at a time when there is much would-be expression of the psyche, that literature is a writer's way of escaping from himself:

The progress of an artist is a continual self-sacrifice, a continual extinction of personality.[2]

A complete escape is, of course, out of the question. Inevitably there is a relation between the written thing and its author's personal experience. There is *some* relation always. The question is what is related to what, and how strongly. And, as far as works in the highest ranks of literature go, the relationship as a rule is tenuous.

These things being so, it would seem a golden rule for critics calling in biographical criticism as a help to literary to call it in only as a last resort. By 'the highest ranks of literature' I mean to distinguish poems, plays and novels from 'prose of thinking', essays and letters. If literature existing as letters does not necessarily provide biographers with the truth about the man himself, much less so does literature existing as novels. Except for drama and epic, the novel kind offers us as little as any. Novels proffer themselves as wholly free of biographical context. If they were published anonymously, that would scarcely affect the conditions of our reading them. There is something badly wrong with a novel that requires its readers to know about particular actual lives as well as about general human life,

---

[1] *Letters*, III, 13.   [2] *Selected Essays*, 1932, p. 17.

18-2

and we should not charge a novel with that defect until in fairness we have given it every chance to prove that it is free. It is already clear that I do not find Thackeray's novels unsatisfactory—and for reasons, too, I hope, that are already clear. But if I saw them in need of explanation, I should not go for it to Thackeray's life until I had knocked at other doors.

Professor Greig, finding difficulties, has gone to the personal life. This is from the last page of his book:

...we cannot rank [Thackeray] among 'the greatest novelists'. Saintsbury is almost certainly right about them. They take hints from experience; they reproduce the quality of it; they re-fashion the details. They are masters of their experience. They shape it into something rich and strange. Thackeray could do the same— sometimes. He re-shaped his experience of the various models— two, three, it does not matter how many there were—that he used for Becky Sharp, so that the woman in the novel became a new creation, unhampered by the accidents of real life. But this he was incapable of doing when his relationship to the living original of a character in fiction was predominantly emotional. The principal witness in support of this charge is his mother. The effect she produced upon his fiction—direct when he chose to portray her as Helen Pendennis; indirect, though little less powerful, when he touched, even lightly, on the Mother-Child theme—was disastrous. Disastrous, too, in varying degrees, were his other obsessions with people—his wife, his mother-in-law, Jane Octavia Brookfield, William Brookfield (after the quarrel), and Sally Baxter.

The process of the reasoning is quite clear: (1) Professor Greig sees Thackeray as 'a novelist *manqué*'—that black phrase comes twice in his book; (2) he has found, then, his faults in the novels; and (3) in this age of psychologists, he flies to the life of Thackeray for his explanation. The novels are spoiled for him because he sees the author as failing to preserve the due aesthetic distance between his quotidian self, which survives in some form or other in his letters and in records, and the selves of his personages. He pictures him as vacillating bumpily between self-involved transcript of his experience as a man and transcript of the life he imagined for his novel.

In defending Thackeray I cannot appeal to Professor

Greig on the ground that I like the novels and would that he liked them as much. But two grounds exist outside personal taste—the grounds of the historical and the judicial —terms which explain themselves as I proceed.

2

We should expect Thackeray's novels to need some explaining since they survive out of the past. They are fixed things; they go on being reprinted as Thackeray left them— apart, of course, from the inevitable crop of accidental errors. Meanwhile they are suffering the fate inevitable for written things that survive: the connotations of their words are changing, and waves of new readers are arising who, without an effort, cannot accord the novelist the simple decency of trying to see his things as he made them and gave them to his first readers. There is evidence that what Professor Greig sees to-day as faults in the novels—leaving aside the question whether his values are the right ones—turn out, after the application of the historical imagination, to be the virtues of a hundred years ago. Professor Greig's historical imagination does exist—that is clear from subsidiary remarks scattered here and there over his book. But he applies it to Thackeray's life without extending its application to Thackeray's times, which are reflected in contemporary literature.

The fault he finds biggest is Thackeray's presentation of the character of Helen Pendennis. He quotes the following passage from the chapter concerned with the meeting of Helen and her son Arthur on the death of her husband:

> What passed between that lady and the boy is not of import. A veil should be thrown over those sacred emotions of love and grief. The maternal passion is a sacred mystery to me. What one sees symbolized in the Roman churches in the image of the Virgin Mother with a bosom bleeding with love, I think one may witness (and admire the Almighty bounty for) every day.[1]

Professor Greig calls the subject here treated 'the mother-child theme'. Improving his case for him, we can narrow

[1] Ch. II.

the name to the mother-son theme. On this particular example of Thackeray's dealing with that theme, his comment runs:

As a piece of emotive writing, this passage is not likely to find favour now, though it may have moved many of the readers it was meant for.

That it did please Thackeray's original readers, we have evidence to hand:

Thackeray's contemporaries...accepted [Helen Pendennis]— as they did his very similar portrait of Laura—at Thackeray's own valuation. The early reviewers of *Pendennis* were united in their admiration of both ladies. Thomas Hood sums up their response, when he inquires: "What can we do but simply bow down reverently before the goodness and sweetness of Helen Pendennis, and the wisdom and womanhood of Laura?"[1]

From this it follows that there is no need to explain the passage in Thackeray by reference to Thackeray himself. If anything calls for explanation, it is something as general as public opinion itself. That opinion, being public, was widely expressed by the writers of the time. I limit myself to three instances: (1) in one of the 'Yellowplush' Papers Thackeray pillories a play of Bulwer-Lytton, *The Sea Captain, or The Birthright* (1839), which, as it happens, contains this passage:

> Hark? she has blessed her son! I bid ye witness,
> Ye listening heavens—thou circumambient air:
> The ocean sighs it back—and with the murmur
> Rustle the happy leaves. All nature breathes
> Aloud—aloft—to the Great Parent's ear,
> The blessing of the mother on her child.[2]

(2) Aurora Leigh recounts a visit to Marian Erle and her (illegitimate) baby: they are standing over his cot:

> While we stood there dumb,—
> For oh, that it should take such innocence
> To prove just guilt, I thought, and stood there dumb;
> The light upon his eyelids pricked them wide,
> And, staring out at us with all their blue,

[1] Ray, *The Buried Life*, p. 56.
[2] *The Memoirs of...Yellow plush*, VIII ('Epistles to the Literati').

As half perplexed between the angelhood
He had been away to visit in his sleep,
And our most mortal presence,—gradually
He saw his mother's face, accepting it
In change for heaven itself, with such a smile
As might have well been learnt there,—never moved,
But smiled on, in a drowse of ecstasy,
So happy (half with her and half with heaven)
He could not have the trouble to be stirred,
But smiled and lay there. Like a rose, I said:
As red and still indeed as any rose,
That blows in all the silence of its leaves,
Content, in blowing, to fulfil its life.

She leaned above him (drinking him as wine)
In that extremity of love, 'twill pass
For agony or rapture, seeing that love
Includes the whole of nature, rounding it
To love...no more,—since more can never be
Than just love. Self-forgot, cast out of self,
And drowning in the transport of the sight,
Her whole pale passionate face, mouth, forehead, eyes,
One gaze, she stood! then, slowly as he smiled,
She smiled too, slowly, smiling unaware,
And drawing from his countenance to hers
A fainter red, as if she watched a flame
And stood in it a-glow.[1]

(3) Among the many who witness to the contemporary cult of the mother, the rebels are as useful for my purpose as the devotees. The arch-rebel seems to be Flaubert, who, in a letter of 11 January 1859 discussing the natures of man and woman, rises to this prophecy:

Le culte de la mère sera une des choses qui fera pouffer de rire les générations futures. Ainsi que notre respect pour l'amour. Cela ira dans le même sac aux ordures que la sensibilité et la nature d'il y a cent ans.[2]

These instances suggest that when Thackeray said of mothers things that a hundred years later we should not quite like to, he was unembarrassedly one of a crowd. And the evidence that he knew this is in 'The Overture' before

[1] E. B. Browning, *Aurora Leigh*, 1857, vi, 581 ff.
[2] *Œuvres Complètes, Correspondance*, Paris 1926–33, iv, 304.

The Newcomes, where he is fancying the critic at work on his story:

"...in what a contemptuous way", may Solomon go on to remark, "does this author speak of human nature! There is scarce one of these characters he represents but is a villain. The fox is a flatterer; the frog is an emblem of impotence and envy; the wolf in sheep's clothing, a bloodthirsty hypocrite, wearing the garb of innocence; the ass in the lion's skin, a quack trying to terrify, by assuming the appearance of a forest monarch (does the writer, writhing under merited castigation, mean to sneer at critics in this character? We laugh at the impertinent comparison); the ox, a stupid common-place—the only innocent being in the writer's (stolen) apologue is a fool,—the idiotic lamb, who does not know his own mother!" And then the critic, if in a virtuous mood, may indulge in some fine writing regarding the holy beauteousness of maternal affection.

For evidence, however, that in writing on this theme Thackeray carried his fellows with him we need not go beyond the passage from *Pendennis* Professor Greig singles out. That passage shows Thackeray sharing with Pope and Wordsworth a sense of the authority of his theme in the midst of the theme of Nature. The test of whether a piece of literature is Natural or not lies in that old saying *quod semper, quod ubique, quod ab omnibus*. Consciously or not, Thackeray appealed to two of these three criteria:

What one [everyone, *omnes*] sees symbolised...I think one [*omnes*] may witness...every day [*semper*].

Even the 'I' of 'I think' invokes the *omnes*: it is the 'I think' of one who is confident that, as Portia says,

> I think and the world thinks so too.

There was a further test for Nature which, in the opinion of Johnson, it was well for a writer to provide against. When he praised Gray's *Elegy*, part of his praise ran as follows:

The four stanzas beginning 'Yet even these bones' are to me original: I have never seen the notions in any other place; yet he that reads them here persuades himself that he has always felt them.[1]

To this test also Thackeray stood up well. As I have already shown, he plucks the secret from the very bosom of Nature

[1] *Lives of the Poets*, III, 441 f.

that a mother feels a sexual[1] jealousy towards the girl her son is in love with.

Thackeray, then, had strong reasons for believing that his idea would interest his readers. And from this it follows that what alone can call for explanation is the expression he gave his idea. Here, too, the principle pertaining to the expression of the Natural offers help. As I have said earlier the 'what oft was thought' was dull unless revived by an expression which seemed the best to date.[2] The first step towards best expression was different expression—whether that difference marked also a betterment was not for the expresser to say. But at least Thackeray fulfilled the condition of difference—he brought in, for expressing old matter, the new image drawn from the material images in Catholic churches. And even here he was not working without companions. 'Roman' imagery was popular in the writings of the time, people having now become more concerned with the Catholic Church than for a long time previously. Some of them were even concerned to link it with the theme under discussion. There is, for instance, Pompilia's speech in the *Ring and the Book* (1868–9), as tender as it is prolonged, and in particular these lines:

> Nobody did me one disservice more,
> Spoke coldly or looked strangely, broke the love
> I lay in the arms of, till my boy was born,
> Born all in love, with nought to spoil the bliss
> A whole long fortnight: in a life like mine
> A fortnight filled with bliss is long and much.
> All women are not mothers of a boy,
> Though they live twice the length of my whole life,
> And, as they fancy, happily all the same.
> There I lay, then, all my great fortnight long,
> As if it would continue, broaden out
> Happily more and more, and lead to heaven:
> Christmas before me,—was not that a chance?
> I never realized God's birth before—
> How he grew likest God in being born.
> This time I felt like Mary, had my babe
> Lying a little on my breast like hers....[3]

[1] In the nineteenth century this word carried a completer sense than it carries to-day.   [2] See above, p. 204.   [3] Lines 1677 ff.

There is one thing more. In the passage from *Pendennis* I am discussing, Thackeray twice used the word 'sacred'. I have already spoken at length of his philosophy and of the sanctity he found in the family affections; all that need be added here is that he would have achieved the interest of novelty only if he had not found it.

3

In the passage from *Pendennis* quoted on p. 277, Thackeray coupled grief with love. When we think of Helen Pendennis, we think of her death. The chapter in which she dies is a furnace of spirituality, but not necessarily because of abnormally excessive feelings private to Thackeray. Turning again to Victorian literature as a whole, we see funeral furnaces lit whenever authors can lay hands on the fuel. Ruskin said of the death of Little Nell that Dickens 'simply killed [her] for the market, as a butcher kills a lamb'.[1] Whether or not this is fair to Dickens, it at least tells us something about the market. To the condition of the market Henry Fitzmaurice Hallam also witnessed on the occasion of the death of Paul in *Dombey and Son*:

I am so hardened as to be unable to look on it in any light but pure 'business'[2]

—he has become hardened through his experience of contemporary literature. A superior part of the market is represented in the same letter of Hallam:

Everybody is pretending that the death of Paul Dombey is the most beautiful thing ever written. Milnes, Thackeray, and your Uncle [Henry Hallam?] own to tears.[3]

Almost all the magnificent best-sellers of the time have protracted death scenes in them, of which I need only mention *Festus*, *The Dream of Gerontius*, and *The Ring and the Book*. Is it not more reasonable to see Thackeray as of his time rather than to see him wrecking his novels with autobiographic excesses that are out of place in fiction?

[1] xxxiv, 275.
[2] Charles and Frances Brookfield, *Mrs Brookfield and her Circle*, 1905, I, 255.   [3] Ibid.

4

I do not say that the course I am taking to keep Thackeray's novels at a distance from his biography has altogether the support of Thackeray himself—or rather, to remember distinctions already drawn, the support of Thackeray the letter-writer and converser. It is partly because of encouragement from the letter-writer that Professor Greig has gone astray. In a letter to Arthur Hugh Clough, Thackeray wrote:

I have been going over some of the same ground (of youth) [as you treat of in *The Bothie*] in this present number of Pendennis.... When you come to London I hope you will come and see me. M[rs.] Pendennis is living with me (She is my mother) and I have a couple of little girls whom you shall hear read if you like.[1]

And there is this report in a letter of Charlotte Brontë:

...his mother who—(he says) is the original of Helen Pendennis.[2]

The letter to Clough is as near as Thackeray comes to identifying the actual and the fictional woman. In his article on Thackeray in the new *Chambers's Encyclopaedia*, Mr Ray has taken the identification as complete, and in *The Buried Life* he writes:

Thackeray intended Helen Pendennis to be a quite literal picture of Mrs. Carmichael-Smyth.[3]

This, surely, is to write like Mudge and Sears, who conclude their dictionary with an 'index of originals', achieving four pages of these equations.

I grant that Thackeray's novels probably existed in a stronger relationship to his personal life than those of certain other novelists: the relationship was no doubt stronger than that between Defoe's personal life and *Robinson Crusoe*. The question is how much stronger. We must not accept Thackeray's remarks on the subject without weighing them. And here I shift to my second ground, the judicial.

[1] *Letters*, II, 457.
[2] *The Brontës*, III, 244; letter of 7 June 1851.   [3] P. 49.

The statement to Clough comes in a letter. It was not a statement made in print for all to see. Its terms are relative between two people; they are extravagant because intended to undergo the limitations of practical experiment. Professor Greig, who lives a hundred years too late to make that experiment, takes these statements for truth; likewise Mr Ray. But the result of the experiment for Charlotte Brontë at least was negative. The sentence I began to quote above ends with this:

> ...came to see me the other day—I liked her better than I thought I should.

This amounts to saying that to know Helen Pendennis was no fit and fair preparation for knowing Mrs Carmichael-Smyth. Certainly, Mrs Carmichael-Smyth did not think so. This is from a letter Thackeray sent to a third person:

> You see by Jane Eyre's letter dont you why we can't be very great friends? We had a correspondence—a little one; and met, very eagerly on her part. But there's a fire and fury raging in that little woman a rage scorching her heart w[hich] doesn't suit me. She has had a story and a great grief that has gone badly with her. 'Tis better to have loved & lost than never to have loved at all.' I said the same thing before I read it in Tennyson. I'm well of that pain now though—only very weak after it requiring soothing & a Sister of Charity. [Mary Holmes, his correspondent, had just entered the Church of Rome.] It gives the keenest tortures of jealousy and disappointed yearning to my dearest old mother (who's as beautiful now as ever) that she can't be all in all to me, mother sister wife everything but it mayn't be—There's hardly a subject on w[hich] we don't differ. And she lives away at Paris with her husband a noble simple old gentleman who loves nothing but her in the world, and a jealousy after me tears & rends her. Eh! who is happy? When I was a boy at Larkbeare, I thought her an Angel & worshipped her. I see but a woman now, O so tender so loving so cruel. My daughter Anny says O how like Granny is to M[rs.] Pendennis Papa—and Granny is mighty angry that I should think no better of her than that.[1]

Mrs Carmichael-Smyth no doubt was not an unprejudiced judge of the case. But the weighty evidence of this letter among others suggests that Thackeray was master of his

[1] *Letters*, III, 12 f.

emotions, warm as all of them were for him always. He recoiled from Charlotte Brontë and her emotions. He recoiled from his mother and hers. He had enough of his own. Thinking of Charlotte Brontë, he said that a novelist should be calm, should not be in a passion with his characters. Thackeray is not in a passion with his passions.

That was also true, I think, of the life of his imagination. That life seems to have existed at a distance from his actual life. After finishing *Esmond* he made one or two references to the sad state of his life at the time it was being written, but suggested also that for all its autumn shadow it lay outside that life:

my book just out is as dreary and dull as if it were true.[1]

And while writing it, he had noted that

It occupies me to the exclusion of the 19th century pretty well.[2]

The process by which the nineteenth century was excluded from his imagination is suggested on many occasions in the letters: as here in one to his young daughters:

Well it's lucky you weren't with me for my gloominess is perfectly awful. I hope something is coming of it: and that I am biling up with something that is worth all this melancholy. What a dreadful stupid letter. I knew it would be, that is why I have not written these 3 or 4 days.

Give my love to my dearest Mother and have her to understand that this Blue Devil of whom I complain is only an artistic blue devil and that he comes always before I get to work: and that there is no other reason; and that it would be just as bad or nearly if you were here and I might be sulking in my own room waiting for the Inspiration and as black, mum, stupid and melancholy, as now when I am my dearest women's affectionate father all the same![3]

He fought, or bore, his blue devils till he found himself looking at a land of sunshine, the Fable-land playfully fancied at the close of *The Newcomes*. All his books could have begun with a version of the beginning of *The Pilgrim's Progress*:

As I walk'd through the Wilderness of this World, I lighted on a certain place, where was a Denn: And I laid me down in that place to sleep: And as I slept I dreamed a Dream....

[1] *Letters*, III, 100.   [2] Ibid. III, 15.   [3] Ibid. III, 57.

Thackeray wrote in a sort of hallucination. It was the same when his mind left the present for the past, a slipping on to another plane, of which there are several instances in the letters, and which provide some remarkable passages in the fiction—notably the account of the house of old Sir George Thrum in *The Ravenswing*, and this much shorter passage in *The Virginians*:

Hearken to Harry Warrington reading out his brother's letter! As we look at the slim characters on the yellow page, fondly kept and put aside, we can almost fancy him alive who wrote and who read it—and yet, lo! they are as if they never had been; their portraits faint images in frames of tarnished gold. Were they real once, or are they mere phantasms? Did they live and die once? Did they love each other as true brothers, and loyal gentlemen? Can we hear their voices in the past? Sure I know Harry's, and yonder he sits in the warm summer evening, and reads his young brother's simple story...[1]

When he wrote his novels, it seems that the personages existed at the further end of a telescope, and the farewell he says to them is like that of Prospero when the pageant fades—I have already quoted from 'De Finibus', which contains the reference to Captain Costigan:

Nothing shall convince me that I have not seen that man in the world of spirits.

It was as if his memory of all he had experienced threw up a golden vapour in which walked, with all the clarity and vigour of the drawings of Doyle, the personages of his fiction. This is how I see the matter, despite all the evidence to the contrary so well presented by Mr Ray.

The identifications of Helen Pendennis with his mother were made for and by people who, knowing Helen Pendennis, knew, or were about to know, Mrs Carmichael-Smyth. In that same 'Roundabout' paper, Thackeray was to tell them what identity between the two they were to find. Thackeray the essayist writing about Thackeray the novelist has left this statement:

I suppose authors invent their personages out of scraps, heel-taps, odds and ends of characters.[2]

[1] Ch. xii.   [2] *The Roundabout Papers*, 'De Finibus'.

He does not deny that the earthly links are firm, but he knows them to be nugatory in proportion to the complete personage. Such scraps were the source of his personages in actual life. And it is also worth noting that he discovered enough scraps to link his personages with actual people whom he had not known until later—after writing *Esmond* he gave the name Viscountess Castlewood to his new friend Mrs Baxter, and the name Beatrix to his new friend Sally Baxter.[1] Further, his debt to literature was as heavy as his debt to life. Perhaps even heavier. Mr Ray has found that the biography of a relation of Thackeray's by marriage has some resemblance to the career of Colonel Newcome. But Thackeray's account of his genesis is literary. No one can read *The Newcomes* without being reminded of Don Quixote and Sir Roger de Coverley. When a friend mentioned this to him, he 'started' with surprise:

'You have touched on the very truth', said he. 'I had been reading the Don's memoirs and the Sir Roger papers in the "Spectator" just before attacking that last task. I tried to make the Colonel a creation of my own, but I was conscious all the while that my beloved old heroes were blending in my mind.'[2]

If Thackeray started, however, it was because he had forgotten, for he makes explicit reference to Don Quixote in chapter VI of his novel, and to Sir Roger in chapter XIX.

I have taken some pains in the body of my book to show that a novelist using 'I' to represent the author cannot make it represent the man, try as he will. Not able to put himself directly into the novels, he cannot put in anybody else. Mr Ray calls his book *The Buried Life*. His title, it seems to me, is more accurate than he allows.

[1] *Letters*, III, 150, 151.
[2] J. G. Wilson, *Thackeray in the United States 1852–3, 1855–6*, 1904, II, 92.

Thackeray and Two Later Novelists

One of the critics I should like to persuade to a more just view of Thackeray is Dr Leavis, and I propose to look at certain things broached in a recent book of his. At least he can be commended for trying to see Thackeray whole, for facing him squarely. And yet how painful the encounter for Thackeray! The paragraph accorded him in *The Great Tradition* is a paragraph of dismissal. Dr Leavis drops a slab of concrete on the novels:

whereas Dickens's greatness has been confirmed by time, it is quite otherwise with his rival.... It seems to me that Thackeray's place is fairly enough indicated, even if his peculiar quality isn't precisely defined, by inverting a phrase I found the other day on an examination-paper: 'Trollope is a lesser Thackeray'.[1] Thackeray is a greater Trollope; that is, he has (apart from some social history) nothing to offer the reader whose demand goes beyond the 'creation of characters' and so on. His attitudes, and the essential substance of interest, are so limited that (though, of course, he provides incident and plot) for the reader it is merely a matter of going on and on; nothing has been done by the close to justify the space taken—except, of course, that time has been killed (which seems to be all that even some academic critics demand of a novel). It will be fair enough to Thackeray if *Vanity Fair* is kept current as, in a minor way, a classic: the conventional estimate that puts him among the great won't stand the touch of criticism.[2]

What I think the misconceptions and misjudgments of this paragraph I have already, I think, made clear enough. Here I shall plead for Thackeray by showing how much was

[1] The examinee was quoting Chesterton's *Victorian Age in Literature*. The comparison of Trollope with Thackeray was inevitable from the start: 'Trollope is a water-colour follower of Thackeray' wrote Charles Knight (*Passages in a Working Life*, 1864–5, III, 186). The comparison is evidence of a tradition, and to me at least of a 'great' tradition. It would be interesting to know if Proust had read Thackeray. I can find no evidence of his having had that pleasure. We know of his debt to George Eliot, which to some extent was a debt to Thackeray.

[2] Op. cit. p. 21.

owed him by two of the three novelists who, with Jane Austen, form the great tradition according to Dr Leavis.

Literary tradition is a process, examined usually at points on the length and breadth of its career, by which a younger writer learns from the writings of an elder the sort of things people do learn from admired or revered associates—what to pay attention to, how to value and interpret this and that, ideas and words. All writers, great or small, receive, and the great ones and some of the smaller, transmit. For me Thackeray is a great writer. What odd positions Dr Leavis forces one into! Thackeray laughed at critics like R. H. Horne who seemed to think that there was something original in asserting that 'Shakespeare is a great poet'.[1] But, confronted with Dr Leavis's criticism, a criticism much given to wide-scale rejection or down-grading, we must make a place once again for such truths. Since the seventeenth century 'Milton is a great writer' has had the leaden obviousness of a truism. Now once again, after the treatment he has received from Dr Leavis, it sparkles as a truth. Once again, also, it is seemly to say that Thackeray is a great novelist. Saying it, one feels like a schoolboy claiming greatness for a mountain sighing through all its pines, for a vast, many-twinkling sea.

2

Thackeray, like any great writer, receives and transmits. He receives from—to name his more immediate and most important English benefactors—Pope, Fielding, Sterne, Scott, Lamb, Carlyle. He transmits—to confine ourselves to the stars in Dr Leavis's impoverished empyrean—George Eliot and Henry James.

Something is made by Dr Leavis of George Eliot's debt, over Thackeray's head, to Jane Austen:

Positively, there is continuity from Jane Austen. It is not for nothing that George Eliot admired her work profoundly, and wrote one of the earliest appreciations of it to be published.[2]

[1] Review of Horne's *A New Spirit of the Age* in the *Morning Chronicle*, 2 April 1844.   [2] P. 9.

Dr Leavis has no footnote to this statement so that we cannot know to what he refers. If, as I guess, it is to the essay
on 'The Lady Novelists', which appeared in the *Westminster Review*, that essay is by George Henry Lewes—it is
wrongly ascribed in the collection *Essays and Reviews of
George Eliot* (Boston, 1887). Whether George Eliot already
admired Jane Austen at that date, we cannot, I think, be
certain. But however that may be, she greatly admired
Thackeray. Continuity, which is indicated by such admiration, is secure from him to her. It is true that in a
letter to her publisher written about her first work she dis-
claimed conscious discipleship. But only to withdraw the
disclaimer in conceding that, like herself, Thackeray valued
truthfulness towards his material, the right and privilege of
a novelist to see it, as it were, with the eyes of a man whom
ordinary people would respect, and to see a vast amount of
it. 'I can hardly believe', she wrote on 11 June 1857,

I can hardly believe that the public will regard my pictures [those
of *Scenes from Clerical Life*] as exceptionally coarse. But in any case
there are too many prolific writers who devote themselves to the
production of pleasing pictures, to the exclusion of all disagreeable
truths, for me to add to their number. In this respect, at least,
I may have some resemblance to Thackeray, though I am not
conscious of being in any way a disciple of his, unless it constitutes
discipleship to think him, as I suppose the majority of people with
any intellect do, on the whole the most powerful of living novelists.[1]

And, since this is George Eliot, she may have intended to
include among 'living novelists' Continental ones. Nor is
her tribute less powerful because by 1857 one of Thackeray's
strongest English rivals was dead—Charlotte Brontë, for
whom he was master and hero—and two, if she had in mind
Emily, whose single novel was not yet much known.

The plane which George Eliot occupied so securely as a
novelist had been won back for contemporary novelists
mainly by Thackeray. It was mainly because of him that
when George Henry Lewes enunciated the qualifications
she would need for writing fiction he included among them
the possession of a philosophy, a qualification he could not

[1] *George Eliot's Life*, ed. J. W. Cross, ch. VII.

but allow she was well equipped with. And such was her debt to Thackeray on this score that the proportions in which she mixes the philosophic with the purely narrative are similar to his. Nor is there in her early writings a great difference between the colours of their philosophies. The difference that strikes us is mainly one of tone and imagery —Thackeray is light and conversational and draws his imagery from familiar sources, George Eliot has a severer sound and gait, and her images are wrested from quarters more difficult of access. This is the opening of Chapter II of *Amos Barton*:

It was happy for the Rev. Amos Barton that he did not, like us, overhear the conversation recorded in the last chapter. Indeed, what mortal is there of us, who would find his satisfaction enhanced by an opportunity of comparing the picture he presents to himself of his own doings, with the picture they make on the mental retina of his neighbours? We are poor plants buoyed up by the air-vessels of our own conceit: alas for us, if we get a few pinches that empty us of that windy self-subsistence! The very capacity for good would go out of us. For, tell the most impassioned orator, suddenly, that his wig is awry, or his shirt-lap hanging out, and that he is tickling people by the oddity of his person, instead of thrilling them by the energy of his periods, and you would infallibly dry up the spring of his eloquence. That is a deep and wide saying, that no miracle can be wrought without faith—without the worker's faith in himself, as well as the recipient's faith in him. And the greater part of the worker's faith in himself is made up of the faith that others believe in him.

Let me be persuaded that my neighbour Jenkins considers me a blockhead, and I shall never shine in conversation with him any more. Let me discover that the lovely Phoebe thinks my squint intolerable, and I shall never be able to fix her blandly with my disengaged eye again.

Thank heaven, then, that a little illusion is left to us, to enable us to be useful and agreeable—that we don't know exactly what our friends think of us—that the world is not made of looking-glass, to show us just the figure we are making, and just what is going on behind our backs! By the help of dear friendly illusion, we are able to dream that we are charming—and our faces wear a becoming air of self-possession; we are able to dream that other men admire our talents—and our benignity is undisturbed; we are able to dream that we are doing much good—and we do little.

The Thackerayan philosophy exists substantially also in her second book—I have not examined her later ones from this point of view. Witness the opening chapter of Book II of *Adam Bede*:

"This Rector of Broxton is little better than a pagan!" I hear one of my readers exclaim. "How much more edifying it would have been if you had made him give Arthur some truly spiritual advice. You might have put into his mouth the most beautiful things—quite as good as reading a sermon."

Certainly I could, if I held it the highest vocation of the novelist to represent things as they never have been and never will be. Then, of course, I might refashion life and character entirely after my own liking; I might select the most unexceptionable type of clergyman, and put my own admirable opinions into his mouth on all occasions. But it happens, on the contrary, that my strongest effort is to avoid any such arbitrary picture, and to give a faithful account of men and things as they have mirrored themselves in my mind. The mirror is doubtless defective; the outlines will sometimes be disturbed, the reflection faint and confused; but I feel as much bound to tell you as precisely as I can what that reflection is, as if I were in the witness-box narrating my experience on oath.

Sixty years ago—it is a long time, so no wonder things have changed—all clergymen were not zealous; indeed there is reason to believe that the number of zealous clergymen was small, and it is probable that if one among the small minority had owned the livings of Broxton and Hayslope in the year 1799, you would have liked him no better than you like Mr Irwine. Ten to one, you would have thought him a tasteless, indiscreet, methodistical man. It is so very rarely that facts hit that nice medium required by our own enlightened opinions and refined taste! Perhaps you will say, "Do improve the facts a little, then; make them more accordant with those correct views which it is our privilege to possess. The world is not just what we like; do touch it up with a tasteful pencil, and make believe it is not quite such a mixed entangled affair. Let all people who hold unexceptionable opinions act unexceptionably. Let your most faulty characters always be on the wrong side, and your virtuous ones on the right. Then we shall see at a glance whom we are to condemn, and whom we are to approve. Then we shall be able to admire, without the slightest disturbance of our pre-possessions: we shall hate and despise with that true ruminant relish which belongs to undoubting confidence."

But, my good friend, what will you do then with your fellow-parishioner who opposes your husband in the vestry?—with your newly-appointed vicar, whose style of preaching you find painfully below that of his regretted predecessor?—with the honest servant who worries your soul with her one failing?—with your neighbour, Mrs Green, who was really kind to you in your last illness, but has said several ill-natured things about you since your convalescence?—nay, with your excellent husband himself, who has other irritating habits besides that of not wiping his shoes? These fellow-mortals, every one, must be accepted as they are: you can neither straighten their noses, nor brighten their wit, nor rectify their dispositions; and it is these people—amongst whom your life is passed—that it is needful you should tolerate, pity, and love: it is these more or less ugly, stupid, inconsistent people, whose movements of goodness you should be able to admire—for whom you should cherish all possible hopes, all possible patience. And I would not, even if I had the choice, be the clever novelist who could create a world so much better than this, in which we get up in the morning to do our daily work, that you would be likely to turn a harder, colder eye on the dusty streets and the common green fields—on the real breathing men and women, who can be chilled by your indifference or injured by your prejudice; who can be cheered and helped onward by your fellow-feeling, your forbearance, your outspoken, brave justice.

So I am content to tell my simple story, without trying to make things seem better than they were; dreading nothing, indeed, but falsity, which, in spite of one's best efforts, there is reason to dread. Falsehood is so easy, truth so difficult. The pencil is conscious of a delightful facility in drawing a griffin—the longer the claws, and the larger the wings, the better; but that marvellous facility which we mistook for genius is apt to forsake us when we want to draw a real unexaggerated lion. Examine your words well, and you will find that even when you have no motive to be false, it is a very hard thing to say the exact truth, even about your own immediate feelings—much harder than to say something fine about them which is *not* the exact truth.

And so this proceeds for several more pages. It is remarkable that so original a thinker should have learned so much from one to whom some of his contemporaries denied the coveted praise of being a thinker at all. Though George Eliot was gifted to make more discoveries than Thackeray in the human stuff, he is her teacher as much as anyone, and his influence stretches over the whole of the human material— from the earliest years of life to the close when, as death approaches their personages, both novelists invoke the tenderness of the Divine Pity.[1] In general, both hold the same things sacred. And again, both are fascinated by the past, though they see it differently—Thackeray as a spectacle, an object blurred and mellowed by the mists of manhood, George Eliot as a field from which something is to be expected, where seeds are sown unwittingly, as well as a field which through our later experience we see as golden.

A further debt exists. Thackeray, as I have shown, was much concerned with the outward and visible signs of character and personality. George Eliot, too, was much concerned with them, but concerned more than he with thoughts that are inner and invisible. To turn to the methods of Elizabethan drama for comparison. Shakespeare will make a personage say

> My way of life
> Is fallen into the sere, the yellow leaf.

He has at his disposal speech as wide as speech can ever be, stretching from that, say, of the odes of Keats to that of the stories of Defoe. He can say anything in speech, leaving it to his actors to repeat as much as they can of the same things in face, posture, clothes, tone of voice. In a novel, speech throughout the Shakespearean gamut is possible on the ground that the novel is what you make it. But it was not possible in the sort of novel written by Thackeray or George Eliot. Thackeray limited himself mainly to the means open to the historian. Speech therefore he could use only as it lies at the Defoe end of the scale, that being the only end available to most of us in ordinary life. To reinforce this speech he could also draw on the bodily signs, which Shakespeare left to his actors—mainly, at least: occasionally a personage will

---

[1] Cf. *Pendennis*, ch. LVII (Helen is dying): 'And once more, oh, once more, the young man fell down at his mother's sacred knees, and sobbed out the prayer which the Divine Tenderness uttered for us, and which has been echoed for twenty ages since by millions of sinful and humbled men'; and *The Newcomes*, ch. LXXIX: 'the old man [Colonel Newcome], whose heart was well nigh as tender and as innocent [as that of Clive's baby son]; and whose day was approaching, when he should be drawn to the bosom of the Eternal Pity'; and *Adam Bede*, ch. XLV, where Dinah is comforting Hetty in prison: 'it was the Divine pity that was beating in [Dinah's] heart'.

describe the bodily signs in another. These signs he discovered in plenty, and read much significance into them. George Eliot, on the other hand, snatched more of Shakespeare's advantages by choosing to be the omniscient sort of novelist. But, as far as speech went, she did not use the whole Shakespearean scale because she chose to limit the speech of her personages—unless it was dialect speech, from which 'poetry' had not been dispelled by social inhibition—to something near that of ordinary people. It is even so in *Romola*, which is a novel set in what we are free to think of as more poetical times not far from Shakespeare's. But though she could not give her personages speech like 'My way of life. . .', she could, being omniscient, give them this part of the Shakespearean scale as the unspoken wording for their thought, writing—to adapt the given instance—something like this:

It came on him that his way of life was fallen as it were into the yellow leaf. "Yes", he said to himself, "life's but a walking shadow...."

The poetry of her personages is expressed in an account of the thinking, not of the speaking. And having no actors to match such thinking in the appearances of the body, she adds or melts into the thinking an account of those appearances. From Thackeray she could learn little about the interior monologue, because his personages, apart from Mr Batchelor, seldom engage in it. But she could learn from him how thought affects the body. On occasion she could even take over weighty details intact, benefiting by the discoveries of her master. I have already called attention to one such detail:[1] the turning, long neck of Ethel in *The Newcomes*[2] and that other neck in *Middlemarch*,[3] Rosamond's, lofty and consciously revolved.[4]

For George Eliot, it is clear, the reading of Thackeray was anything rather than a mere 'going on and on'.

[1] *Criticism and the Nineteenth Century*, 1951, p. 32.
[2] Ch. xxv.   [3] E.g. in ch. LVIII.
[4] Contemporary fashions of women's dresses, which exposed the neck and part of the shoulders, facilitated this means of expression. But the neck is an organ of character, whether clothed or bare—witness 'Martinus Scriblerus', who in the *Memoirs*, ch. x, 'charg'd all Husbands to take notice of the Posture of the Head of such as are courted to Matrimony, as that upon which their future happiness did much depend'.

3

What Henry James derived from Thackeray is partly distinct and partly indistinguishable from what he derived from George Eliot.

For the young James, Thackeray's giant figure stood well in the foreground. In a review written in 1864, when he was twenty, he spoke of *Vanity Fair* as a novel read not once but, it is suggested, habitually. Reviewing a volume of Thackerayiana some ten years later, and finding it a bad piece of workmanship, he drew the obvious comparison:

It really strikes us as sad that this is the best that English literature should be able to do for a genius who did so much for it.[1]

Even for James in middle age admiration is complete. Speaking, as late as 1884, of 'a short time ago', when

the English novel...had no air of having a theory, a conviction, a consciousness of itself behind it—of being the expression of an artistic faith, the result of choice and comparison,

he did not leave the point without adding:

I do not say it was necessarily the worse for that; it would take much more courage than I possess to intimate that the form of the novel, as Dickens and Thackeray (for instance) saw it, had any taint of incompleteness.[2]

I have collected as many references to Thackeray as I could find in the writings of James. They are always those of an admirer, and some of the later ones alone make reservations. A partial defection was inevitable in those later years when James came to write novels of a cathedral-like objectivity and shapeliness. In the Preface to *The Tragic Muse* defection on the grounds of form went as far as it ever did:

A picture without composition slights its most precious chance for beauty, and is moreover not composed at all unless the painter knows *how* that principle of health and safety, working as an

[1] *The Nation*, New York, 9 Feb. 1875, p. 376.
[2] 'The Art of Fiction', in *Longman's Magazine*, IV, May–Oct. 1884, p. 502.

absolutely premeditated art, has prevailed. There may in its absence be life, incontestably, as "The Newcomes" has life, as "Les Trois Mousquetaires", as Tolstoi's "Peace and War" have it; but what do such large loose baggy monsters, with their queer elements of the accidental and the arbitrary, artistically *mean*?[1]

Nevertheless his debts early and late are considerable, and stand on all the scores possible.

First, the score of the material. That there is much in common between the 'worlds' of Thackeray and Henry James is attested by a remark James made to William Dean Howells in answer to a criticism of his *Hawthorne* (1879). After discussing the question of provinciality, he proceeds as follows:

I sympathise even less with your protest against the idea that it takes an old civilization to set a novelist in motion—a proposition that seems to me so true as to be a truism. It is on manners, customs, usages, habits, forms, upon all these things matured and established, that a novelist lives—they are the very stuff his work is made of; and in saying that in the absence of those 'dreary and worn-out paraphernalia' which I enumerate as being wanting in American society, 'we have simply the whole of human life left', you beg (to my sense) the question. I should say we had just so much less of it as these same 'paraphernalia' represent, and I think they represent an enormous quantity of it. I shall feel refuted only when we have produced (setting the present high company—yourself and me—for obvious reasons apart) a gentleman who strikes me as a novelist—as belonging to the company of Balzac and Thackeray. Of course, in the absence of this godsend, it is but a harmless amusement that we should reason about it, and maintain that if right were right he should already be here. I will freely admit that such a genius will get on *only* by agreeing with your view of the case—to do something great he must feel as you feel about it. But then I doubt whether such a genius—a man of the faculty of Balzac and Thackeray—*could* agree with you! When he does I will lie flat on my stomach and do him homage—in the very centre of the contributor's club, or on the threshold of the magazine, or in any public place you may appoint![2]

In the Thackerayan world of 'manners, customs, usages, habits, forms' James was permanently a denizen, both as

[1] Op. cit., New York ed., 1909, I, x.
[2] F. O. Matthiessen, *The James Family*, New York, 1947, p. 502. The date of the letter is June 1879.

man and writer. He lived in it avidly, and like Thackeray was much struck with the part played in it by money. Included in the general debt are several smaller ones, chief among which is the 'international situation' of which in *The Virginians* Thackeray had been a sensitive and thorough explorer. A particular debt on this score of matter well attests the individuality of the debtor—James's way of contenting himself with a single coin since he can raise a good round sum from it. In 'The Bedford-Row Conspiracy' (the plot of which Thackeray tells us he borrowed from the French of one Charles de Bernard) a Liberal M.P. takes the highest moral grounds and advises a novice against accepting a sinecure arranged for him by his Tory uncle—whereupon the M.P. gets it for his own nephew. The incident has no more and no less prominence in Thackeray than a thousand others, but in James it forms the core of a *nouvelle*: in 'The Lesson of the Master' the young aspirant is a writer, and on the noble advice of the Master puts his art before his prospective happiness in marriage—only to see the Master marry the girl himself.[1]

Still on this score of matter, I cannot but think that James learned from Thackeray—as also from Pope's *Rape of the Lock*—how piquant a subject lies in the woman who does not defeat or outrage our moral judgment—moral in the widest sense—so much as baffle it with the aesthetic fascination of the changes on the surface. Becky Sharp and Blanche Amory may well have helped James to make his Daisy Miller and Verena Tarrant. And, like Thackeray again, James knows the ill effects ascribable to good people who are not well enough versed in the psychology of the less good: the virtues of Rachel Castlewood breed vices in her son, and it is partly because Isobel Archer is so good a person that she marries the wrong man.

---

[1] Perhaps James was indirectly indebted to Thackeray for the theme of 'Sir Dominick Ferrand'. When at his death Thackeray's furniture was sold, a broker bought for a few shillings an old bureau, and found an overlooked bundle of his letters in one of the drawers (see Thackeray's *Letters*, IV, 301 f.). In James's story the letters in the desk compromise an eminent politician.

Then there is the heavy debt for the conception of the frustrated middle-aged male personage. Mr Lionel Trilling has recently noted a strand in nineteenth- and twentieth-century literature which he has called that of 'the defeated hero'.[1] This sort of personage he sees emerging in the Arthur Clennam of *Little Dorrit*, the parts of which novel Dickens began to publish in 1855. Perhaps *Pendennis* (1848–50) and *Esmond* (1852) helped towards the forming of the type, but in any event it exists with an Athene-like completeness in the Mr Batchelor of *Lovel the Widower* (1860). That personage is the Captain Touchit (Jamesian name!) of *The Wolves and the Lamb* (1854), but in that discarded drama there is no hint of the Mr Batchelor to be, who is as complete an instance of the type as the Prufrock of Mr Eliot: parted by eighty years, the two almost speak the same language. Here is Mr Batchelor ruminating over his inaction at a crisis of the story—he has witnessed through the window the amatory attack made on Elizabeth, the governess whom all the men are in love with:

I was just *going* to run in,—and I didn't. I was just going to rush to Bessy's side to clasp her (I have no doubt) to my heart: to beard the whiskered champion who was before her, and perhaps say, "Cheer thee—cheer thee, my persecuted maiden, my beauteous love—my Rebecca! Come on, Sir Brian de Bois Guilbert, thou dastard Templar! It is I, Sir Wilfred of Ivanhoe." (By the way, though the fellow was not a *Templar*, he was a *Lincoln's Inn man*, having passed twice through the Insolvent Court there with infinite discredit.) But I made no heroic speeches. There was no need for Rebecca to jump out of window and risk her lovely neck. How could she, in fact, the French window being flush with the ground floor? And I give you my honour, just as I was crying my war-cry, couching my lance, and rushing *à la recousse* upon Sir Baker, a sudden thought made me drop my (figurative) point: a sudden idea made me rein in my galloping (metaphorical) steed, and spare Baker for that time.

Suppose I had gone in? But for that sudden precaution, there might have been a Mrs. Batchelor. I might have been a bullied father of ten children. (Elizabeth has a fine high temper of her own.)[2]

[1] 'A Portrait of Western Man', *The Listener*, 11 June 1953.
[2] Ch. v.

In James's fiction the middle-aged and frustrated and much-thinking are recurrent figures—witness 'The Diary of a Man of Fifty', 'The Middle Years', and *The Ambassadors.* Mr Batchelor forecasts in particular the prying hero of *The Sacred Fount*—one chapter in *Lovel the Widower* is entitled 'In which I play the spy'.

The quotations I have made from *Lovel the Widower* here and in the body of my book, and from Thackeray's authorial commentary, are evidence that he had something to teach James, and others earlier and later, about the nature of the stream of consciousness, as also—to anticipate my comments on methods of writing—how the stream of consciousness might be put into written words.

Midway between the matter of a novel and its form we can conveniently place the felt presence of the author. James's presence is not unlike Thackeray's. In his earlier novels there is even something of the Thackerayan commentary, but to the end persists that indulgent, fondling tone in the recurrent epithets James took over from his master—'little', 'queer', 'dear', 'pretty'—even in verbs like 'wail', 'quaver', 'piped', which, while describing as if objectively the tone of spoken words, also suggest the author's attitude towards the speaker. Even in the latest work James, like Thackeray, will refer to a personage as 'our hero', an expression which is unthinkable, say, in a later novel of Virginia Woolf, who had no wish to draw on many sources of power available to her predecessors. Such expressions, when used by Thackeray and James, *are* sources of power. For them they are no mere synonyms for a hero's name but rather nodal points of commentary—and, despite the restrictions James placed on Thackeray, nodal points of irony.[1] Taking over much of Thackeray's field of interest,

[1] During the later years when James was pulling away from Thackeray's influence he contrasted the satire of Thackeray with that of H. G. Wells, whom he was praising with characteristic generosity:

we are starving, in our enormities and fatuities, for a sacred satirist (the satirist *with* irony—as poor dear old Thackeray was the satirist without it), and you come, admirably to save us...You have written the first closely and intimately, the first intelligently and consistently ironic and satiric novel. In everything else there has always been the

James took over much of his attitude to it, and was indebted to him for tone, angle, vivacity, high spirits, satirical laughter, and the admired 'humour...so complex and refined'.[1] More than was possible for a writer of George Eliot's heavier cast of genius, James achieved something of the light, lithe, subtle, poetic quality of Thackeray's commentary. When it comes to form, James owes nothing to Thackeray for the structure of his later novels—we cannot imagine Thackeray fore-thinking the shape of *The Ambassadors* any more than of imitating the shape of *Tom Jones*, which he admired so heartily, but there are one or two debts of a smaller but vital kind. The shape of the *nouvelle* 'Three Meetings' seems to remember that of the *nouvelle* 'Dennis Haggarty's Wife'. And the fully-expanded image which gives the title to *The Golden Bowl* and which, as it expands, helps to organize the mental and psychological progress of its personages must have come from *The Virginians*: I quote the long climax of the scene in question not only to illustrate the immediate point, but also to show the general similarities between Thackeray and the earlier and middle Henry James. There is a psychological crisis in the family: Madam Esmond has authorized Mr Ward, the boys' tutor, to beat the elder of them in return for the last of a series of insubordinations. Passions banked up behind the haughty graces are breaking them down:

In the midst of his mother's harangue, in spite of it, perhaps, George Esmond felt he had been wrong. "There can be but one

---

sentimental or conventional interference, the interference of which Thackeray is full.

(*Letters*, ed. Percy Lubbock, 1920, II, 39 f.) The best instance of Thackeray's irony in the use of 'our hero' comes in *Pendennis*:

On this the two ladies went through the osculatory ceremony which they were in the habit of performing, and Mrs. Pendennis got a great secret comfort from the little quarrel—for Laura's confession seemed to say, "That girl [Blanche Amory] can never be a wife for Pen, for she is light-minded and heartless, and quite unworthy of our noble hero. He will be sure to find out her unworthiness for his own part, and then he will be saved from this flighty creature, and awake out of his delusion."

(Ch. xxv.)

[1] The review of *Thackerayana*, in *The Nation*, New York, 9 Feb. 1875, p. 376.

command in the house, and you must be mistress—I know who said those words before you," George said, slowly, and looking very white—"and—and I know, mother, that I have acted wrongly to Mr. Ward."

"He owns it! He asks pardon!" cries Harry. "That's right, George! That's enough: isn't it?"

"No, it is *not* enough!" cried the little woman. "The disobedient boy must pay the penalty of his disobedience. When I was head-strong, as I sometimes was as a child before my spirit was changed and humbled, my mamma punished me, and I submitted. So must George. I desire you will do your duty, Mr. Ward."

"Stop, mother!—you don't quite know what you are doing," George said, exceedingly agitated.

"I know that he who spares the rod spoils the child, ungrateful boy!" says Madam Esmond, with more references of the same nature, which George heard, looking very pale and desperate.

Upon the mantel-piece, under the Colonel's [Henry Esmond's] portrait, stood a china-cup, by which the widow set great store, as her father had always been accustomed to drink from it. George suddenly took it, and a strange smile passed over his pale face.

"Stay one minute. Don't go away yet," he cried to his mother, who was leaving the room. "You—you are very fond of this cup, mother?"—and Harry looked at him, wondering. "If I broke it, it could never be mended, could it? All the tinkers' rivets would not make it a whole cup again. My dear old grandpapa's cup! I have been wrong. Mr. Ward, I ask pardon. I will try and amend."

The widow looked at her son indignantly, almost scornfully. "I thought," she said, "I thought an Esmond had been more of a man than to be afraid, and"—here she gave a little scream as Harry uttered an exclamation, and dashed forward with his hands stretched out towards his brother.

George, after looking at the cup, raised it, opened his hand, and let it fall on the marble slab below him. Harry had tried in vain to catch it.

"It is too late, Hal," George said. "You will never mend that again—never. Now, mother, I am ready, as it is your wish. Will you come and see whether I am afraid? Mr. Ward, I am your servant. Your servant? Your slave! And the next time I meet Mr. Washington, Madam, I will thank him for the advice which he gave you."

"I say, do your duty, sir!" cried Mrs. Esmond, stamping her little foot. And George, making a low bow to Mr. Ward, begged him to go first out of the room to the study.

"Stop! For God's sake, mother, stop!" cried poor Hal. But

passion was boiling in the little woman's heart, and she would not hear the boy's petition. "You only abet him, sir!" she cried. "If I had to do it myself, it should be done!" And Harry, with sadness and wrath in his countenance, left the room by the door through which Mr. Ward and his brother had just issued.

The widow sank down on a great chair near it, and sat awhile vacantly looking at the fragments of the broken cup. Then she inclined her head towards the door—one of half-a-dozen of carved mahogany which the Colonel had brought from Europe. For a while there was silence: then a loud outcry, which made the poor mother start.

In another minute Mr. Ward came out bleeding, from a great wound on his head, and behind him Harry, with flaring eyes, and brandishing a little couteau-de-chasse of his grandfather, which hung with others of the Colonel's weapons, on the Library wall.

"I don't care. I did it," says Harry. "I couldn't see this fellow strike my brother; and, as he lifted his hand, I flung the great ruler at him. I couldn't help it. I won't bear it; and, if one lifts a hand to me or my brother, I'll have his life," shouts Harry, brandishing the hanger.

The widow gave a great gasp and a sigh as she looked at the young champion and his victim. She must have suffered terribly during the few minutes of the boys' absence; and the stripes which she imagined had been inflicted on the elder had smitten her own heart. She longed to take both boys to it. She was not angry now. Very likely she was delighted with the thought of the younger's prowess and generosity. "You are a very naughty disobedient child," she said, in an exceedingly peaceable voice. "My poor Mr. Ward! What a rebel, to strike you! Papa's great ebony ruler, was it? Lay down that hanger, child. 'Twas General Webb gave it to my papa after the siege of Lille. Let me bathe your wound, my good Mr. Ward, and thank Heaven it was no worse. Mountain! Go fetch me some court-plaster out of the middle drawer in the japan cabinet. Here comes George. Put on your coat and waistcoat, child! You were going to take your punishment, sir, and that is sufficient. Ask pardon, Harry, of good Mr. Ward, for your wicked rebellious spirit,—I do, with all my heart, I am sure. And guard against your passionate nature, child—and pray to be forgiven. My son, O, my son!" Here, with a burst of tears which she could no longer control, the little woman threw herself on the neck of her eldest born; whilst Harry, laying the hanger down, went up very feebly to Mr. Ward, and said, "Indeed, I ask your pardon, sir. I couldn't help it; on my honour I couldn't; nor bear to see my brother struck."

The widow was scared, as after her embrace she looked up at George's pale face. In reply to her eager caresses, he coldly kissed her on the forehead, and separated from her. "You meant for the best, mother," he said, "and I was in the wrong. But the cup is broken; and all the king's horses and all the king's men cannot mend it. There—Put the fair side outwards on the mantelpiece, and the wound will not show."

Again Madam Esmond looked at the lad, as he placed the fragments of the poor cup on the ledge where it had always been used to stand. Her power over him was gone. He had dominated her. She was not sorry for the defeat; for women like not only to conquer, but to be conquered; and from that day the young gentleman was master at Castlewood. His mother admired him as he went up to Harry, graciously and condescendingly gave Hal his hand, and said, "Thank you, brother!" as if he were a prince, and Harry a general who had helped him in a great battle.[1]

There is a debt, finally, on the score of manner of proceeding. From Thackeray James learned a particular means towards the establishment of continuity, a means which I have noted above[2] the device of disclosing the whole of an object by stages, of enriching a thing at the same time as you make a return to it.

In the *nouvelles* the debt for manner of proceeding is particularly heavy. James himself might have been the author of the following:

One winter he took his family abroad; Cecilia's health was delicate, Lovel told me, and the doctor had advised that she should spend a winter in the south. He did not stay with them: he had pressing affairs at home; he had embarked in many businesses besides the paternal sugar-bakery; was concerned in companies, a director of a joint-stock bank, a man in whose fire were many irons. A faithful governess was with the children; a faithful man and maid were in attendance on the invalid; and Lovel, adoring his wife, as he certainly did, yet supported her absence with great equanimity.

In the spring I was not a little scared to read amongst the deaths in the newspaper:—"At Naples, of scarlet fever, on the 25th ult., Cecilia, wife of Frederick Lovel, Esq., and daughter of the late Sir Popham Baker, Bart." I knew what my friend's grief would be.

---

[1] Op. cit. ch. v.   [2] See above, pp. 32 ff.

He had hurried abroad at the news of her illness; he did not reach Naples in time to receive the last words of his poor Cecilia.

Some months after the catastrophe, I had a note from Shrublands. Lovel wrote quite in the old affectionate tone. He begged his dear old friend to go to him, and console him in his solitude. Would I come to dinner that evening?

Of course I went off to him straightway. I found him in deep sables in the drawing-room with his children, and I confess I was not astonished to see my Lady Baker once more in that room.

"You seem surprised to see me here, Mr. Batchelor!" says her ladyship, with that grace and good breeding which she generally exhibited; for if she accepted benefits, she took care to insult those from whom she received them.[1]

Might he not also have written this from the same work?

Lady Baker appeared at the second dinner-bell, without a trace on her fine countenance of that storm which had caused all her waves to heave with such commotion at noon.[2]

Or this from *The Book of Snobs*?

Well—I rang the bell at a little low side-door; it clanged and jingled and echoed for a long, long while, till at length a face, as of a housekeeper, peered through the door. . . .[3]

Counting such small items, the debts are innumerable. I call them small, but who can measure importance in things of this sort? If they are small, it is as jewels are. In *Esmond* we get the phrase 'an almost wild smile',[4] which is quintessential James.

Finally, I should not be surprised if a close reading of both writers would not disclose debts in James of the somnolent shop-lifting sort. Thackeray describes the 'faint smile playing on [the] features' of the Reverend Charles Honeyman as 'like moonlight on the façade of Lady Whittlesea's chapel';[5] and of Olive Chancellor James writes;

a smile of exceeding faintness played about her lips—it was just perceptible enough to light up the native gravity of her face It might have been likened to a thin ray of moonlight resting upon the wall of a prison.[6]

---

[1] *Lovel the Widower*, ch i.   [2] Ch. iv.
[3] Ch. xxviii.   [4] Bk ii, ch. vi.
[5] *The Newcomes*, ch. xix.   [6] *The Bostonians*, bk i, ch. i.

I have already indicated, I think, that a study of Thackeray and James together would yield substantial results. The debt of the latter to the former was of filial intimacy. There can be no question that a place for Thackeray must be found in any tradition of the novel, whatever our standards of admission.

INDEXES

INDEX OF THACKERAY'S WRITINGS

Barry Lyndon, The Memoirs of, 133, 208, 212–15; quoted briefly, 208; quoted at length, 125 f., 206, 212 f., 213 f., 214

'Bedford-Row Conspiracy, The', 298

Book of Snobs, The, 18, 36, 121, 186, 223, 240, 249, 305

Catherine, 120, 133–7, 186, 208, 211, 239, 246; quoted briefly, 91, 136, 246; quoted at length, 135 ff., 199

Cornhill to Cairo, From, 36, 151, 181, 182, 236–9

'Daddy, I'm Hungry...', 186 f.

Denis Duval, 2, 122, 189, 265; quoted briefly, 36; quoted at length, 46, 176 f.

'Dennis Haggarty's Wife', 186, 212, 301

English Humourists of the Eighteenth Century, The, 11

Esmond, The History of Henry, ix, 2, 12, 16, 38, 39, 50 ff., 81, 122, 126, 188, 240, 268, 271, 285, 299; quoted briefly, 268, 305; quoted at length, 193, 247 f.

'Going to See a Man Hanged', 125

Great Hoggarty Diamond, The, and *The History of Samuel Titmarsh*, 204

Irish Sketch Book, The, 233 f.

Letters, 124, 273, 287, 298; quoted briefly, 3, 13, 18, 21, 50, 56, 136, 163, 174, 206, 207, 208, 245, 269, 275, 283, 285; quoted at length, 16, 131, 220–5

'Lever's St Patrick's Eve—Comic Politics', 216–20

'Little Dinner at the Timmins's, A', 163

Lovel the Widower, 172, 182, 299 f.; quoted briefly, 37, 43, 67, 189, 191, 201; quoted at length, 29 ff., 32, 45, 241 f., 304 f.

Mr. Brown's Letters to his Nephew, 21

'Mrs. Perkins's Ball', 3

Newcomes, The, 2, 11, 18, 54, 56, 63, 75 f., 112, 122, 158, 251, 255, 279, 285; quoted briefly, 5, 13, 16, 35, 42, 44, 75, 94, 96, 130, 149, 154, 164, 165 f., 189, 201, 202, 250, 251, 294, 305; quoted at length, 26 f., 27 f., 33 f., 76 f., 79 f., 87 f., 88 f., 92 f., 94 f., 97 ff., 177, 189 f., 194 f., 195 f., 200 f., 203, 234 f., 280

Our Street, 186

Paris Sketch Book, The, 181, 188, 228 f.

Pendennis, The History of, 2, 21, 44, 74, 124, 157, 173, 179, 189, 299; quoted briefly, 19, 35, 38, 42, 43, 65, 70, 81, 86, 93, 187, 189, 199, 206, 243, 294; quoted at length, 37, 46 f., 66, 115, 123 f., 152 f., 155 f., 183 ff., 197, 246 f., 277, 301

Philip, The Adventures of, 2, 18, 38, 74, 91, 171, 172, 182, 191, 251; quoted briefly, 35, 39, 75, 90, 93, 150, 164, 201, 267; quoted at length, 26, 34, 40 f., 42, 43, 87, 149 f., 178 f., 200, 202, 232, 251

20-2

'Proposals for a Continuation of "Ivanhoe"', 18

Ravenswing, The, 36, 211, 245, 249, 286

Rebecca and Rowena, 45

Rose and the Ring, The, 201

Roundabout Papers, 14, 55 f., 113, 188, 205, 226, 231, 269; quoted briefly, 93, 110, 187, 232, 286; quoted at length, 11, 14, 17, 21, 114, 233, 244 f., 269–71

Second Funeral of Napoleon, The, 119

'Thieves' Literature of France', 114, 206

Shabby Genteel Story, A, 6, 187

Vanity Fair, ix, 2, 16, 23, 58, 74, 75, 82 ff., 96, 117, 122, 131, 150, 164 f., 174, 189, 208, 208 f., 209–20, 220, 225 f., 240, 251, 255, 296; quoted briefly, 35, 36, 39, 44, 113, 188, 191, 201, 225, 244; quoted at length, 39 f., 57, 63 ff., 82, 83 f., 128 f., 159, 193, 251

Virginians, The, ix, 2, 38, 50, 91, 122, 146, 158, 201, 298; quoted briefly, 3, 9, 36, 68, 78, 179, 200; quoted at length, 42, 48, 66, 68 f., 101–8, 146–8, 202, 286, 301–4

Wolves and the Lamb, The, 299

Yellowplush, Memoirs of Mr. Charles J., 278

INDEX OF THACKERAY'S PERSONAGES

Amory, Blanche (*christened* Betsy), 86, 262, 298

Anne, Queen, 81, 145, 229

Baker, Lady, 37

Batchelor, Charles, 29, 241 f., 295, 299 f.

Baughton, Miss, 87 f.

Baynes, Charlotte, 35, 171

Bell, Helen Laura, 86, 169, 230, 250

Bolton, Fanny, 38, 124–33, 156, 167 ff.

Bows, Mr, 141, 156

Brown, Bob, 111, 271

Browns, Joneses, Smiths, 111

Bullocks, the, 160

Castlewood, Rachel, Viscountess, 12, 86, 126, 154 f., 230, 287, 298

Clavering, Lady, 35

Costigan, Captain J. Chesterfield, 140, 142, 156, 241, 286

Costigan, Emily, *known as* 'The Fotheringay', 35, 137–44, 239

Crawley, Sir Pitt, 16

Crawley, Colonel Rawdon, 16, 35, 83 f., 159

Dobbin, Major William, 209

Eaves, Tom, 191

Esmond, Beatrix, 39, 144–8, 158, 172, 172 f.

Esmond, Colonel Henry, 12, 126, 145, 146, 154 f., 172, 214

Esmond, Lady Maria, 36, 38, 146, 172

Esmond, Madam Rachel, 6, 145, 301

Firmin, Dr George Brand, 38, 86 f., 151, 196

Firmin, Philip, 35, 171

Fitz-Boodle, George Savage, 191, 212 ff., 243

Franklin, Benjamin, 81

Gashleigh, Mrs, 163

Hayes, Catherine, 135 ff.

Honeyman, Charles, 5, 95, 177, 194, 305

Joneses, Smiths, Browns, 111

Kew, Frank, Earl of, 35

Kew, Louisa Joanna Gaunt, Dowager Countess of, 5, 35, 36, 243

Lambert, Mrs Martin, 86, 173
Lovel, Adolphus Frederick, 172
Lyndon, Barry, 114, 119 ff., 151, 243 f.

Mackenzie, Mrs, 92 f.
Motte, M. de la, 176, 178

Newcome, Barnes, 27, 37, 94 f., 250 f.
Newcome, Sir Brian, 149
Newcome, Clive, 6, 27, 35, 37, 108 f., 197
Newcome, Ethel, 27, 295
Newcome, Sophia Alethea (Mrs Hobson Newcome), 26 f., 195
Newcome, Colonel Thomas, 149, 153 f., 173, 194, 231, 235, 287

Pendennis, Arthur, called Pen, 37, 62, 124–33, 138–44, 156, 167 ff., 182–5, 197, 230, 239, 240, 255–62
Pendennis, Major Arthur, 35, 46 f., 86, 141, 142, 239, 267
Pendennis, Helen, 156 f., 169, 250, 277–82, 284, 286
Pinkerton, Barbara and Jemima, 9, 165
Pretender, The (Chevalier de St George), 81, 193
Prior, Elizabeth, 32, 172, 299

Ridley, John Hames, 197
Ringwood, John George, Second

Baron and First Earl of, 35, 149

Sampson, Mr, 160
Saverne, Comte de, 45
Saverne, Comtesse de, 178
Sedley family, the, 194
Sedley, Amelia, 159 f., 164 f., 173, 209
Sedley, Joseph, 16
Sharp, Rebecca, called Becky, 9, 16, 26, 35, 39, 75, 83 f., 86, 94, 122, 131, 159, 163, 164 f., 173, 232, 245, 251, 298
Sherrick, Mr, 5, 86
Sherrick, Julia, 35
Smiths, Joneses, Browns, 111
Steyne, George Gustavus, Marquis of, 5, 16, 57, 84, 128, 158, 193
Swallowtail, Colonel, 239

Thrum, Sir George, 249, 286
Tregarvan, Sir John, 149
Twysdens, the, 149

Ward, Mr, 301
Warrington, George, 6, 182–5, 197, 255–62
Warrington, Henry Esmond, 146, 158, 160 ff., 171, 172
Washington, General George, 81
Woolcomb, Grenville, 85

Yellowplush, Charles James Harrington Fitzroy, 186

GENERAL INDEX

Addison, Joseph, 50, 51, 53, 228, 269, 287
Allen, John, 222
Allingham, William, 205
Andersen, Hans, 207 f.
Arabian Nights, The, 38
Arnold, Matthew, 52, 55, 58, 109 f., 191, 264, 274
Athenæum, The, 210
Austen, Jane, 41, 87, 289

Bacon, Francis, 85
Bagehot, Walter, 19
Bailey, Philip James, 282
Balzac, Honoré de, 5, 7
Baudelaire, Charles, 250
Baxter, Mrs George, 287
Baxter, Sally, 131, 287
Beerbohm, Max, 118
Beethoven, 269, 271
Berkeley, George, 232

Bernard, Charles de, 298
Bible, 38, 45
Blackmore, Sir Richard, 55
Blackwood, John, 227
Blomfield, Charles James, Bishop of London, 223
Brimley, George, 154, 172
Brontë, Charlotte, 23, 61 f., 87, 245, 283–5, 290
Brontë, Emily, 151, 290
Brookfield, Charles and Frances, 282
Brookfield, William, 220–4
Brown, H. K. ('Phiz'), 117
Brown, Dr John, 207
Brownell, William Crary, 24, 112, 115 f., 191, 203
Browning, Elizabeth Barrett, 7, 278
Browning, Robert, 7, 171, 174, 281, 282
Bulwer, *see* Lytton
Bunyan, John, 38, 163, 285
Burne-Jones, Edward, 255
Butt, John E., 14

Cardus, Neville, ix
Carlyle, Thomas, 46, 53 f., 111, 226, 239, 240, 289
Carmichael-Smyth, Mrs, 283–6
Cervantes, 13, 287
Chaucer, Geoffrey, 85, 151, 228
Chesterton, Gilbert Keith, 6, 231, 267, 288
Chopin, 268
Clough, Arthur Hugh, 283 f.
Collins, Wilkie, 22
Cornhill, The, 4, 14, 29, 124, 127, 182
Court Gazette, The, 188

Daily Journal, The, 239
Daily Post, The, 239
Defoe, Daniel, 41, 172, 283, 294 f.
Dickens, Charles, ix, 2, 3, 7, 11, 14, 18, 50, 110 f., 151, 211, 231, 246, 271, 282, 299
Disraeli, Benjamin, 5, 12
Dixon, Richard Watson, 55

Dobell, Sydney, 58 f.
Dodds, John W., 192, 243, 273
Doyle, Richard, 117, 286
du Maurier, George, 23 f.
Duffy, Charles Gavan, 187
Dumas, Alexandre, 11, 21, 113

Eastlake, Lady, 210, 252
Edgeworth, Maria, 225
Eliot, George (Mary Anne Evans), 13, 151, 163, 187, 191, 192, 198, 262, 288, 289–306
Eliot, T. S., 275, 299
Elliott, Ebenezer, 186
Ennis, Lambert, 273

Fielding, Henry, 5, 11, 13, 41, 44, 70, 124, 130, 150, 188, 231, 232, 289, 301
Flaubert, Gustave, 71 ff., 279
Forster, John, 225
Forsythe, R. S., 81
Fraser's Magazine, 23, 133, 212
Friswell, J. H., 9
Froude, James Anthony, 57
Fulton, Robert, 181

Gainsborough, Thomas, 112
Gaskell, Elizabeth Cleghorn, 187
Georges I–IV, 230
Goldsmith, Oliver, 52, 228
Gray, Thomas, 205, 269, 280
Greenwood, Frederick, 119
Greig, J. Y. T., 11, 125, 131, 240, 273, 276–87

Hallam, Henry Fitzmaurice, 282
Hannay, James, 53, 154, 163, 190, 226, 232
Hardy, Thomas, 166, 264
Harrison, Frederic, 50
Henley, William Ernest, 51 f.
Hertford, Seymour-Conway, Francis Charles, third Marquis of, 57
Hodgson, Ralph, 264
Hogarth, William, 188
Holmes, Mary, 265, 284
Homer, 41, 42, 46, 203
Horne, Richard Hengist, 289

Howell, James, 113
Howells, William Dean, 297
Hume, David, 85
Hutton, Richard Holt, 19

Jack, A. A., 3
James, Henry, 4, 8, 24, 49, 50, 70, 80 f., 93, 144, 232, 289, 296–306
Johnson, Samuel, 52, 53, 70, 163, 178, 188, 202 f., 204, 215, 228, 274

Keats, John, x, 228, 268, 294

Lamb, Charles, 55, 65, 264, 289
Langland, William, 228
Laurel and Hardy, 271
Law, William, 97
Leavis, F. R., 25, 117, 175, 288–306
Lemon, Mark, 206, 220, 223
Lever, Charles James, 216–20
Lewes, George Henry, 290 f.
Louis XIV, 188
Lowry, H. F., 274
Lowther, Lord, 187
Lubbock, Percy, 71 ff., 79 f., 82 ff., 90, 301
Lytton, Edward Bulwer, first Lord Lytton, 278

Matthiessen, F. O., 297
Mitford, Mary Russell, 186
Montaigne, 113
Morning Chronicle, The, 216–19, 289
Mozart, 269
Mudge, Isadore Gilbert, 6, 283
Muir, Edwin, 174

Nation (New York), The, 296, 300
Newman, John Henry, 52, 178, 205, 238, 265–6, 271, 274, 275, 282

Oxford and Cambridge Magazine, The, 255

Pater, Walter, 65, 109 f., 231

Peacock, Thomas Love, 12
Pope, Alexander, 38, 43, 44, 46, 85, 145, 155, 192 f., 204, 215, 246, 249, 266, 280, 289, 298
Porter, Mrs Gerald, 227
Powles, H. H. P., 181
Pritchett, V. S., 273
Proctor, Mrs Bryan Waller, 223 f.
Proust, Marcel, 288
Punch, 117, 183, 223–5
Purcel, Peter, 187

Quarterly Review, The, 210, 252 f.
Quiller-Couch, A. T., 24, 52 f.

Ray, Gordon N., 62, 179, 209–27, 273, 278, 283–7
Reeve, Henry, 222
Richardson, Samuel, 5, 41, 130, 150
Ritchie, Anne Thackeray, 16
Roscoe, William Caldwell, 19, 23, 121 f., 144, 175–83, 188, 198, 203, 204 f., 223, 225, 230, 232, 243, 253–5, 263–6
Rousseau, Jean-Jacques, 250
Rowlandson, Thomas, 51
Ruskin, John, 7, 164, 233, 282

Saintsbury, George, 2 (bis), 51, 121 f., 128, 173, 231, 240, 267 f.
Sand, George, 228 f.
Schubert, 53
Schumann, 269
Scott, Sir Walter, 41, 75, 289
Scriblerus, Martinus, 295
Sears, M. Earl, 6, 283
Shakespeare, William, 5, 38, 48, 85, 112, 117 f., 163, 171, 172, 228, 243, 271, 280, 286, 294 f.
Sharp, M. W., 9
Stanfield, Charles, 237
Stannard, Mrs Arthur, 8
Steele, Richard, 50
Stein, Gertrude, 113
Stephen, James Fitzjames, 191 f., 196, 240
Sterne, Laurence, 70, 205, 228, 289
Sue, Eugène, 114, 206

Swift, Jonathan, 53, 227, 246

Taine, Hippolyte, 226
Tennyson, Alfred, 20, 205, 271
Thackeray, Harriet Marian, 221
Tilford, J. E., 126
Tillotson, Kathleen, 14
Times, The, 53, 118, 126, 128
Tinker, Chauncey B., 274
Trilling, Lionel, 299
Trollope, Anthony, 5, 14, 91, 124, 127, 229, 288

Virgil, 41, 45, 46

Walpole, Horace, 51
Webster, John, 118
Wellek, René, 85
Wells, H. G., 300
Wilson, Edmund, 25, 37
Wilson, J. G., 287
Winkworth, Catherine and Susanna, 224
Woolf, Virginia, 215, 231, 300
Wordsworth, William, 88, 192 f., 228, 232, 280

Young, G. M., 78

Printed in Great Britain
by Amazon